Mental Maps
of the Founders

Mental Maps
of the Founders

How Geographic Imagination
Guided America's Revolutionary Leaders

MICHAEL BARONE

BOOKS

First American edition published in 2023 by Encounter Books,
an activity of Encounter for Culture and Education, Inc.,
a nonprofit, tax-exempt corporation.
Encounter Books website address: www.encounterbooks.com

Manufactured in the United States and printed on
acid-free paper. The paper used in this publication meets
the minimum requirements of ANSI/NISO Z39.48–1992
(R 1997) (*Permanence of Paper*).

FIRST AMERICAN EDITION

LIBRARY OF CONGRESS CATALOGING-IN-PUBLICATION DATA IS AVAILABLE
Information for this title can be found at the Library of Congress
website under the following ISBN 978-1-64177-351-5 and LCCN 2023942654.

CONTENTS

INTRODUCTION

MENTAL MAPS

"If you want to really learn about a subject," my friend Lou Cannon, the great *Washington Post* reporter and Ronald Reagan biographer, once told me, "write a book about it." So one explanation of why I decided to write this book is that I wanted to learn more about the American Founders. Over the past three decades I have read many of the wonderful proliferation of books about the Founders, most of them by brilliant academics tenured in that golden age when American universities wanted faculty specializing in the history of colonial America and the early republic, and many others by gifted and learned amateurs. All these writers were immersed in the history and scholarship of the period. What could I, a journalist writing about politics and demographics, sometimes in historical perspective, add?

At sometime during the Covid lockdowns, an answer occurred to me: maps. Not just the physical maps available to them—there are already good accounts of these—but of their mental maps, their geographical orientation, the maps in their minds. "The urge to map is a basic, enduring human instinct," writes historian Jerry Brotton. "From early childhood onwards, we make sense of ourselves in relation to the wider physical world by processing information spatially."[1] When we go to the store, go to work, go to school, we start off with an idea of how we will get there and how we will get back. And we have maps of larger scale in our minds as well, from the child's maps we develop of how to get to school to adults' maps of the routes to workplaces, shopping malls, restaurants, airports, summer vacation spots. Americans have a sense of where their state capital is, and Washington, DC, and New York and Los Angeles and Orlando. Mapping apps may be reducing our need to keep our mental maps up to date, just as earlier technologies reduced our need to develop them, and some individuals have much better senses of direction than others, but the need for geographic orientation seems to be primary. "Every animal on earth knows how to navigate," writes Kathryn Schulz in *The New Yorker*, including "cats, bats, elephant seals, red-tailed hawks, wildebeests, gypsy moths, cuttlefish, slime mold, emperor penguins."[2] Polynesians developed a sense of where they were in the Pacific Ocean. Tupaia, the Polynesian navigator whom Captain Cook picked up in the Society Islands, showed Cook the way to New Zealand and drew a chart showing hundreds of islands in the Polynesian triangle linking New Zealand, Hawaii, and Easter Island. In the 1970s, the scientist John O'Keefe located "place neurons" in the hippocampi[3]—the parts of the brain that scientists have found to be enlarged in London cab drivers who have memorized "The Knowledge," the names and courses of 25,000 streets within six miles of Charing Cross and every shop and restaurant on each one of them.

I cannot claim to have an enlarged hippocampus, but I have always been aware, more than I think most people are, of the maps in my mind. I grew up in northwest Detroit, on flat farmland set off into square mile sections—in accordance with a plan first developed by Thomas Jefferson and included in adapted form in the Founders' Northwest Ordinance of 1787. With the explosive development of the auto industry in the 1910s and 1920s, the farmlands of the square miles in Greenfield and Redford Townships, a dozen miles from downtown Detroit, were laid out in straight streets running north and south between each mile road. In this geometrically regular setting, I found it easier to learn north, south, east, and west than to distinguish right from left, and I memorized the names of each cross street on Seven Mile Road as we returned on Sunday nights from my grandmother's house. To that early map I made additions. On a family trip driving back from Florida when I was six, at a small town traffic circle, I said we should take one road while my parents insisted on taking another. After eight or ten miles it was apparent they'd made the wrong choice, and from there on in, I was in charge of the maps on excursions and vacations.

The Founders had no such reliable maps to guide them. They lived in Atlantic seaboard colonies whose boundaries were not all clearly defined and whose backlands had never been accurately mapped. They were aware of the colonies'—and then the states'—rapid demographic growth, at a time when Europeans assumed static populations was the norm and population decline due to disease or famine was an ever-present possibility. Nor was it clear what the boundaries would be of the entity declaring itself independent in July 1776. The slaveholders in the colonies of the Caribbean, the Bahamas, and Bermuda were more interested in British aid to suppress slave rebellion than in seeking independence, while the French-speaking Catholics of Canada were, after their cultural independence was guaranteed by the Quebec Act of 1774, content enough with British rule to repel the invasion of the Protestant rebels in 1775 and 1776. Nor were all the seaboard colonists joining the Patriot cause. An estimated one-third were Loyalists, and half or more in New York, the essential geographic link between fiercely rebellious New England and the Chesapeake colonies on the other side of the Delaware River. Indigenous North Americans—the Indian tribes—were certainly not on board. The Iroquois Federation, whom the British had courted during what was called in North America the French and Indian War, stayed mostly loyal to the Crown, and multiple tribes chafed at the possibility of colonists, released from British restrictions like the Proclamation of 1763, surging in large numbers across the Appalachian chain and occupying lands where they farmed and hunted. How and under what terms would the Founders maintain their independence amid the colonial claims of the far larger and militarily more formidable British, French, and Spanish empires? These were vexing questions during the Revolutionary War, in the early republic which faced a world war between France and Britain for all but a few months between 1793 and 1815, and even in the years beyond.

The maps in traditional historic atlases, showing thick dotted lines demarking political sovereignty in North America, convey an impression of certainty and settledness which the Founders could not have shared. Their mental maps were full of contingencies, of what the new nation they hoped they were creating would look like and be like. The essays that comprise this book are attempts to understand what these extraordinary individuals' mental maps looked like, how they changed in response to events and circumstances, actions, and responses.

The Founders were extraordinary people, of strong character, penetrating intellect, and impressive self-discipline—more even than I had thought while embarking on this project, and after writing, for publication and for pay, about American politics, American demography, and American history for sixty years. It is astonishing that men of such stature emerged from a society of some three or four million people in the late eighteenth century. They had certain things in common. One was legislative experience. Benjamin Franklin, George Washington, and Thomas Jefferson were elected to and served in the Pennsylvania Assembly and the Virginia House of Burgesses, and James Madison, Alexander Hamilton, and Albert Gallatin were elected to and served in the independent Virginia, New York, and Pennsylvania legislatures. These legislatures were, to a perhaps surprising extent, meritocracies, where young men of extraordinary talent were recognized and advanced by experienced leaders. Another thing they had in common: They were really smart—and amazingly adaptable. Benjamin Franklin and George Washington were largely self-educated, but Franklin

became a pioneering scientist by pursuing his ever-vigilant curios-
ity, and Washington became a general capable of fashioning a successful strategy for an irregular army and an executive confident
enough to harness the astonishing talents, seldom equaled in any
era's history, of Alexander Hamilton and Thomas Jefferson. James
Madison was a political theorist of the highest caliber and also a
legislative leader able to assemble coalitions and fashion compromises, and Albert Gallatin in his always French-accented English,
was adept at frontier electioneering, governmental financing, and
treaty making—and compiling a dictionary of North American
Indian languages.

The enterprise of these extraordinary individuals could not have
succeeded as it did without multiple astonishing contingencies.
One was the survival of the colonial legislatures in which they got
their practical political education and developed their sophisticated
political philosophies. In the 1680s, the Catholic King James II
embarked on a project of abolishing the colonial legislatures—
indeed, neither French nor Spanish nor other British colonies had
freely elected legislatures with governmental powers. King James's
project was frustrated by his ouster in what has generally been
referred to as the Glorious Revolution of 1688–89, whose importance for American history inspired me to write a book on it.[4] His
successors, his Protestant son-in-law (and nephew) and daughter,
William III and Mary II, restored the colonial legislatures, and the
principles their actions were taken as establishing were invoked
repeatedly by the Founders. But as I found when researching that
book, the expedition of William of Orange, as he then was, could
have been frustrated if one of a dozen things had not chanced
to go right. Another contingency without which the history the
Founders made might never have come to be was the success of
the lawsuit prosecuted in England's Privy Council between 1732
and 1743 by Thomas Fairfax, the sixth Baron Fairfax of Cameron.
This established Lord Fairfax's claim to the Fairfax Grant, initially

made by an exiled and money-hungry teenage King Charles II in 1649, which covered 5.2 million acres between the Rappahannock and Potomac Rivers from Chesapeake Bay to the rivers' sources west of the Blue Ridge—the largest landholding grant not just in Virginia but in any of the seaboard colonies. In 1747, Lord Fairfax moved to Virginia to superintend his property, and in the next year, he hired a sixteen-year-old, six-foot-two neighbor to help survey some of his lands west of the Blue Ridge. Without this and subsequent ventures into Lord Fairfax's backlands, George Washington would not likely have been sent (with a map recently published by Joshua Fry and Peter Jefferson, father of Thomas Jefferson) to the Forks of the Ohio River to repel French advances in 1754, in the course of which he started a world war and accumulated the military experience that made him the inevitable choice of the Continental Congress to command the Continental Army in 1775. Other eighteenth-century hazards—smallpox, shipwreck—could easily have ended the careers of any of the Founders, leaving his deeds undone and his unique contribution unreceived.

There is a tradition, still revived occasionally in campaign oratory but mostly scorned, of attributing the success of the American Revolution and the launching of the American republic as due to the hand of what the Founders may have referred to as Divine Providence. I do not take that view. But anyone who does can find evidence for it in the unlikely contingencies that abound in the lives of the Founders and in these little essays on their mental maps.

ONE

BENJAMIN FRANKLIN
Join or Die

In 1746, Benjamin Franklin ordered from William Strahan a map of North America and another map of the world. Both men were printers, Franklin in Philadelphia and Strahan in London, and close friends; Franklin at Strahan's suggestion had hired David Hall as his foreman and would turn over his printshop to him on his retirement two years later. Franklin was also at this time the publisher of the *Pennsylvania Gazette*, compiler of *Poor Richard's Almanack*, which sold 10,000 copies a year, and postmaster of Philadelphia, in which capacity he could send copies of the *Gazette* to other colonies free of charge. For a decade he had been clerk of the Pennsylvania Assembly, the colony's elective legislature, even though he was at odds with the two competing political forces. The Assembly was dominated by Quakers, whose pacifism prevented them from supporting measures to protect the colony during the ongoing war with France, while the governor was appointed by the proprietor Thomas Penn, son of the man who had founded the colony six decades before, who would block attempts to tax proprietorship property. Franklin opposed both stands. The two maps, he told Strahan, were "to be hung, one on each side of the Door in the Assembly Room," as historian Edmund Morgan writes, to "remind members of the Assembly that Pennsylvania was not an island, a fact they were still exasperatingly slow to grasp."[1]

At age forty, Franklin was familiar with much of the territory depicted on the maps. He was born the fifteenth of seventeen children of a candlemaker in Boston, apprenticed at age twelve in his brother James's print shop, where he wrote and sneaked unto print fourteen droll essays supposedly written by a country widow named Silence Dogood. Balking at his brother's mistreatment, he sailed away at age seventeen to New York and, finding no printing work there, to Philadelphia. In his *Autobiography*, written many years later when he was internationally famous, Franklin with characteristic self-mockery portrays himself as an almost penniless youth disembarking in Philadelphia, with "three great puffy rolls" of bread, two under each arm, seen by his future wife, who "thought I made, as I certainly did, a most awkward, ridiculous appearance."[2] The young Franklin was induced, by promises never fulfilled, to sail to London to buy printing equipment, and so had exposure, before he was twenty, to a metropolis which, with 600,000 people, was perhaps the world's largest city and the focus of literary giants Addison and Steele, Swift and Defoe, Richardson and Fielding. In 1726 he returned to Philadelphia, and in 1728, at twenty-two, quietly set up his own print shop, with no outward indication that he would in another twenty years retire as one of the richest and most famous men in British North America.[3]

Philadelphia in those years was the fastest-growing city in the North American colonies, and Franklin contributed much to its growth. He soon acquired the *Pennsylvania Gazette* and his humorous articles helped make it the highest-circulation newspaper in the colonies. In 1732, he began publishing the annual *Poor Richard's Almanack*, whose humorous storytelling and virtue-promoting proverbs helped it outdo its rivals and sell 10,000 copies a year.[4] With other tradesmen who met for modest dinners regularly, he established a subscription library in 1731,[5] the Union Fire Company in 1736,[6] in 1749 the Academy, a college that became the University of Pennsylvania, and in 1751 a hospital for which he raised private contributions and got the Assembly to agree to contribute another £2,000—thus inventing the matching grant.[7] He proposed a constable patrol to be paid by a graduated property tax, which the Assembly adopted years later, and he organized a militia to protect Pennsylvania when it appeared vulnerable to French and Indian invasion during King George's War in 1747.[8] In 1739, when the evangelical minister George Whitefield came to North America in what became known as the Great Awakening, Franklin, though not a believer, promoted his preaching in colonies from Georgia to New England, built a large hall for him to speak in Philadelphia, published volumes of his sermons and ten editions of his journals.[9] As his printing business prospered, he set up, with printing presses and type, younger men as partners in print shops from Charleston to Newport, Rhode Island, and even in the Caribbean island of Antigua, typically receiving one-third of the profits for five or six years. He secured the printing business of the Pennsylvania Assembly, was named its clerk in 1736, and became its official printer of "the Votes, Laws, Paper Money, and other occasional Jobbs [*sic*]."[10] In time he became the public printer also for Delaware, New Jersey, and Maryland. In 1737, he became postmaster of Philadelphia, with a small salary but the right to mail his newspaper for free[11] and "to afford me a very considerable income," he noted.

"Despite all of his unpretentiousness he could not help making money. He had a natural genius for business,"[12] writes historian Gordon Wood. "Franklin's print shop had by then grown into a successful, vertically integrated media conglomerate," writes biographer Walter Isaacson. "He had a printing press, publishing house, newspaper, an almanac series, and partial control of the postal system. The successful books he had printed ranged from Bibles and psalters to Samuel Richardson's novel *Pamela*, a tale whose mix of raciness and moralism probably appealed to him.[13] He owned eighteen paper mills and may have been the "largest paper dealer in the English-speaking world,"[14] owned multiple rental properties in Philadelphia and coastal cities, collected payments for hundreds of pounds of loans and speculated in western lands in the Ohio River valley. Wood estimates that his printing business brought him £600 a year, more than what George Washington was earning from Mount Vernon, and estimated his total annual income at £2,000, twice that of Pennsylvania's governor. "He became a very wealthy man, perhaps one of the richest colonists in the northern part of the North American continent."[15] By 1748, when he formally retired from his printing business but retained streams of income from it and his investments and partnerships in multiple printing businesses, including £650 a year for eighteen years from his share in the Philadelphia print shop.[16]

In the course of becoming rich, Benjamin Franklin accumulated more knowledge of the British North American colonies than perhaps any other person. With that knowledge, and as "master of my own time," as he told his friend the New York official and scientist Cadwallader Colden, he had "leisure to read, study, make experiments, and converse at large with such ingenious and worthy Men as are pleas'd to honour me with their Friendship or Acquaintance on such Points as may produce something for the common benefit of Mankind, uninterrupted by the little Cares and Fatigues of Business."[17] Franklin was an uncommonly curious observer who was prompted incessantly to learn how and why the world worked as it did. This was a man who noticed that "nor'easter" storms came not from the northeast but the southwest, and why; who on his Atlantic voyages noticed differences in ocean temperatures and identified the Gulf Stream current; who noticed that dark fabrics absorb heat more than light fabrics and recommended that the walls of fruit stands be painted black. In the early 1740s, in a North America that then had a measurably colder climate than in the twentieth and twenty-first centuries, he observed that warm air expands to take up more space than cold, and devised a stove with pipes that drew cold air from below and minimized cold drafts and smoke.[18]

Later in the 1740s, Franklin, intrigued by a traveling lecturer's displays with electricity, conducted his own experiments, with glass tubes to generate static electricity, with small electrified iron balls and nearby corks, with Leyden jars filled with electrified liquids and covered with electrified metal foil and in 1752, famously, with a silk kite fitted with a sharp wire on top and a suspended key on the bottom, which drew sparks and sent a charge to a Leyden jar. From his experiments with electricity, he made theoretical discoveries—positive and negative charges, capacitors and batteries, insulators and conductors, electrical grounding—and a practical invention—the lightning rod—all of which have endured. "Franklin's law of the conservation of charge," writes the historian of science I. Bernard Cohen, "must be considered to be of the same fundamental importance to physical science as Newton's law of conservation of momentum."[19] While admitting that he "was a practical experimenter more than a systematic theorist," biographer Walter Isaacson adds, "He was one of the foremost scientists of his age, and he conceived and proved one of the most fundamental concepts about nature: that electricity is a single fluid." And his practical invention, the lightning rod, remains in universal use nearly three centuries later, with never any pecuniary return to Franklin, who, as with the Franklin stove, refused to take out a patent on his invention.[20] But Franklin's work on electricity won him international fame and academic respect. This dropout from Boston Latin School received honorary M.A. degrees from Harvard and Yale in 1753 and William and Mary in 1756, and in that year became a member of the Royal Society in London.

In the eighteenth century, when savants such as Goethe and Humboldt could strive to master every field of human learning, Franklin's gift for observation and invention was not limited to scientific studies. He could apply it to geography and demographics as well.

The maps he ordered from William Strahan in 1746 were his attempt to share his learning with others, in a time of crisis. For two years, Britain had been at war with France in the conflict known in Europe as the War of Austrian Succession and in North America as King George's War. In 1745, Massachusetts volunteers, aided by the Royal Navy, had seized the fortress of Louisbourg, on the tip of Cape Breton Island, northeast of Nova Scotia and commanding the Gulf of St. Lawrence and the rich cod fisheries off Newfoundland. But British colonists were vulnerable on land. Indians allied to the French had attacked coastal Maine and the Hoosac valley in western Massachusetts and had seized Saratoga, just two dozen miles north of the British fur trading depot of Albany, New York.

The maps Franklin ordered showed the larger strategic picture. France claimed sovereignty over vast lands, from the St. Lawrence valley north of New England and New York and the Mississippi River valley, west of seaboard colonies. The thickly populated British seaboard colonies were surrounded, on the north and the west, by much larger expanses of land thinly populated by Indians and officially claimed by France. There was a concentration of French settlers around the citadel of Quebec, founded by Samuel de Champlain in 1608, and a much smaller number of French fur traders, explorers, and Jesuit missionaries who ranged over the St. Lawrence valley, the Great Lakes, and the Mississippi valley. These far-flung territories were connected by forts in Detroit and New Orleans, established in 1701 and 1718, and populated by Indian tribes with which the French had friendlier relations (and much more frequent intermarriage) than the vastly more numerous British settlers typically had with their indigenous neighbors. The maps illustrated the danger of French and Indian invasion on the British colonies, protected from overseas invasion by the British Navy but vulnerable on their lightly defended western frontiers not many miles inland. Their strategic weakness prompted Franklin to bypass Pennsylvania's pacific Quaker legislators and their indifferent and taxophobic proprietor, Thomas Penn, and create an active militia in 1747. The war ended in 1748, but in peace negotiations, the British returned Louisbourg to France in return for France's reinstatement of British allies in the Austrian Netherlands and the return of the East India Company's colony of Madras—a trade that infuriated the colonists who had raised troops and funds to evict the French.

This Treaty of Aix-la-Chapelle was signed in 1748, the year of Franklin's retirement. But the years that followed were not times of leisure but of increasing activity and fame for the man who, though he no longer appeared in his leather apron, still signed himself simply "B. Franklin, printer." In 1749, he wrote his proposal for what would become the University of Pennsylvania. In 1751, he published his paper on electricity, which, together with his 1752 experiment with the kite, would make him internationally famous. In 1751, he was elected to the Pennsylvania Assembly and handed down his position as clerk to his son William (whose illegitimate birth he acknowledged without ever divulging the name of his mother). In 1753, he was named, with a less active nominee from Virginia, joint postmaster of North America. "He applied all that he had learned running the Philadelphia post office to the colonial post office," writes historian Edmund Morgan. "He introduced strict accounting and increased the speed and reliability of mail delivery, and he made the post office profitable.[21] With the experience he had gained as postmaster in Philadelphia, he plunged into a flurry of activity. "Franklin drew up typically detailed procedures for running the service more efficiently, established the first home-delivery system and dead letter office, and took frequent inspection tours," writes Walter Isaacson. "Within a year, he had cut to one day the delivery time of a letter from New York to Philadelphia."[22] And in 1754, he finally agreed to the publication of a pamphlet he had written three years earlier and circulated in letter to English friends,[23] entitled *Observations Concerning the Increase of Mankind, Peopling of Countries, etc.,* which stands as the first serious analysis of the demographics of what would become the United States of America.

He was inspired to write this, Morgan tells us, in 1749, while preparing the 1750 edition of *Poor Richard's Almanack*, when "he had noted that the colonies were thought to be doubling in population every thirty years and that the increase was attributed to immigration."[24] But that struck him as not quite right. "People increase faster by Generation in those Colonies," he wrote. He had certainly observed a population increase in the city of Philadelphia, from less than 5,000 when he disembarked there in 1723 to almost 13,000 (the largest in the colonies) as he was drafting the pamphlet 1751.[25] But he was also very much aware that more than nine-tenths of the British colonists lived outside cities. His work as a publisher and journalist and postmaster, his partnerships in print shops in multiple colonies, and his work promoting George Whitefield's rallies from South Carolina to New England—all these experiences gave this perspicacious observer a closer acquaintanceship with British North America than anyone else, and no one else in an era that lacked systematic statistics was better able to generalize from what he observed. He sought out particularly men with notable expertise. "There had always been a few in Philadelphia, men like James Logan, the learned fur trader, and John Bartram, the self-taught botanist. And there were men of large minds he encountered incidentally in his visits to other colonies as deputy postmaster: John Mitchell, the cartographer in Virginia[, and] Jared Eliot, the experimental farmer in Connecticut," notes Morgan, plus science buff Cadwallader Colden, later governor of New York, and John Perkins of New York.[26] "As a postmaster he had helped bind America together," writes Isaacson. "He was one of the few men equally at home visiting the Carolinas as Connecticut—both places where he had once franchised print shops—and he could discuss, as he had done, indigo farming with a Virginia planter and trade economics with a Massachusetts merchant."[27] His experience was unduplicated. "No one had seen more of America," Gordon Wood writes, "and no one knew more important people in the colonies, than he."[28]

Observations consisted of just twenty-four numbered paragraphs, in pedestrian prose unadorned by Franklin's characteristic irony and humor. "People increase in Proportion to the number of Marriages, and that is greater in Proportion to the Ease and Convenience of supporting a Family," he leads off his second paragraph. "In countries full settled," he observes in paragraph four, lands are occupied and improved, and "Labourers are plenty, their Wages will be low" and "this Difficulty deters many from Marriage." Therefore in Europe, "generally full settled with Husbandmen, Manufacturers, &c.,...there cannot now much increase in people." In contrast, he writes in the sixth paragraph, "Land thus being plenty in *America*, and so cheap that a labouring man, that understands Husbandry, can in a short Time save Money enough to purchase a Piece of new Land sufficient for a Plantation, whereon he may subsist a Family, such are not afraid to marry." He observes that marriage is more common "and more generally early" in America than in Europe. Logic tells him that will result in more children and that "our People must at least be doubled every 20 years." Extending this logic not just to his home colony of Pennsylvania, but to all of Britain's Atlantic Seaboard colonies, he looked far ahead. "There are suppos'd to be now upwards of One Million English Souls in North America (tho' 'tis thought scarce 80,000 have been brought over Sea," he observes. "This million doubling, suppose but once in 25 years, will, in another Century, be more than the People of *England*, and the greatest number of *Englishmen* will be on this Side of the Water." Which is exactly what happened: By 1851, there were more people living in the United States than in England.[29]

It is notable that Franklin was primarily concerned with the proliferation in the colonies of people of English descent. In his thirteenth paragraph, he lists as one of the "Things that must diminish a Nation" the "Introduction of Slaves." In the 1750s, Franklin continued to own slaves and did not yet share his Quaker neighbors' support of abolition of slavery; it was not until the 1770s that he came out against the slave trade and in the 1780s for the abolition of slavery itself.[30] In the last two paragraphs of *Observations,* he expressed his preference for British immigrants over those especially from Germany, expressing fears that "Palatine boors," offspring of the German pacifists attracted to Pennsylvania by agents of William Penn, would "Germanize us instead of our Anglifying them," and called for "excluding all Blacks and Tawneys [and] increasing the lovely White and Red." These sentiments, obnoxious to twenty-first century readers, were part of his conviction, strong at the time, that the North American colonies were and should be British and indeed would in a century be the largest component of the English-speaking world.

Franklin circulated this paper to the Quaker merchant and scientist Peter Collinson and other epistolary friends in London. It was widely read and cited by Adam Smith in *The Wealth of Nations* (1776) and Thomas Malthus in his *Essay on the Principle of Population* (1798).[31] Presumably he wanted well-informed people at the center of the empire to realize that the colonies were growing more rapidly, and contained a greater percentage of Englishmen, than was usually appreciated—and that their growth was threatened by the geographically vast but thinly settled French territories to the north and west. As historian A. W. Brands put it, "the future of America, and with it of the British empire, depended on the availability of land [which] was what made the contest with France so important."[32] The longer-run implication, contemplated then by almost no one in London, was that in time the majority of the English-speaking population would live not in the cramped British Isles but in the broad geographic expanse of North America. His extrapolations also challenged the conventional wisdom that regarded population as something that tended not to increase but to remain static, except when reduced by calamities, which Franklin listed—"being conquered," "Loss of Trade," "Loss of Food," "Bad Government and insecure Property." In fact, population growth was just starting to accelerate in Europe, at a rate imperceptible to most observers in an era with no regularly scheduled official censuses. But the European-descended population was growing more rapidly in North America, as Franklin observed and explained. Collinson was dazzled by *Observations*. "I wish, my Dear Friend, you'll oblige the ingenious part of mankind with a public view of your observations &c. on the increase of mankind," he wrote. "I don't find anyone else has hit it off so well."[33] Franklin replied that he wanted to revise the text, perhaps to make it more comprehensible, perhaps to inject some of his characteristic humor. But for three years, other business obtruded. Finally, in 1754, he had it printed in Boston, and it attracted attention not only in the colonies but in London, even as Britain's contest with France had resumed in lands beyond the Appalachian mountains.

The struggle between Britain and France in North America continued after the 1748 treaty restored the fortress of Louisbourg to the French and raised their hopes of expanding their empire in the thinly populated lands of North America. In 1753, they set their eyes on the Ohio River valley and built a series of small forts heading south from Lake Erie—Fort Presque Isle, in present-day Erie, Pennsylvania; Fort LeBoeuf, fifteen miles south; and Fort Venango, fifteen miles farther east. They were clearly heading toward the Forks of the Ohio, where the Allegheny and Monongahela Rivers joined to form the Ohio River, the second largest tributary of the Mississippi. This was territory scarcely known to British colonists, depicted inaccurately in the map published in 1751 by the Virginians Peter Jefferson (father of Thomas Jefferson) and Joshua Fry.[34] In 1753, King George II ordered that a British emissary demand the French leave or force them out, and Virginia authorities selected for the assignment a twenty-one-year-old planter who had worked as a surveyor west of the Blue Ridge. George Washington trudged along Indian trails and across icy rivers to Fort LeBoeuf but was rebuffed by the French, and his report of his mission together with a hand-drawn map was published in London.[35] Washington's mission surely came to the attention of Benjamin Franklin, who for some time "had envisioned two new colonies being created in the West 'between the present frontiers of our colonies on one side, and the lakes and Mississippi on the other.' These colonies, he said, would lead 'to the great increase of Englishmen, English trade, and English power.'"[36]

From the maps he had ordered, he could see how the French advance into the Ohio Country and their alliance with Indians there would block the British from expanding into the heart of the continent. But he had a hard time convincing others of the need for colonial unity. It was a goal he had cherished for some time. He was familiar with the Six Nations federation of the Iroquois, which had conducted something in the nature of diplomatic relations with colonial authorities in New York and with Britain's Indian agent, Sir William Johnson. "It would be a very strange thing," Franklin wrote his New York friend James Parker in 1751, "if six Nations of ignorant Savages could be capable of forming a scheme for such a union...and yet that a like union should be impracticable for ten or a dozen English colonies, to whom it is more necessary."[37] In October 1753, he was one of three Pennsylvania commissioners attending a conference in Carlisle, amid the first Appalachian chains, with Indian tribes, including not only the nearby Delaware but also the Iroquois representatives from lands west of Albany, New York; the Pennsylvanians heard but did not quite agree to pleas to prevent white settlers from venturing beyond the mountain ridges.[38] In April 1754, as Washington embarked on a second expedition as lieutenant colonel commanding 150 Virginia militiamen, charged with capturing the Forks of the Ohio, and as the French were building Fort Duquesne there, the Assembly in Philadelphia ignored Franklin's argument that the fort was within the boundary of Pennsylvania and rejected his proposal that the colony aid the Virginia effort.[39] But the Assembly did respond positively to an order of the Board of Trade in London that the colonies send delegates to a conference in the frontier fur trading post of Albany, New York, in June 1754. At least one Iroquois leader was urging the breaking of the Covenant Chain alliance with the British, entered into in the 1670s, which "would mean that the colonies, stripped of their Iroquois buffer, would become frontiers."[40] Franklin was named one of four Pennsylvania delegates, together with the Assembly speaker, the colony's secretary, and a member of the Penn family.[41]

In May 1754, the news came to Philadelphia of the first disastrous results of Washington's expedition. In an encounter with the French, an Indian ally had slain the French diplomat Jumonville, an act of war in French eyes—which turned out to be the beginning of what became known in North America as the French and Indian Wars and in Europe and India as the Seven Years' War. In London, Horace Walpole, inveterate diarist and son of the long-serving (1721–42) first prime minister, wrote, "The volley first by a young Virginian in the backwoods of America set the world on fire."[42] For Franklin, colonial unity became even more urgent. In the *Pennsylvania Gazette*, he wrote an editorial blaming French advances "on the present disunited state of the British colonies." More vividly, and of more lasting importance, as biographer Walter Isaacson recounts, "he printed the first and most famous editorial cartoon in American history: a snake cut into pieces, labeled with the names [actually, the abbreviations] of the colonies, with the caption: 'Join, or Die.'"[43] This was a more radical proposal than most twentieth and twenty-first century Americans may appreciate. The colonies had separate origins and separate cultures—the separate "folkways" that David Hackett Fischer has famously described in *Albion's Seed*.[44] This diversity reflected in part religious differences at a time when memories were still fresh of catastrophic religious warfare in Britain and Europe: The New England colonies were founded by Calvinists, Virginia and the Carolinas by Anglicans, Maryland by Catholics, Pennsylvania by Quakers, and New York by the Dutch. Their economic interests were varied as well. The idea that an as yet undetermined number of these diverse colonies should act as a political unit was novel, even exotic, and in the 1750s unrealistic. In advancing it, Franklin showed the same originality in politics as he had shown in his work on electricity in science. And Franklin being Franklin, he had a plan for how the colonies could unite. He proposed a multi-colony General Council, to be appointed by the colonial assemblies, and a President General to be appointed by the Crown, to "provide for a common defense for the increasingly connected and costly frontiers."[45] It would meet at multiple sites and would have revenues raised by a tax on liquor. At first he expected this arrangement to arise locally, but later suggested it be authorized by an act of Parliament.[46] What is startling is how much this plan resembles not so much Franklin's own preferences—the Pennsylvania Constitution he shepherded in 1776 had a unicameral legislature and a collective executive—as it anticipates the basic features, forged through compromise, of the Constitution proposed, with Franklin's support, in 1787 and ratified in 1788.

On his way to the Albany conference, he ran this proposal by friends in New York City. In Albany, after the inconclusive negotiations with the Iroquois were finished, he persuaded a majority of delegates to adopt his latest version of the plan. Some New York delegates opposed it (as two of three New York delegates would oppose the Constitution in 1787), as did Pennsylvania's Quaker speaker, while it was supported with some vigor by Thomas Hutchinson, the future Massachusetts governor who would oppose the American Revolution. It passed easily, but with no political effect: It was the act of a commission with no power to enforce its writ and to which Virginia, the largest colony, had not bothered to send any delegates. The colonial assemblies, bypassed as the state legislatures would be by the Constitutional Convention, were all opposed, and so was the British Parliament and Privy Council, fearing a possible move toward colonial independence. Franklin understood it was opposed for different reasons, as he wrote in his *Autobiography*. "The assemblies did not adopt it as they all thought there was too much *prerogative* in it, and in England it was judged to have too much of the *democratic*."[47] Nevertheless, he traveled to Boston afterward and met with Governor William Shirley and corresponded with him in December 1754. Franklin said he distrusted royally appointed governors, who had no property in America, to represent local interests, and he agreed to Shirley's suggestion that Americans might elect representatives to the British Parliament. But he added the proviso that that should happen only after repeal of current British navigation and trade laws—a step British leaders in those pre–free trade days were unwilling even to contemplate. And he added a warning, in language that would be echoed in the decades ahead: "It is suppos'd an undoubted Right of Englishmen not to be taxed but by their own Consent given thro' their Representatives."

In his *Autobiography*, Franklin argued that his Albany Plan could have prevented the Revolution and resulted in a harmonious trans-Atlantic British empire. "The colonies so united would have been sufficiently strong to have defended themselves [in 1754–63]. There would then have been no need of troops from England; of course the subsequent pretence for taxing America, and the bloody contest it occasioned, would have been avoided."[48] But this is not entirely convincing. The two goals that Franklin relentlessly pursued during his retirement were, if not irreconcilable, then at least in tension with each other. One was colonial unity. As he wrote in a letter to Peter Collinson, "Britain and her Colonies should be considered as one Whole, and not as different States with separate interests."[49]

The other was his calculation that a unified North America was "a potentially equal part of the British Empire"[50] indeed, one that would grow larger than any other country—as he wrote in his *Observations* pamphlet, published in the critical year of 1754 and in his talks with Governor Shirley in December of that year. The colonies moved toward unity in objecting to British taxes and in the opening, some twenty years after the adjournment of the Albany conference, of the First Continental Congress in September 1774. But authorities in London, despite Franklin's considerable fame and constant advocacy during his many years there (1757–62 and 1764–75), never came close to taking seriously his arguments that the colonies should be given equal weight with the home country in an English-speaking empire. As historian Edmund Morgan summarizes, "This long-term goal of an Anglo-American empire of equals directed Franklin's public service until he was obliged to give it up in 1775."[51]

★ ★ ★

Franklin spent the next twenty years seeking to advance a relationship between the colonies and Great Britain, and then the next fifteen years after that in asserting the independence of a North American republic—what Thomas Jefferson called "an empire of liberty." In Philadelphia, he remained a dominating figure, though at odds with the proprietor-appointed governor and the pacifist Quakers, as General Edward Braddock arrived in the spring of 1755 to lead an attack on Fort Duquesne. At Braddock's request, he obtained needed horses and wagons for his expedition, giving farmers his personal bond for payment. After Braddock's defeat and death—he was buried on the retreat of the remnants of his army by his aide George Washington—Franklin was reimbursed with army funds only through the intervention of Governor Shirley.[52] Then in 1756, despite his rage at the proprietors' refusal to be taxed, he organized a military unit, patrolled the frontier, and in uniform marched his troops through Philadelphia. In early 1757, the Assembly voted to send him to London as colonial agent, to lobby the proprietors to accept taxation and, failing that, to oust them and make Pennsylvania a royal colony.[53] He sailed in June 1757 and spent most of the rest of his life across the Atlantic, from 1757–62 and 1764–75 in London, and 1776–85 in Paris.

In Britain, Franklin pursued a course that flowed logically from his conclusions in *Observations*, confident that the North American colonies should continue to be part of the British Empire, but insisting they must also be partners in an as yet undefined relationship with the Crown, perhaps with representation in the Westminster Parliament or perhaps with a colonial parliament of their own. To pursue this goal, the colonies would need to act in unity, of the sort that he had espoused successfully to the delegates at the Albany conference but without success beyond, and to achieve that unity it would help if Pennsylvania should shed the Penn proprietorship—the goal for which the Assembly had sent him across the Atlantic—and gain, like all the others except Maryland, a royal charter. As he stayed on, however, and ultimately became agent (or lobbyist) for other colonies—Georgia in 1768, New Jersey in 1769, Massachusetts in 1770—he had no success in his campaign to abolish the proprietorship but turned his attention to the deteriorating relationship between Britain and the colonies.

From his arrival, Franklin had some reason to expect success. He was a celebrity for his writings and his discoveries about electricity. He was awarded honorary degrees by St. Andrews and Oxford—and was known ever afterward as Doctor Franklin—and settled into a comfortable domestic situation just two minutes' walk from the bustling Strand and five minutes from the seat of Parliament. In the Seven Years' War, started as the French and Indian War with Washington's retreat in 1754, Franklin supported the aggressive strategy of the guiding minister William Pitt,[54] which produced resounding victories in 1759 in India and in the Plains of Abraham outside Quebec, where both commanding generals died amid a British victory that resulted in France's expulsion from Canada. When George III sought peace after coming to the throne in 1760, Franklin opposed proposals that Britain retain the rich sugar island of Guadeloupe and hand back Canada and Louisiana to France. He remembered how Britain had relinquished Louisbourg in peace negotiations in 1748, and he drew on his demographic projections in *Observations*, in making his case. "All the country from the St. Lawrence to the Mississippi will in another century be filled with British people. Britain itself will become vastly more populous, by the immense increase of its commerce; the Atlantic will be covered by your trading ships; and your naval power, thereby continually increasing, will extend your influence around the whole globe, and awe the world."[55] His argument prevailed, and the 1763 Treaty of Paris gave Britain both Canada and Spanish Florida, while the Bourbon King of France compensated his cousin the Bourbon King of Spain by ceding him an enormous and undefined swathe of North America west of the Mississippi River called Louisiana. Franklin was also able to get his illegitimate son William Franklin appointed royal governor of New Jersey that year.

Trouble came when the king and his ministers got Parliament to impose a stamp tax on the North American colonies to provide revenue for imperial expenses. Franklin opposed the 1765 Stamp Act, not as an assault on colonists' rights but as unduly unpopular, and proposed instead a land bank which would lend cash at interest, with profits to the Crown.[56] "In the surviving papers that came from his hand in the next nine or ten years, the greater part of them having to do with the empire," historian Edmund Morgan writes, "Franklin can be seen year after year trying to patch up the empire, trying to undo the mistakes of a heedless ministry, trying to guide colonial protests in constructive ways, trying to interpret them constructively to an uncomprehending English public."[57] His efforts to promote accommodation rather than confrontation over supposed rights had flagged by 1770, and he encouraged American correspondents to continue their 1769 boycott of British goods. In 1773, he secretly released a letter from his Albany Plan ally, Massachusetts Governor Thomas Hutchinson, opposing colonial protests. In January 1774, when news of the Boston Tea Party's destruction of taxed East India Company tea reached London, he stood silent in a room called the Cockpit in Whitehall as he was denounced in vitriolic terms by Solicitor General Wedderburn—a purposeful humiliation of a man who, despite his professions of humility, was proud of his accomplishments. The next day, he was dismissed from his lucrative postmastership. Over the rest of the year, he sought a change of ministry, gaining support from the long-out-of-office William Pitt, who visited Franklin at his house exactly a year after his humiliation in the Cockpit and then squired him around Westminster Palace before speaking out for conciliation of the colonies. But Pitt's initiative made no headway among ministers who "appear'd to have scarce discretion to govern a Herd of Swine."[58] In March 1775, Benjamin Franklin sailed for Philadelphia.

After almost two decades of living comfortably in London, during which he ignored pleas to return home by his wife, who died in 1774, Franklin returned from the metropole to the periphery to begin the process that the historian Gordon Wood used as the title of his biographical study, *The Americanization of Benjamin Franklin*. By this time, Franklin had abandoned his view that the colonies should strive for practical compromises rather than insist on recognition of their rights, and his sincerity was attested by his refusal to intervene against the ouster and imprisonment of his son William for his Loyalism. Almost instantly he was chosen as a member of the Second Continental Congress, which would meet in the Pennsylvania State House—now Independence Hall—across the street from the house which his late wife had designed and furnished. In the fall of 1775, he served on secret committees to buy arms and seek a foreign alliance, and from March to May 1776, at age seventy, he made an arduous overland trip to Montreal, which General Benedict Arnold's New England troops were occupying, to see if Canadians would be interested in joining the Revolution (the French Canadians, promised continued recognition of the province's Catholic Church and French language by Britain's 1774 Quebec Act, were not).[59]

Franklin saw coming into existence something very much like the union of the colonies he had recommended at the Albany conference more than twenty years before. The thirteen seaboard colonies were acting in unity in the Continental Congresses, starting in 1774, when he was still in England, although the invitations he contemplated for "the West India Islands, Quebec, St. Johns, Nova Scotia, Bermudas, and the East and West Floridas"[60] went unanswered. The states—no longer colonies—could maintain their separate customs and laws, and Franklin worked successfully for a Pennsylvania constitution providing for a unicameral legislature and a group executive—features dropped when a new constitution was written and approved in 1790 and which were not much admired or imitated elsewhere. His constitution also provided for representation according to population—a novel idea, in an era lacking regularly conducted censuses, but one which Franklin managed to get adopted in Pennsylvania and which was adopted into federal legislation for congressional districts in 1842. But it was not adopted for the Confederation Congress, due in part to the opposition of Pennsylvania's John Dickinson, a native of Delaware, then as now an entity with an institutional interest in equal representation of each state.[61] Soon it was apparent that Franklin's talents and fame could better be employed overseas. In October 1776, Congress voted to send him to Paris, to negotiate for French support for the American Revolution. Five days later, he was on board a ship headed to Paris.

There, he was an even greater celebrity than he had been in London. With his stringy long natural hair and with a marten fur cap he had picked up on his way to Montreal, he symbolized the simplicity of the New World, concealing "a profound and crafty mind" with a subtle appreciation of a long-demonstrated capacity to shape public opinion. "The American virtuoso," writes diplomatic historian Samuel Flagg Bemis, "was the greatest man whom the New World had yet produced, and he was, with the possible exception of Voltaire, the best-known person in the world. His name, on every lip as soon as his arrival in France was announced, and his face, which soon appeared on every lady's snuff-box, served to retrieve the prestige which the American cause had lost in French public opinion by the defeat of Long Island."[62] Franklin established a cordial relationship with the French foreign minister the Comte de Vergennes and left himself and his papers open to spies both French and British. Early on, he won moral and monetary support for the American cause, and after news of the October 1777 British defeat at Saratoga reached Paris, he cemented a formal alliance.

Four years later, after the October 1781 British defeat at Yorktown, events called into play his knowledge of geography. To the unofficial British envoy Richard Oswald, a merchant and slavetrader with whom he was long acquainted, Franklin laid down in July 1782 his requirements for a peace treaty with Britain. Leading his list was an acknowledgment of American independence which his American colleagues John Jay and John Adams wanted (but later did not quite insist on) as a prerequisite for beginning negotiations, followed by a settlement of boundaries with Canada and fishing rights in the cod banks off the shore of Newfoundland. Franklin got Vergennes to agree to parallel rounds of negotiations—the United States versus Britain, France with its ally (but not America's ally) Spain versus Britain—in violation of Congress's resolution that the Americans must act only in concert with France, a requirement Jay and Adams considered ridiculous but which Franklin managed to unostentatiously avoid. This enabled Franklin to stand fast on Jay's insistence on the Mississippi River as the United States' western boundary; French attempts to suggest lines much farther east were simply brushed aside. Franklin, who by 1751 had foreseen the surge of American settlers west of the Appalachian chains, would not give up the territory that he was sure awaited them and rejected Spain's attempt 'to coop us up within the Alleghany Mountains.'" He strove to hold open the possibility of including Canada in the new union, but when that proved a nonstarter, he insisted on the provision dear to John Adams's heart, assuring American rights to the Newfoundland fisheries, including the right to dry fish on the shore. Agreement between the Americans and the British was reached in November 1782, but the final treaty was delayed until after the French persuaded the Spanish to give up on their effort to gain Gibraltar from Britain and was finally ratified only in September 1783.[63] It is a measure of Franklin's subtle persuasiveness that both the British and the French were satisfied with the settlement; only Spain, which had refused to recognize American independence, was displeased. "The historian now privileged to read documents unknown to the members of the Continental Congress can have nothing but praise for the work of their plenipotentiaries at Paris," writes the historian Bemis. "The greatest victory in the annals of American diplomacy was won at the outset by Franklin, Jay, and Adams."[64]

In September 1785, Franklin sailed across the Atlantic one last time. He was elected three times as president of Pennsylvania under the state constitution he had done so much to write, and he remodeled his house, with a larger dining room and library spacious enough for forty thousand volumes. He presided over the American Philosophical Society he had founded; wrote papers on smokeless stoves and smoking chimneys, on the design of ships and the course of the Gulf Stream; gave advice to Noah Webster on phonetic spelling, to Robert Fulton on steam engines for ships, and to his British friend Benjamin Vaughn on the toxicity of lead. He joined the antislavery society sponsored by Philadelphia Quakers and was pleased that Pennsylvania had passed a gradual abolition act and disappointed that the federal government did not do so.[65] He was naturally elected to the Constitutional Convention, which like the Second Continental Congress, but under more peaceable conditions, assembled just steps from his house. At the Convention, his dogged pursuit of the main issue and his willingness to acquiesce in the contrary and strongly held views of others were readily apparent. His comment as he emerged from the signing to a woman who asked what the document produced—"a republic, if you can keep it"—showed his own optimism but also his sense, developed perhaps during his long and frustrating stay in London, that his ability to understand how things work was superior to his ability to determine the course of public affairs. His insight into the demographic future of North America, of how the mostly empty space on his maps between the Appalachians and the Mississippi would be filled with Americans, thanks to the compounding effects of higher birth rates and economic growth, was unique among his own generation and only slowly appreciated among the next. His anticipation of the course of political events was in many respects more hopeful than prescient, but throughout a long and eventful life, he showed the capacity to reinvent himself and a willingness to defer to others openly on tactics, while continuing to pursue silently his overarching strategy. His vision of a united trans-Atlantic, English-speaking polity has only been approximated during the occasional high points of what American and British leaders have, optimistically or calculatingly, called a special relationship, but the span and scope of the influence—political, military, cultural—of the English-speaking powers has exceeded even his most optimistic visions. And his vision of the seaboard colonies as a unit, and of their people filling the lands beyond the Appalachians he negotiated, has been realized and extended by the citizens of the republic he did so much to establish, who have managed, despite continual diversity and deep divisions, to keep it.

TWO

GEORGE WASHINGTON
West by Northwest

George Washington was not always the tight-lipped icon of the Gilbert Stuart portraits or the dazzlingly uniformed general mounted on a white steed. He was once a young man with red-brown hair from an outer corner of Virginia with limited prospects, a fine horseman with a knack for meticulous diary entries and precise calculations, the younger son of the second marriage of a Virginia planter whose death when he was eleven deprived him of the English education received by his older brothers. There was no indication that his early military exploits would bring him to the attention of one British king or that his leadership of a rebellion against his successor—and his subsequent renunciation of power—would lead that monarch to hail him as "the greatest man in the world." His accomplishments and his rise to fame owe much to the territory on the map which he always considered his home, from his birth in the narrow Northern Neck between northern Virginia's two great rivers, to his boyhood home overlooking the Rappahan-nock and his mansion, Mount Vernon, overlooking the Potomac.

George Washington's career—and the American Revolution—would not have occurred as they did absent a royal land grant made almost a century before by a teenage monarch in exile. For all this land on which he was born, lived, and died, the 5.2 million acres of the Fairfax Grant, comprised the lands between the

Rappahannock and the Potomac Rivers from the Northern Neck jutting into Chesapeake Bay to the rivers' sources beyond the first and second ridges of the Allegheny Mountains. In Washington's time, this vast territory was the property of Thomas Fairfax, the 6th Baron Fairfax of Cameron, the only member of the British House of Lords to settle in the North American colonies.[1] The grant's history went back to September 1649, when King Charles II granted the land between the two rivers to Sir John Culpeper and six associates who had supported his father, King Charles I, in the English Civil War. This was a declaration with no practical effect: Charles I had been beheaded in January 1649, and Charles II was only a claimant to the throne, a teenager in exile since September 1648 in the Dutch Republic dependent on his sister Mary and her husband, the Stadtholder William II, Prince of Orange. Granting land over which he had no effective sway was one way a desperate young pretender could gain support. After Charles was restored to the throne in 1660, the grantees negotiated a twenty-one-year renewal, following which the second Lord Culpeper bought out five of the other owners, while he effectively controlled the interest of the sixth, a Culpeper cousin. Culpeper obtained a perpetual renewal of the grant in 1688 from King James II, just before his ouster later that year in the Glorious Revolution and one year before Lord Culpeper's death: a stitch in time that prevented the grant from unraveling. His widow, Margaret Culpeper, inherited his five-sixths share, while the Culpeper cousin's one-sixth was inherited in 1694 by their daughter Catherine Culpeper, who was married to Thomas the 5th Baron Fairfax. A series of deaths—of the 5th baron, his mother-in-law, and her daughter—resulted in consolidation of the ownership of the grant. Just as multiple inheritances in 1715 fell in on his precise contemporary Thomas Pelham Holles at age twenty-one, so in 1719, the multiple shares of the Fairfax Grant fell in on Thomas the 6th Baron Fairfax of Cameron at age twenty-five. As the Duke of Newcastle, Pelham Holles became the patronage master and political fixer of the Whig grandees who were the king's ministers for almost every year between 1715 and 1761, with his younger brother Henry Pelham as prime minister for eleven years and serving in that position himself as the theoretical superior of the brilliant war minister William Pitt.

Lord Fairfax had a more dilettantish career, attending Oxford, holding a commission in the Horse Guards, and contributing to Addison and Steele's pioneering journal *The Spectator*. He never married and took great delight in fox hunting. In his first years as proprietor of the Fairfax Grant, he was content to let his agent, Robert "King" Carter, sell parcels and collect quitrents. But when Carter died, in 1732, Fairfax was astounded to learn that the agent had accumulated 300,000 acres and £10,000 in cash for himself (ie.: Carter), enough to maintain a London townhouse and a landed estate in the English countryside. So Fairfax set out to make sure the estate's largesse came into his own hands. In 1732, he launched a lawsuit in England's Privy Council to overcome challenges to his ownership by Virginia authorities who coveted the rents and land sales. At the same time he sent his cousin William Fairfax to act as his agent in Virginia, and he made an extended visit to the colony himself from 1735 to 1737. After eleven years, he prevailed in the Privy Council, and in 1747, now past fifty, he returned to Virginia permanently and installed himself at the Belvoir mansion William had built on the Potomac six years before.

This was the year George Washington turned fifteen. Belvoir was three or four miles downriver from the Little Hunting Creek farm of Augustine Washington, George's father, which on his death in 1743 was inherited by his oldest son, Lawrence, four-teen years George's senior. Lawrence promptly married William Fairfax's daughter Anne and expanded his father's house, which he renamed after Edward Vernon, the admiral who commanded his Royal Navy squadron in the siege of Cartagena in 1741. Into this vicinage George Washington gravitated, away from the farm farther south where his severe mother, Mary Ball Washington, for more than forty years maintained her home on property that, under his father's will, was technically his. These lands were not at the edge of settlement, but near enough, and the Fairfax Grant extended far to the west and northwest. Its full extent was not established until a survey was conducted in 1746 by Peter Jefferson (father of three-year-old Thomas Jefferson) and Thomas Lewis, who penetrated far into what is now the westernmost point of Maryland and its border with West Virginia and there planted a Fairfax Stone at the western end of the North Branch of the Potomac. Connecting that line with the headwaters of the Rappahannock finally established the Grant's area as some 5,200,000 acres (larger than Wales) and home to some 3,400,000 people as this is written. Lord Fairfax was keen to capitalize on this enormous domain, selling out chunks or leasing farmsteads, and for that he needed someone to survey it in detail.

George Washington was then approaching his full height of more than six feet and had already become a gifted horseman whose command in the saddle was so often noted later in his life. Deprived of his elder brothers' English education, he had little formal schooling, but studied ancient rules of etiquette and mastered Euclidean geometry and studied astronomy. He kept copious notes of all his reading and activities, and in his copybooks, the "calligraphy and mathematical diagrams show conscious artistry as well as care," as his biographer James Thomas Flexner notes.[2] He was careful in his appearance, quiet and respectful of his elders, fourteen years younger than Lawrence, eight years younger than William Fairfax's son George William Fairfax, and thirty-nine years—almost two full generations—younger than Lord Fairfax. Even at that age he seemed possessed of good judgment and self-confidence when he finally felt moved to speak: habits he maintained when he reached the highest levels of military and civil office. In March 1748, when Lord Fairfax needed a surveyor to lay out farm lots in the Shenandoah Valley, on the other side of the Blue Ridge, he sent out George William Fairfax and, as his assistant, the sixteen-year-old George Washington.

Surveying was seasonal work, conducted almost entirely in cold weather months, "as you could not sight through your theodolite when leafage blocked the view." It meant trudging through uneven terrain and "tangled, gloomy forest,"[3] following Indian trails and risking encounters with unfriendly Indians, and it meant standing steady and still to make accurate measurements. This was hard work. One antiquarian describes how "'chain men' stretched iron chains with a fixed number of links between poles to measure distance, sixty-six feet at a stretch. Surveyors determined bearings with a compass, and... the line-of-sight technology required cutting a straight line through brush, swamps and virgin forests to sight the poles, so whatever hills and valleys were on the way had to be crossed rather than bypassed."[4] A surveyor needed a strong sense of direction, the ability to discern the position of the sun even with the view blocked by overhanging trees, the ability to discern faint Indian trails, traverse treacherous terrain, and then to remain immobile for extended periods. And it meant meticulously recording his work. "In his field notes," writes the scholar of George Washington's map making, "the surveyor recorded the boulders, trees or other features that defined the corners of the tract, and he produced a plat, a small map that was part of the final survey document."[5] Maps: The young George Washington was carefully imposing a mathematical order on disorderly nature, converting virgin land into economic capital, promoting civilized settlement of uncharted wilderness. "Swift appraisal of the tangible world," as Noemie Emery writes in her insightful Washington biography, "would always be his mental forte."[6]

Washington recorded his adventures in a diary titled "A Journal of My Journey over the Mountains," which described his exploits in "fording swollen rivers, fending off hungry bears, shooting wild turkey and sleeping rough under the stars." He decried one night's bed infested with "vermin, such as lice, fleas, etc.," and his relief at obtaining the next night a "good feather bed with clean sheets."[7] He happened upon a crowd of thirty Indians brandishing a single scalp, shared liquor with them, and watched their war dance. This was the first of several journeys by George Washington to the mostly unsettled land beyond the Blue Ridge: more than twenty-five years before Daniel Boone would lead settlers westward through the Cumberland Gap. In 1749, at seventeen, the Fairfaxes hired him to survey the plat of the small city of Alexandria they were founding on the Potomac, ten miles upriver from Mount Vernon, and later that year, he ventured out alone beyond the Blue Ridge to the Shenandoah Valley. In the spring of 1750, he brought his instruments there again, laying out forty-seven tracts and earning the hefty sum of £140. That fall the eighteen-year-old bought 1,459 acres on Bullskin Creek, a tributary of the sinuously winding Shenandoah River. This, followed by the purchase of another 550 acres in 1752, was the beginning of a lifelong quest: As historians Stanley Elkins and Eric McKittrick explain, Washington "was obsessed with the idea of amassing lands in the West, tremendous amounts of it, putting it all under cultivation and bringing commerce and people there.... He was fully determined that it should bring him wealth, possessions and status. He would in fact expend much time and effort on this, revealing considerable executive capacities."[8]

That summer of 1750 also brought tragedy to the Washingtons. Lawrence Washington seemed headed for a distinguished career. Home from naval service and intermarried into the Fairfax family, he was readily elected a member of Virginia's House of Burgesses, the colonial legislature, which King James II threatened to abolish before his ouster in the Glorious Revolution of 1688–89, and he was appointed adjutant general of Virginia. But he contracted a stubborn cough which turned out to be tuberculosis: A trip to England did not help, nor did a visit with George in the summer of 1750 to the warm springs across the Blue Ridge—today Berkeley Springs, West Virginia. In September 1751, Lawrence and George sailed to the sugar-producing island of Barbados. This was George's only travel outside the later limits of the United States, and there he made his first visit to a theater, which he enjoyed ever afterward, and survived an attack of smallpox, which gave him immunity from the often deadly disease. He sailed back to Virginia in January 1752, and six months later, Lawrence died at Mount Vernon at age thirty-four. Lawrence deeded Mount Vernon to his widow and child and, if they died without heirs, to George who was obviously his favorite brother. After his widow remarried months later and moved away, George rented the property from her. He also managed to get himself chosen as adjutant general for the northernmost of the four districts the House of Burgesses created. That same year Lord Fairfax moved to a new mansion, Greenway Court, which he built in the Shenandoah Valley west of the Blue Ridge near where George Washington had installed a white post, a facsimile of which still stands today.[9] In his early twenties, Washington was living in a mansion overlooking the Potomac, a dominant figure in the Fairfax Grant and a prominent figure in the colony of Virginia.

For most of what some historians call the long eighteenth century, between 1688 and 1815, Britain and France were at war or on the brink of war, at first in Europe and on adjacent waters, but later increasingly on distant oceans and in faraway lands from South Asia to North America. In the late 1740s, the War of the Austrian Succession in Europe and King George's War in North America were winding down, without any resolution of the two nations' land claims in North America. The conflict was apparent in contrasting maps. Many mid-eighteenth-century maps of North America[10] showed the British seaboard colonies confined to the narrow space between the Atlantic and the Alleghenies, with the name of New

France emblazoned over a wide expanse almost entirely empty of European settlers to the north and west. But in the British Anti-Gallican Society's 1755 map, "vibrant color exaggerates the British colonial claims to the west while the French are relegated to a small area of Canada and their 'encroachments,' as signified in anemic milky white."[11] The difference between the maps is emblematic of the conflict, sometimes open and sometimes covert, in eighteenth-century North America between these two great powers. In the first half of the century, French alliances with Indians in interior North America[12] and the voyages of *métis* fur trappers and Jesuit missionaries supported French claims to the large swath of territory west of the Allegheny Mountains connecting the French settlements along the St. Lawrence River with the Great Lakes and the Mississippi Valley south to New Orleans. In the 1750s, the French were hoping to break the Covenant Chain alliance of the Iroquois with the British and to check the westward expansion of the British colonies, whose population was then probably the fastest-growing in the world. In that effort, they dispatched small military units to build outposts in the Ohio Country in what is now western Pennsylvania.

Suddenly the Fairfax Grant, as the farthest interior extension of settlement of the British North American colonies with its recently surveyed boundaries west of the Allegheny Mountains, was on the political and religious frontier between Protestant Britain and Catholic France. Prominent Virginians took notice of France's claims to the Ohio River basin and in 1747 formed the Ohio Company to stake claims in the area. British investors included Virginia's Lieutenant Governor Robert Dinwiddie (the nominal governor was an absentee who never appeared in the colony) and the Duke of Bedford, then First Lord of the Admiralty; Virginian principals included members of the Fairfax family and their in-law Lawrence Washington. This was an enterprise of young men, looking to profit from decades of growth: The Duke of Bedford was thirty-eight, Lawrence Washington was twenty-nine, and George William Fairfax was twenty-three. In 1749, the Ohio Company obtained a royal grant of half a million acres, contingent on building a fort in the Ohio Valley and establishing at least two hundred families there.

Meanwhile, the French were pushing forward, building a chain of forts to connect Lake Erie with the Ohio valley—at Fort Presque Isle, present-day Erie, Pennsylvania; Fort Le Boeuf, fifteen miles to the south; and Fort Venango, another fifteen miles to the east, on the Allegheny River, which flowed down to the Forks of the Ohio—the confluence with the Monongahela River, which is now downtown Pittsburgh. By 1753, this looked to the highest level of the British government like a strategic offensive that must be countered with British forts on the Ohio. King George II himself ordered that a British emissary tell the French to retire from what he considered British soil. If they refused, "We do strictly command and charge you to drive them out by force of arms." Who could deliver this message? Dinwiddie, notified of the king's command in August 1753, consulted the King's Council, of which William Fairfax was a member. In October 1753, George Washington galloped to the colonial capital of Williamsburg to offer his services. He was chosen as, in the words of a London magazine, a "youth of great sobriety, diligence, and fidelity" who was also "used to the woods," one of the few Virginians who knew the western country.[13]

Washington made three ventures in three successive years into the Ohio Country beyond the Blue Ridge. This was largely unmapped territory. Washington undoubtedly studied the map prepared by Peter Jefferson (the father of Thomas Jefferson) and his colleague Joshua Fry, which they had submitted to the Governor's Council in October 1751.[14] Its eastern half was fairly accurate, but the northwestern corner, covering the Ohio River and Lake Erie, "reflected only a bare knowledge of the frontier."[15] Departing in

October, the twenty-one-year-old Washington encountered cold weather in the mountains. He rode his horse across the Allegheny River to reach the Forks of the Ohio—now Pittsburgh's Golden Triangle—which he found "extremely well situated for a fort, as it has the absolute command of both rivers."[16] Downstream on the Ohio, he met with Indian chieftains, including the Iroquois Tanacharison, known to the British as the Half King. Proceeding upstream on the Allegheny through rainy weather, he reached Fort Venango and Fort LeBoeuf, just fifteen miles from Lake Erie. There he presented Governor Dinwiddie's order to withdraw to the French commander, who did not hide his disdain. Washington's return was fraught with peril; he fell off a raft in the floe-laden Allegheny River and spent hours in the icy water before reaching the farther bank. His hand-drawn map of his route and plan of Fort LeBoeuf were forwarded to London, and his hastily written report to Dinwiddie was published in the colonies and read in London as evidence of France's dangerous aggression. Even King George II knew his name.[17]

Washington was promptly named lieutenant colonel and deputy commander of a force of Virginia militia charged with repelling the French from the Ohio Country. He set off in April 1754 with 150 recruits. Aware that several thousand French and Indian allies had set up Fort Duquesne at the Forks, he set up a camp which he named Fort Necessity at Great Meadows on Laurel Hill, the westernmost Appalachian ridge, and set out to find and attack a French force of thirty-five men. The attack resulted in the death of the French diplomat Jumonville, who had been assigned to demand that the British evacuate the Ohio valley. To his brother John Augustine, the twenty-two-year-old George Washington wrote in May, "I have heard the bullets whistle, and believe me, there is something charming in the sound." But the denouement of this campaign was anything but charming. In the Great Meadows, Washington had his men build a stockade, on what turned out to be indefensible ground when in July 1754 a larger French force, headed by Jumonville's brother, overran the fort and killed one-third of Washington's forces. Washington surrendered and, in what he later said was confusion, signed a document admitting that Jumonville was assassinated. For that he received some criticism and a downgrade of rank, in response to which he resigned his commission. But in Virginia and in London, he was praised for leading the first charge against French aggression in what came to be known in North America as the French and Indian War and in Europe as the Seven Years War. In London, the diarist Horace Walpole wrote, "The volley first by a young Virginian in the backwoods of America set the world on fire."[18]

The British were not about to concede the Ohio Country to the French, and in the next year dispatched General Edward Braddock and two regiments of redcoats to Virginia. Braddock asked Washington to serve as his *aide-de-camp* but scornfully rejected his advice to adopt the informal tactics of the French and Indians. But Braddock did agree with Washington's advice to leave behind much of his cumbersome artillery train and ordered his troops hack out only a narrow right of way under the forest canopy from Fort Cumberland in Maryland toward the Forks of the Ohio, portions of which can be seen today. There on July 9, just ten miles upriver from the Forks, on the bottomlands along the Monongahela River, Braddock's army was attacked by the French and their Indian allies, whose war whoops and shooting from behind trees disheartened and slaughtered the redcoats in their tight formations. Braddock's other aides and then the general himself were shot, while Washington, seemingly immune to the four bullets that pierced his clothes and the two that killed his horses, tended him and led the remnants of the army on an all-night retreat. Four days later, Braddock died. Washington supervised his burial in the roadway, camouflaging his grave which neither the French and Indians nor later historians have ever found.[19]

In August 1755, Washington was appointed commander with the rank of colonel of a newly formed Virginia Regiment charged with protecting the long frontier of the colony from the French and Indians. Dissatisfied with his subordination to regular British officers of inferior rank, he traveled to Philadelphia, New York, and Boston in February 1756 and again to Philadelphia in the spring of 1757. The spring of 1758 saw the arrival in Philadelphia of General John Forbes, ordered to seize Fort Duquesne from the French. Recognizing Washington as "a good and knowing officer in the back country," Forbes recruited him as an aide, while Virginia's House of Burgesses named Washington as commander of an augmented force of 2,000 men. Washington urged Forbes to follow Braddock's Road, a trail he had helped blaze, from Virginia over the mountain to the Forks, but Forbes insisted on proceeding overland entirely within Pennsylvania. Washington led one of the attacking forces that found Fort Duquesne abandoned and burned by the French, and took possession of what would become Fort Pitt and Pittsburgh. Virginia was no longer in the French line of attack, and the British victory at Québec in 1759 would lead to the end of the French empire in North America.

The year 1758, when he turned twenty-six, was a turning point in George Washington's life. His active military service was over, and he resigned his commission in November. He had already begun remodeling Mount Vernon, adding to Lawrence's mostly one-story house and buying nearby farms which ultimately totaled 8,000 acres. The voters of Frederick County in the Shenandoah Valley, site of his Bullskin Creek property, elected him in July to the House of Burgesses, where he was immediately respected for his military service and for his sound judgment, enunciated rarely and only after long hours of listening carefully to others. In March 1758, he began his courtship of Martha Dandridge Custis, reputed to be the richest young widow in Virginia. With the marriage in January 1759, biographer Ron Chernow writes, "Washington swiftly achieved the social advancement for which he had struggled in the military. Almost overnight he was thrust into top-drawer Virginia society and could dispense with the servility that had sometimes marked his dealings with social superiors."[20] As he turned twenty-seven years old, he had survived smallpox, pleurisy, malaria, dysentery, and hundreds of bullets aimed at his direction, and he was embarking on what turned out to be his longest period, nearly seventeen years, of domestic tranquility at his beloved Mount Vernon— legally his property when Anne Fairfax Washington Lee died in March 1761. George and Martha Washington had a large circle of acquaintances—Mount Vernon hosted dozens for dinner and on extended stays—but Washington himself "lacked a large number of close friends or confidants" and "didn't have many true intimates," as Chernow writes.[21] Earlier in his life, he had mostly deferred to his elders and superiors. Now, with few contemporaries and with hard-earned respect, he tended to maintain his customary silence, listening to others' opinions and keeping his judgments to himself until they were fully formed. "The objective," writes Chernow, "was to learn the maximum about other people's thoughts while revealing the minimum about your own."[22]

Did he appreciate that he had played a key part, one recognized explicitly by King George II, in setting off a world war? Did he think that the tide of events had passed him by, leaving him to the pursuit of domestic happiness? Did he appreciate that he was quickly singled out by fellow burgesses as "one of those young men of high ability placed on important committees, even chairmanships, relatively soon after their first appearance in the House?"[23] Did he sense he might have still a greater destiny? Unusually for a colonial leader, he had traveled over the mountain barriers. His trips to protest his subordination to British military officers had brought him to Pennsylvania,

New York, and Massachusetts during 1756 and 1757. He had become acquainted with the different cultures and situations of the Northern seaboard colonies. But he had never traveled any significant distance south of Virginia's southern border, and he remained rooted in the Fairfax Grant and the lands farther west and northwest which he had begun traversing at age eighteen. As he remodeled Mount Vernon, he moved the door from the east front, where his sailor brother Lawrence had it overlooking the Potomac, to the west front, looking out over past his 8,000 acres to the vast expanse of Fairfax lands and the pathway leading west by northwest to the Forks of the Ohio.

In October 1770, he set off on a nine-week tour of the Ohio Country, from the Forks of the Ohio, where he met an Indian chief who remembered how he had seemed impervious to bullets fifteen years before and, as he recorded in his diary, "spoke of a fine piece of land and beautiful place for a house, and in order to give me a more lively idea of it, chalked out the situation upon his deer skin."[24] He proceeded down the Ohio River to the junction with the Great Kanawha River in what is now West Virginia. There he purchased land, just as he had bought the 200-acre plot at the Great Meadows including the site of his defeat at Fort Necessity. He "remained attentive to the commercial prospects of this sparsely populated region," as Ron Chernow notes, retaining timber and mineral rights from the farmers who leased his lands, and noted that "the coal seems to be of the very best kind, burning freely and abundance of it."[25] This Tidewater Virginia farmer seemed alert to the possibility that the lands west and northwest of the Fairfax Grant would become America's coal-and-iron industrial heartland—and to the possibility that the Potomac River, breaking through one after another of the Appalachian ridges, could be the vital link between the seaboard lands and the vast interior of the Ohio Country and beyond.

★   ★   ★

When George Washington arrived at the Continental Congress in May 1775 wearing the blue and buff uniform of the Fairfax County militia, he was making a point, and one beyond just his fondness for elaborate and carefully fitted clothing. The other Virginia delegates—Peyton Randolph, Edmund Pendleton, and Benjamin Harrison—were all older men, but even among his own generation no one at the Congress had anything like the military experience of the forty-three-year-old Washington. "Colonel Washington appears at Congress in his uniform," John Adams wrote, "and by his great experience and abilities in military matters is of much service to us."[26] The Congress was already aware of the clash between British soldiers and Massachusetts militia men at Lexington and Concord on April 19—"the shot heard 'round the world," in Ralph Waldo Emerson's words[27]—and in late May, members heard that British troops led by three British generals had just landed in Boston Harbor. On June 14, the Congress authorized ten companies from Pennsylvania, Maryland, and Virginia to march north and support the New Englanders. The next day, nominated by John Adams of Massachusetts and elected by unanimous vote, George Washington was chosen as the commander of what was grandly styled the Continental Army.

Colonial Americans were very much aware of the different origins and character—what the historian David Hackett Fischer would two centuries later in his book *Albion's Seed* call the folkways—of the various North American colonies. The members of the Continental Congress were aware as well of differing attitudes toward the revolutionary cause. Massachusetts in particular and New England in general were adamantly opposed to what their people regarded as British tyranny, and in June, before Washington managed to get to Cambridge, the rebels, though defeated, had shown they could inflict severe losses on the redcoats at Bunker Hill. The Virginia elite, as indicated by the Burgesses' choices for delegate at the Continental Congress, was solidly in the revolutionary camp, as were the leaders of its Chesapeake Bay neighbor Maryland. Pennsylvania, despite or perhaps because of the political quietude of its many Quakers, was supporting the Congress that was meeting in its State House, now known as Independence Hall.

But Loyalists or Tories—supporters of the British Crown and opponents of the rebellion—were thick on the ground elsewhere. "How many loyalists were there? They have been estimated at the highest of half the population: perhaps one-third is nearer the mark," writes the British military historian Piers Mackesy.[28] The colonies, he argues, were split on ethnic lines. "The Tories were weakest where the colonists were of the purest English stock. In New England they may have been scarcely a tenth of the population; in the South a quarter or third; but in the Middle Colonies including New York perhaps a half." New England was indeed populated almost entirely by descendants of settlers from England, with large numbers from East Anglia, whose rigid principles and intolerance of religious dissent repelled others. Pennsylvania, whose Quaker proprietor, William Penn, actively recruited German-speaking pietists, was ethnically more diverse. New York, founded by the Dutch, with much of its land still owned by Dutch-ancestry patroons, its polyglot population of Huguenots and Jews in New York City, and its British-allied Iroquois federation still occupying the terrain west of Albany, was even more diverse and proved especially problematic in the revolutionary cause.

After Washington took command in Cambridge, he moved quickly up the learning curve in dealing with prickly New England Yankees. His artillery commander, the Boston bookseller Henry Knox, hauled fifty-nine cannon from Fort Ticonderoga north of Albany on oxen-driven sledges over the Berkshire mountains to

Boston Harbor, where its positioning on the South Boston peninsula by Washington in March 1776 prompted the British troops to evacuate unremittingly hostile Massachusetts, never to return. The British moved their dominant navy with 10,000 sailors and some 32,000 British and Hessian troops to New York,[29] where Washington's attempts to dislodge them utterly failed, forcing humiliating retreats—lucky escapes—from Brooklyn and Upper Manhattan. But Washington also fought back. As British forces fanned out over New Jersey, he launched surprise attacks in Trenton on Christmas night and Princeton in the first week of 1777. Thenceforward, Washington's course was to avoid major battle but to retain the capacity to hinder and harass British forces. He was at some disadvantage because the British had superior maps, particularly the Charles Blaskowitz and Claude Joseph Sauthier maps of New York,[30] while Washington depended on dated sources like the 1762 Rocque map of North America[31] and maps commercially printed in Britain and forwarded by French purchasers. And so, "In every locale, Washington sought detailed maps that could provide more information than the more general published maps in his collection."[32]

Both sides' leaders saw New York as pivotal. The British sent General John Burgoyne south from Montreal to join Sir William Howe moving up the Hudson from New York City, with a view toward separating reprobate New England from the rest of the colonies. That failed after Howe set out on a protracted campaign to capture Philadelphia, which finally succeeded in September 1777, and after Burgoyne was defeated and surrendered at Saratoga in October 1777. By that point it seemed clear that Britain would never regain New England. This opened the way for Benjamin Franklin to inveigle the French government to sign an alliance with the United States in February 1778, which prompted both Britain and France to fight for their lucrative Caribbean sugar colonies. And it prompted Howe to evacuate Philadelphia in June 1778 and return to New York.

For George Washington, New York remained, in John Adams's words, "the Nexus of the Northern and Southern Colonies, a kind of Key to the whole Continent."[33] Early on, it seemed clear to Washington that New York would not embrace the revolutionary cause. As James Thomas Flexner describes his thinking in May 1775, "New York, formerly considered a Tory stronghold, was said now to be 'zealous' in the patriot cause, 'but, as I never entertained a very high opinion of your sudden repentances, I will suspend my opinion till the arrival of the [British] troops there.'"[34] For seven years, from his flight across the Hudson in November 1776 until the British left in November 1783, New York "would be a festering sore in Washington's side."[35] After rallying his troops from their 1777–78 winter quarters in Valley Forge, just outside Philadelphia, Washington stationed his headquarters and his forces in New Jersey and the Hudson Valley of New York. The aim was to preserve a land connection, however tenuous, between New England and Pennsylvania and, farther south, Maryland and Virginia, and to be positioned to take advantage of any opportunity to move the British out of New York.

For New York City, with its polyglot population, its Dutch heritages of support of commerce and tolerance but also indifference to principle, in this as in later wars was skeptical of the national purpose. New York City was Loyalist and resistant to Washington during the Revolution, reluctant to ratify the Constitution in 1788 (the Federalist papers were written specifically to persuade reluctant New Yorkers), Copperhead and opposed to Lincoln during the Civil War, and the prime locus of skepticism in the early days of the Cold War, when almost one-half the votes cast nationally for the Soviet-supported Henry Wallace in 1948 were cast in the five boroughs of New York City.

Washington's fixation on New York became apparent when the British embarked on their southern strategy. Their goal was to detach from the revolutionary cause Georgia and the Carolinas, in whose coastal regions whites were vastly outnumbered by slaves, and whose upcountry counties were said to be full of Loyalists and of Indians who had reason to consider the British more sympathetic than the Americans. In December 1778, a small British force captured the Georgia port of Savannah and then took most of Georgia. In May 1780, a larger British force assembled to capture Charleston, the only significant city south of Baltimore, and took it together with 5,500 Continental soldiers. What followed were a series of quick raids, pitched battles, local massacres, bloody reprisals in the upcountry Carolina—the most vicious fighting in the Revolutionary War. Though all this, Washington rejected advice to send large numbers of troops to the South. He dismissed the British capture of Savannah as "certain to 'contribute very little'" to the British war effort. After the losses at Charleston and Camden, he said that the American goal was to "oblige them to ... relinquish a part of what they now hold." As military historian John Ferling writes, "Judging from his correspondence, Washington was only dimly aware of what was occurring in the South Carolina back country in the second half of 1780." In contrast, he goes on, "Since the arrival of the first French fleet under d'Estaing two years earlier, Washington had fixated on New York, intransigently refusing to move his army from its shadow, lest he lose the opportunity to attempt its conquest should another French squadron happen by." At his three-day meeting with the French ground forces commander Rochambeau in Wethersfield, Connecticut, in May 1781, Washington once again "intransigently insisted on a campaign to retake New York," to which Rochambeau seemed to agree, while concealing from Washington the fact that Admiral de Grasse had been ordered to bring his French fleet up from the Caribbean that fall, and in his report to de Grasse ordering him to sail not to New York Harbor but to Chesapeake Bay.[36] Only in July, while he and Rochambeau were on reconnaissance pondering an invasion of New York, the city's enemy's continuing strong position there and the news that Cornwallis, the British commander in the South, was headed to the Chesapeake evidently changed Washington's mind and he suddenly decided that the best course was "an operation to the Southward."[37] He and Rochambeau, after parading their troops ostentatiously in New Jersey opposite New York, then suddenly headed south, where boats at the head of the Chesapeake waited to ferry them south toward Yorktown. There in October, Cornwallis, hemmed in by the French fleet and the French and Continental armies, surrendered Britain's last serious fighting force in the seaboard states.

Washington's apparent indifference to the British campaign in the South, and his continuing preoccupation with capturing New York, suggests that he was pondering what the new nation would look like after the war. Even as he maintained his tactics keeping his Continental forces together and harassing the British troops, he was aware that the results of military action could determine the nation's metes and bounds. When he took command in May 1775, it was not obvious what these would be. As the leftist historian Alan Taylor points out in *American Revolutions*, by no means all of Britain's colonies in the Western Hemisphere supported the revolution. The slaveholders of the sugar colonies of Jamaica and Barbados did not want to surrender preferred access to the British market and defense against slave rebellions. The Continental Congress's authorization of expeditions against Montréal and Québec proved unsuccessful; the province's French speakers were content with Britain's Quebec Act of 1774, which let them preserve their French language and culture and the power of the Jesuit order. Nova Scotia, without a legislature of its own and dependent on the Royal Navy, wasn't interested either, and neither were the sparsely settled East and West Floridas. By 1778, the British knew that New England was lost, and by 1779, they sensed that the chances that the middle colonies from Pennsylvania to Virginia might return to the empire were low but above zero so long as New York stayed loyally in British hands. In addition, they evidently hoped that the Carolinas and Georgia, whose coastal economies so nearly resembled those of their sugar-producing bonanzas in the Caribbean, could be separated and saved for Britain or a pliant European power, as indeed Florida was until 1819; and Washington was evidently less troubled by this possibility than by the possibility of losing a chance to take New York. The South Carolina and Georgia low country along the seacoast was, demographically, not much different from Barbados and Jamaica: the 1790 Census found that only 24 percent of their residents were whites and 75 percent were black slaves. Barbados may have been an attractive model for the original settlers of Charleston; it was not George Washington's.

This seems to have been connected with his changing attitudes toward slavery. He had inherited his first three slaves at age eleven, when his father died, and as a young man he seems to have taken the institution for granted. He lamented his slaves' laziness and, while deploring flogging, sometimes ordered multiple lashes. But these conventional attitudes evidently changed in the revolutionary years, though as usual he mostly kept his own counsel. After his marriage to Martha Custis and his purchase of new lands, he purchased new slaves as well. But as he reduced the production of tobacco, which had been destroying the fertility of so much soil in Tidewater Virginia, and instead planted wheat, oats, and barley, his slaves had significantly less work to do, even as their numbers rose through natural increase. He stopped buying new slaves in 1772, the year he turned forty, and he refused to break up slave families, as so many Virginia planters and executors of decedents' or bankrupts' estates did. He was "tireless in his medical treatment of slaves" and, by 1775, made a regular practice of inoculating them against smallpox. He "allowed selected slaves to keep firearms and hunt wild game in the woods" and allowed slaves to till their own garden plots, keep poultry, and sell eggs, chickens, fruit, and vegetables. On Sunday mornings, he permitted them to travel with passes to Alexandria and peddle their wares in the open marketplace.[38]

Washington's long experience of surveying the Fairfax Grant and traversing the Ohio Country to the west and northwest took him to territory not so obviously adaptable to intensive slave labor as the Tidewater lands in the milder climate of the Chesapeake. Leases on the lands he accumulated and managed to lease in the Upper Potomac, the Ohio Country, and the Great Kanawha were taken up and worked mostly by yeoman farmers, with few or no slaves. He was evidently not dismayed when states—Pennsylvania in 1780, Connecticut and Rhode Island in 1784—enacted laws for the gradual abolition of slavery, when Massachusetts and New Hampshire courts in that decade ruled slavery invalid under their state constitutions, or when the Continental Congress voted in July 1787 to abolish slavery in the Northwest Territory across the Ohio River. By the 1780s, Washington was pursuing his dream of making the Potomac River and a parallel canal the major transportation artery between the Atlantic Coast and the vast interior. Joel Achenbach, whose book *The Grand Idea* is centered on this quest, sees the point clearly. "When Washington insisted that the country had a particular need to bind 'the Middle States with the Country immediately back of them,' he showed not only his provincial thinking (for this was the terrain he'd spent much of his life surveying) but also his latitudinal observation. His eyes read a map from east to west. He thought horizontally. He viewed the East-West political divisions (particularly those more or less along the 40° parallel) as the most threatening to the Union. He had little interest in the migration of Georgia farmers into Choctaw territory, for example. As if by reflex, he tended to look more or less due west from Mount Vernon."[39]

This vision is apparent in Washington's letter to the Marquis de Lafayette on his plans after Yorktown. "I have it in contemplation, however, to make a tour through all the eastern states, thence into Canada; thence up the St. Lawrence, and through the Lakes to Detroit; thence to lake Michigan by land or water; thence through the western country by the river Illinois, to the river Mississippi, and down the same to New Orleans; thence to Georgia by way of Pensacola; and thence through the two Carolinas home."[40] His geographical focus was similar when he contemplated the defense of the new nation, as the author of *George Washington's America: A Biography Through His Maps* makes clear: "Washington correctly anticipated that the border posts in the Northwest would be a zone of contention with the British after the war. He also recommended establishing posts in the following locations, from east to west and north to south: the Penobscot or St. Croix River; the northern end of Lake Champlain; the Connecticut River near the 45° parallel; Ticonderoga; Niagara; Oswego; Fort Erie; Detroit; the straits between Lake Huron and Lake Superior; Fort Pitt; the mouth of the Scioto; the mouth of the Kentucky River; the mouth of the Ohio River; the heights at the mouth of the Illinois River; and on the frontiers of the Carolinas and Georgia."[41]

When Washington took the oath of office in New York in April 1789, the United States still lacked control of many of these lands. The British, citing American failure to compensate Tories for property losses, still occupied what were referred to as the Northwest posts, key forts including Detroit and Vincennes. Indian tribes, many of which had supported the British during the Revolutionary War, had effective control of most lands north of the Ohio River and some in western New York state. Settlers from Virginia and North Carolina had made their way in large numbers to the Bluegrass country of Kentucky around Lexington and to the Cumberland River valley of Tennessee around Nashville, while the territory running south to the disputed boundaries of East and West Florida was Indian country, and Spain, owner of the Louisiana Territory, was blocking Americans from navigation on the Mississippi River and access to the port of New Orleans. Nor were the nation's northeastern boundaries firmly established. Vermont still maintained its claim to be an independent republic and would relinquish that only when granted statehood in 1791, and the British and Americans disagreed on the northern boundary of Massachusetts's Maine territory and would remain so for more than fifty years.[42]

For the moment, the new president concentrated on setting up a government, keeping tight reins over a cabinet with leading members—Alexander Hamilton, Thomas Jefferson—whose brilliance would not be exceeded in the two-hundred-plus years to come. Based in the temporary capital of New York, the city whose capture has been his tantalizing and unreachable goal from 1777 to 1781, Washington was familiar from his Revolutionary War service with nearby New Jersey and Pennsylvania and from his travels homeward with Delaware and Maryland. But after a stubborn illness threatened his life in the spring of 1789, he decided to make personal inspection of well-settled American states, starting off in October 1789 by journeying northward and visiting Connecticut, Massachusetts, and New Hampshire, crossing the Piscataqua River to Kittery in Maine, which was still part of Massachusetts. He set sail for Newport and Providence, Rhode Island, in August 1790, after it had ratified the Constitution earlier in that year. Only in the next year, in April 1791, did he head south from Mount Vernon and visit, for the first time, North Carolina, South Carolina, and Georgia.[43]

The contrast with the northern colonies struck him deeply. "Early in his presidential term he had rolled his way by carriage across New England," writes Joel Achenbach, "marveling at the industriousness of the Yankees, their rapid adoption of manufacturing, and the cleanliness and bustle of their towns. But he would not find such sights in the South, a region of desolate fields, shabby homes, scenes of poverty. He would be taken aback. To a degree he couldn't quite grasp, he had become, over the years, less and less of a southerner."[44] The trip was hectic and may have strengthened Washington's existing distaste for the South and for its peculiar institution of slavery. The historian Henry Adams cites a letter Washington wrote in 1796 to the British agronomist (and coiner of the word "statistics") Sir John Sinclair. He started off praising the Shenandoah Valley, where he had first purchased land, as "the garden of America." Not so the lands farther south. "The uplands of North and South Carolina and Georgia are not dissimilar in soil," he wrote, "but as they approach the lower latitudes are less congenial to wheat, and are supposed to be proportionately more unhealthy. Towards the seaboard of all the Southern States, and farther south more so, the lands are low, sandy, and unhealthy; for which reason I shall say little more concerning them, for as I should not choose to be an inhabitant of them myself, I ought not to say anything that would induce others to be so."[45]

As Adams explained, "For this inferiority, he suggested, among other reasons the explanation that Pennsylvania had made laws for the gradual abolition of slavery, and he declared nothing more certain than that Virginia must adopt similar laws at a period not remote." As president, Washington avoided negative references to slavery, if only to avoid ruptures with southern members of Congress. Personally, he and Martha Washington were angered when, as they prepared to leave Philadelphia for Mount Vernon in 1797, their household slaves ran away, and they took steps to bring them back.[46] Yet in his retirement, Washington spent considerable time and trouble in freeing his slaves in his will and arranging for those owned by Martha Washington to be freed as well. Alas, Virginia did not follow his example. Its 1782 manumission law facilitating the freeing of slaves was revised in 1806 to make manumission more difficult and to require freed slaves to leave the state. The banning of the international slave trade, taking effect at the first moment permissible under the Constitution in 1808, had the tragic result of making Virginia a major exporter of slaves, to the cotton-growing lands farther south and west.

★ ★ ★

Just as Washington looked at his maps during the Revolutionary War and concluded that he must concentrate on recapturing New York, the essential geographic link between patriotic New England and the patriotic Chesapeake colonies, so as president he could look at the map at the boundaries established by the treaty ending the war in 1783 and see how substantial parts of the territory that were theoretically part of the United States were actually under the control or malign influence of America's colonial neighbors, Britain to the north and Spain to the west and south. Establishing full sovereignty was the primary task of his foreign policy and diplomacy well into his second term in office. Washington concentrated on advancing effective American control in the Northwest Territory, where British forces remained in possession of frontier posts it had agreed to give up in 1783, and Indians with whom the British were in contact refused to recognize US authority. In contrast, he did little about exerting control in the territory south of Kentucky and west of Georgia, lands occupied by Indians and subject to influence by Spain, which controlled East and West Florida and the Mississippi River port of New Orleans. Washington's initial offensives against Indians in the Northwest were unsuccessful. A small force under Josiah Harmar was defeated near modern Fort Wayne, Indiana, in October 1790, and in November 1791, a larger force, under Northwest Territory Governor Arthur St. Clair, was defeated, with many massacred, about one hundred miles north of the frontier settlement of Cincinnati.[47] In the Southwest, there was no major military offensive in the 1790s and settlements were limited to small clusters in east Tennessee, around Nashville and in scattered parts of Georgia.

But only small numbers of Americans in that decade were affected by Indian, British, or Spanish threats on the frontier. Many more Americans were affected by policies affecting trade with major European powers, primarily its recent enemy Britain but also its recent ally France. Secretary of State Thomas Jefferson, in his ardent and naïve enthusiasm about the French Revolution, beginning with the storming of the Bastille in July 1789 when he was still the American minister in Paris, and his ally Congressman James Madison, who strove unsuccessfully to pass lower tariffs on French goods, wished to continue a French alliance and maintained that the 1778 treaty was still in effect. Alexander Hamilton, whose financial policies were starting to produce an upswing in trade and perceptible economic growth, argued that trade with Britain would always be much larger than trade with France. As the French Revolution progressed to the Terror predicted by the British parliamentarian Edmund Burke, relations between the two nations, which had been military rivals over much of the previous century, deteriorated. After the execution of Louis XVI in January 1793, Revolutionary France declared war on royalist Britain and Spain in February. Washington, after weighing contrary advice from Jefferson and Hamilton, issued in April a Neutrality Proclamation, a document passed over quickly in many accounts but which was one of the few acts he singled out for specific mention by name in his Farewell Address in September 1796. Washington had fought the French in the 1750s and the British in the 1770s and 1780s; he seems not to have entirely trusted either power and he blanched at what he called the "self-created" Democratic Societies that sprang up, with the encouragement of the undiplomatic ambassador Citizen Genêt, to support France against Britain. He understood from Hamilton the economic importance of trade with Britain, and he knew as well that Britain and Spain were the two nations threatening American frontiers, as France had threatened British colonial frontiers at the start of his career.

The Proclamation effectively rendered the 1778 treaty with the royalist regime of France a dead letter and "leaned toward Great Britain," argues historian Robert Wiebe. "Washington, no partisan of Britain, inclined as he did because of his anxiety for the nation's [north]western territory, a teetering appendage that the United States could never defend against Britain and its Spanish ally."[48] But, as he argued to Jefferson when he was leaving office and returning to Monticello in December 1793, he sought to change Britain's behavior, including not just its retention of the Northwest posts but also its trade restrictions and seizures of merchant ships in the West Indies. For that purpose, in April 1794 he appointed Chief Justice John Jay, who had been foreign affairs minister for eight years in the Confederation government, as a special envoy to Britain to negotiate a new treaty. He also pressed his aggressive military commander in the Northwest Territory, "Mad Anthony" Wayne, who won a decisive battle against British-supported Indians at Fallen Timbers, near present-day Toledo, Ohio, in August 1794.[49] Negotiations then began in which Indians ceded large expanses of land in Ohio and Indiana in the August 1795 Treaty of Greenville. In August 1795, when Jay was trying to negotiate with British officials who had little time for American issues, Washington ordered minister to Britain Thomas Pinckney to travel from London to Spain to negotiate a treaty. Under the previous king, Charles III, recognized as one of eighteenth-century Europe's "enlightened despots,"[50] Spain had been a vigorous power, protective of its cordoned-off empire, but his successor, Charles IV, who succeeded him in 1788, was a less determined monarch, delegating diplomacy to his young minister (and reputed lover of the queen) Manuel Godoy. Pinckney, a Charleston aristocrat, spent months traipsing after the royal household in multiple palaces and finally gained agreement with Godoy in October 1795 on the Treaty of San Lorenzo, which granted three major concessions. Spain agreed to recognize the southern boundary of the United States at the 31° parallel rather than farther north at the junction of the Yazoo River, granted full navigation rights on the Mississippi, and allowed Kentuckians and Tennesseeans floating their agricultural products down the river to deposit their goods in New Orleans.[51] Pinckney's Treaty, as it was known, was so obviously advantageous to the United States that it was ratified without controversy, and Washington did not feel obliged to send large numbers of troops to the southern and southwestern frontiers.

The next month, in November 1794, Jay reached agreement with the British on the Treaty of Amity, Commerce and Navigation, in which the British again promised—effectively, this time, after Fallen Timbers and the August 1795 Treaty of Greenville— to evacuate the Northwest posts and provided limited access for American merchant ships in the British West Indies. Jay's Treaty, its terms kept secret, was ratified by just the required two-thirds vote in the Senate in June 1795, and James Madison's move to oppose appropriations needed to carry out its terms were defeated in March 1796. At first initially unpopular, opinion shifted in its failure as frontier areas from the west end of New York through western Pennsylvania and Virginia came to appreciate its removal of threats of British and Indian violence. The success of the treaty also owed something to external factors. America's commercial trade, mainly with Britain, had been mildly increasing when Washington appointed Jay in April 1794; when Madison's final attack on the treaty flagged in April 1796, it had nearly doubled.[52] During the same period, developments in France—the overthrow of Robespierre's Jacobin regime, the installation of the cynical and corrupt Directory government— sapped the enthusiasm of Jefferson's and Madison's Republican followers. Wayne's military victory at Fallen Timbers and the Treaty of Greenville had opened up settlement in the Northwest Territory, with "the towns of Cleveland, Dayton, Youngstown,

Chillicothe, and Conneaut...spring[ing] into existence in a manner of months, threatening to match, as in time it did and more, the fast-growing populations of slaveholding Kentucky south of the Ohio River." Populating the Ohio Country, long an objective of Washington, was being accomplished, though in a less orderly manner than he had hoped.[53] There was a shift in the balance of the partisan politics, which every major public figure lamented and prosecuted lustily. Just after the elections of 1794, Madison's Republicans seemed to have a secure majority in the House of Representatives; by the fall of 1796, that majority had evaporated and the Federalists would win a clear majority in the elections for the next Congress. It had come time for George Washington to retire, as he had hoped to do after his first term. No longer surrounded by Thomas Jefferson, who resigned in December 1793, and with whom he never again had friendly relations, or by Alexander Hamilton, who resigned in January 1795 but continued to advise the president, Washington continued to lament "the baleful effects of the spirit of party," as he put it in his September 1796 Farewell Address,[54] but he indicated his partiality for one side over the other. He lamented also "a passionate attachment of one Nation for another," and in his own mind had leaned no more toward Britain than to France. "In relation to the still subsisting war in Europe, my Proclamation of the 22d of April 1793, is the index to my Plan," he wrote. "After deliberate examination, with the aid of the best lights I could obtain, I was well satisfied that our country, under all the circumstances of the case, had a right to take, and was bound in duty and interest to take, a neutral position." The United States was an infant nation struggling for legitimacy and survival amid a world war between the two great powers of Europe, maritime Britain and revolutionary France, a war that raged for all but a few months of the two decades between February 1793 and June 1815. It was a major fear keeping the United States reasonably neutral and out of risk of destruction during this period—especially during the first several years, when this conflict appeared to be an ideological struggle between a republic that many believed was based on American ideals and a limited monarchy that shared cultural roots and trade ties with English-speaking and maritime Americans.

Washington insisted that he maintained neutrality not only as to warring foreign nations but also to different parts of the nation. "The name of American, which belongs to you, in your national capacity, must always exalt the just pride of Patriotism, more than any appellation derived from local discriminations," he wrote in the Farewell Address. He went on to cite, at some length and with obvious defensiveness, Pinckney's Treaty as evidence of his regional neutrality. "The inhabitants of our western country have lately had a useful lesson on this head; they have seen, in the negotiation by the Executive, and in the unanimous ratification by the Senate, of the treaty with Spain, and in the universal satisfaction at that event, throughout the United States, a decisive proof how unfounded were the suspicions propagated among them of a policy in the General Government and in the Atlantic States unfriendly to their interests in regard to the Mississippi." More briefly, even offhandedly, he refers to the not unanimously approved Jay's Treaty. "They have been witnesses to the formation of two treaties, that with Great Britain, and that with Spain, which secure to them every thing they could desire, in respect to our foreign relations, toward confirming their prosperity."

But he protested too much. As during the Revolutionary War and in the years immediately afterward, so in his presidency Washington was much more engaged with the states to the north of the Ohio and the Potomac than those to the south. In the unfulfilled plans for a national tour that he shared with Lafayette, and just as in the military expeditions he authorized as president, he was continually referring often and with considerable specificity to the lands north of Mount Vernon, while remaining hazy or silent about those farther south. To Lafayette, he fastened on sites that would become critical nodes in industrial America: Buffalo, Detroit, Pittsburgh, the Mackinac Straits. This was a United States whose expansion would not provide a greater theater for slavery but one in which slavery might be placed on the road to extinction. The Virginian who had taken slavery for granted in the middle of the eighteenth century was looking forward to its decline in the nineteenth century, whose dawn he missed seeing by just a few days. Thomas Jefferson recalled that Edmund Randolph, who served in Washington's administration as attorney general and secretary of state, said that Washington once admitted "that if there were ever to be a division between the North and the South, Washington would align himself with the North."[55] That is consistent with his mental map of the nation of which he was the uniquely important Founding Father, and with what Chernow describes as his "life-long fascination with westward expansion" that made him "the founder best able to visualize the ample contours of the American future, making the notion of a continental empire more than a mere abstraction."[56]

It is not a great leap to say that Washington's mental map closely resembles the map of the states that provided the manpower and materiel that enabled Abraham Lincoln to suppress the Rebellion. It was a nation in which New England was cemented to other Northern states by a New York whose Upstate was settled by the westward onrush of New England Yankees, who kept New York state faithful to the Union despite the dubious loyalties of the always commercial and tolerant, but never unduly principled metropolis of New York City. The Yankee westward rush had continued across Ohio and Illinois, Michigan and Iowa; railroads running roughly parallel with Washington's canal linked the seaboard ports with the burgeoning industries of Pittsburgh and the river metropolises of Cincinnati and Louisville and St. Louis—tiny settlements in Washington's lifetime but which by Lincoln's ranked among the nation's largest cities; the Great Lakes, which Washington had approached within fifteen miles in 1753, were now lined with cities like Cleveland and Detroit, Chicago and Milwaukee, not yet so large as the river cities but dedicated even more unreservedly to the Union, as commemorated by the Soldiers and Sailors Monuments in Cleveland's Public Square and Detroit's Campus Martius. Virginia had seceded, but Washington's own Alexandria and Mount Vernon, located near the capital he had personally located on his beloved Potomac, remained Union territory, as did Arlington Cemetery, established by Lincoln on land once owned by Martha Washington's grandson George Washington Parke Custis. Much of the 50,000 acres Washington had accumulated and then dispersed in his will were in Pennsylvania or the fifty-five counties which formed West Virginia in 1863, facing across the Ohio River the five free states and a sliver of the sixth formed from the free soil of the Northwest Territory. Just as the military strategist George Washington strived to capture New York City to connect New England with the lands just to the west, so the surveyor and land speculator George Washington looked west by northwest from the front door of his beloved Mount Vernon to the continental nation he did more than anyone else to establish.

THREE

THOMAS JEFFERSON

From the Top of the Little Mountain

"Illustrated with A MAP, including the States of Virginia, Maryland, Delaware and Pennsylvania." So reads the title page of the first English language edition, and the first edition carrying the author's name, of the only book Thomas Jefferson ever wrote, *Notes on the State of Virginia*, published in London in July 1787. It is a peculiar book, begun in 1781, the final year Jefferson's terms as governor of Virginia, when he barely escaped British attack. It was fashioned not as a narrative or an argument but in response to a series of questions propounded to the Continental Congress by a French diplomat. Its first chapter is a dry description of Virginia's boundaries, and the text contains tables of the Productions Mineral, Vegetable and Animal of Virginia; the Birds of Virginia; the county militias of Virginia; the Indian Tribes of Virginia; and an eighteen-page list of Histories, Memorials, and State-Papers of Virginia. It begins, importantly, with a map, one that Jefferson declared was of more value than the entire book, and one that was certainly of great personal value to the author.[1] For it was a map engraved by Samuel J. Neele of London, based on Jefferson's revisions of a map drawn by his father, Peter Jefferson, and his surveying partner, Joshua Fry, in 1751. Its inclusion was not just an act of filial devotion, for the Jefferson-Fry map was, in fact, the most frequently used map from its publication up through the American

Revolution. It shows with some precision the shores of the broad rivers flowing into Chesapeake Bay, where boats could dock and load tons of tobacco for sale in Britain; it shows the parallel ridges of Appalachian mountains, "not solitary and scattered confusedly over the face of the country," as Jefferson wrote, but "disposed in ridges one behind another, running nearly parallel with the sea-coast" from Pennsylvania southwest through Virginia to the North Carolina line.[2]

Peter Jefferson traversed much of this territory on horseback and on foot. He was "a man of huge stature and legendary strength,"[3] of minor gentry stock with a small inheritance of horses, livestock, and two slaves. His wife was a daughter of the large and prominent Randolph family. He moved to virgin land upriver from Richmond, where the land, "when viewed from one of its many eminences, appeared as a vast forest, interspersed with plantations four or five miles apart and resembling small villages."[4] It remained wild enough as he developed his land that wolf bounties—70 pounds of tobacco for a young wolf, double for an old one—were issued at sessions of the county court.[5] Peter Jefferson amassed several hundred undeveloped acres on the Rivanna River in Albemarle County near what became the county seat of Charlottesville. He rose to be country sheriff, county lieutenant, a member of the House of Burgesses, even as he remained an active surveyor, accustomed to traverse undeveloped forested land, riding "over successive ranges of mountains that were 'prodigiously full of fallen timber and ivey,' up and down precipices where the horses slipped and fell and through swamps of laurel which appeared impenetrable."[6] In 1746, he and Joshua Fry were employed to locate and connect the sources of the Potomac and Rappahannock Rivers, the western end of the 5.2 million-acre domain of Lord Fairfax that stretched east to Chesapeake Bay. Their journey out and back over heavily forested lands took seven weeks[7] and was capped by their implantation of the Fairfax Stone, the successor of which can still be glimpsed at the headwaters of North Branch of the Potomac River in what is now West Virginia, near the western tip of Maryland.

Thomas Jefferson never ventured that far west. His earliest recollection, he wrote, "was of being caried on a pillow by a mounted slave,"[8] and he grew up in comfortable manor houses. Though his father had little or no formal education, he insisted on a classical education for his son, who readily acquiesced, and delighted in learning Latin and Greek, playing the violin, and reading history. Early deaths were common in the Jefferson family, and Peter Jefferson in 1757 died at age forty-nine, when Thomas was fourteen. To this oldest son, he left half his estate and made a point of bequeathing him his books, surveying instruments, cherry-tree desk and bookcase, and his most valuable slave.[9] They were appreciated: Thomas did not inherit his father's taste for military activities or wilderness explorations, "but he was interested in surveying throughout his maturity. In spirit at least, he could follow the trail across untrodden mountains; and as a draftsman, drawing plats and house plans, he was also his father's son," wrote his admiring biographer Dumas Malone.[10] "In spirit" gets it right: Jefferson spent negligible time exploring new territory in person, but spent hours poring over maps in his study. "Jefferson grew up with maps in his head," writes Joel Achenbach in his study of efforts to build a canal inland from the Potomac, "and they remained there his entire life and into his presidency, when he began filling in the blank spaces, sending Lewis and Clark up the Missouri."[11]

His father's death left teenage Thomas Jefferson a rich man and heir to a place as leader of his community, the dominant male in a house full of adoring women who seemed never to have sought or taken direction from his mother or wife. Unlike other prominent American Founders, he was free, unencumbered by need or duty, to do what he wanted and live the life he chose. "At fourteen years of age," he later wrote, "the whole care and direction of my self was thrown on my self entirely.[12] He worked diligently, scheduling his time meticulously and avoiding frivolity, to pursue manifold intellectual and aesthetic interests and accumulated so much knowledge that in 1961 his successor John Kennedy told a dinner for Nobel Prize recipients that never had so much talent been assembled in the White House except perhaps "when Thomas Jefferson dined alone." In a century when a talented man could pursue the ambition of mastering every branch of knowledge, as Benjamin Franklin and Johann Wolfgang von Goethe seemed to do, or bringing together all learning, as the French editors of the *Encyclopédie* and the Scottish editors of the *Encyclopaedia Britannica* sought to do in 1751 and 1768, Thomas Jefferson throughout his life was interested in seemingly everything: in music and architecture, history and geology, mathematics and botany. Yet he ranked below other Founders in specific areas. He was a less creative scientist than Benjamin Franklin, not as commanding a lawyer as Alexander Hamilton, not at all possessed of the military instincts and confidence of George Washington, not as profound a student of the history and politics of republics ancient and modern as his friend James Madison. Yet he was no less driven or disciplined than any of them. Ron Chernow, the great biographer of Jefferson's enemy Hamilton, notes that despite his apparently secure wealth and social position, "Jefferson was a fanatic for self-improvement. He rose before dawn each morning and employed every hour profitably, studying up to fifteen hours each day. Extremely systematic in his habits, Jefferson enjoyed retreating into the sheltered tranquility of his books, and the spectrum of his interests was vast. . . . Whether riding horseback, playing the violin, designing buildings, or inventing curious gadgets, Thomas Jefferson seemed adept at everything."[13] To this he brought an apparently in-born aesthetic sensibility, an appreciation of beauty, and a preference for symmetry, unusual in colonial Virginia and indeed in pre-Georgian England. "He fairly reveled in what he believed to be beautiful, and his writings often betrayed subtle feeling for artistic form,—a sure mark of intellectual seriousness."[14] And in one important respect he outshined all his contemporaries—as a writer, a fashioner of phrases and practitioner of prose, with a gift that on occasion rose to Shakespearean level. "We hold these truths to be self-evident," he wrote at age thirty-three, "that all men are created equal, that they are endowed by their creator with certain unalienable rights, that among them are life, liberty, and the pursuit of happiness." Who can improve on those words that gave birth to and set the course of a nation?

Not that many years before, when he was seventeen, he decided like so many other sons of Virginia plantation gentry to enroll at the College of William and Mary, where, unlike most of his fellows, he set his own grueling pace, critiquing his teachers, and in Williamsburg, with its 2,000 people the closest thing to a city he had ever seen, savaged the architecture, which the Rockefeller family strove to restore and which millions of grateful Americans have come to regard as a fitting representation of their nation's colonial heritage. Jefferson was a serious student, always eager to get to his books and his violin. He made a favorable impression on the college's leading professor, William Small, and was soon a frequent guest at dinners with Small; the colony's most prominent lawyer, George Wythe; and Virginia's acting Governor Francis Fauquier, a director of the South Sea Company and member of the Royal Society of Arts. This was dazzling company, in intellectual achievement and widespread knowledge the apex of Virginia society, and the fact that the significantly younger Jefferson was repeatedly included indicates that his capacity to charm others with his recondite knowledge and musical flair was already well developed. "At these dinners, Jefferson said long afterward, he heard 'more good sense, more rational and philosophical conversations,' than at any other time in his life," writes his biographer Dumas Malone. "At the Governor's table he heard highly stimulating conversation, and in this court he acquired graces which adorned his life."[15] Yet at the same time, Williamsburg was not unreachably far from the frontier, as Jefferson was reminded when the Cherokee chief Outacity and his warriors visited in the spring of 1762.[16] After graduation later that year, Jefferson stayed on in Williamsburg and read law under George Wythe, who led him through readings in history and philosophy as well as parliamentary and civil law.[17] Jefferson was Wythe's favorite student and he had great admiration for the older teacher, even when they argued opposite sides of a case after his admission to the bar in 1767. His sole travel outside Virginia was prompted by his interest in science: His first trip outside the colony was when he traveled to Philadelphia in 1766 to get a variolation inoculation against smallpox, and gained his first exposure to what was then, with 20,000 people, the largest city in British North America, and he even ventured beyond to travel to the polyglot, Dutch-founded port of New York.[18] He sailed back to Virginia, and in 1768, he ran unopposed for a seat in the House of Burgesses, treating his Albemarle County neighbors to drinks, as was expected, and was elected at age twenty-five.

In 1770, his mother's house, with all his books and papers, burned down, and Jefferson, at twenty-seven and still unmarried, decided to build his own house. Virginia planters' houses were typically built on rivers from which tobacco could be shipped to England and manufactures and luxuries from England could be readily unloaded, and Jane Randolph Jefferson's house was situated on low ground near the Rivanna River, whose waters flowed into the James River and ultimately into Chesapeake Bay. Thomas Jefferson had a different idea. He had read Edmund Burke's *Philosophical Enquiry into Our Ideas of the Sublime and Beautiful*,[19] and had perused the sixteenth-century Italian architect Andrea Palladio's *I quattro libri dell'architettura*.[20] Palladio had designed villas for Venetian merchants on the Veneto's *terra firma*, which struck Jefferson as much more agreeable than the houses he frequented in Virginia. He wanted a house that would be beautifully symmetrical on a site with a view that was breathtakingly sublime. On the extensive property he owned, he chose a hill that rose 900 feet above the Rivanna, with a splendid view once the trees were felled, of hundreds of acres of Virginia Piedmont. To the practical difficulties, he seemed indifferent. A switchback road would have to be built up the mountainside, water would have to be carted up in wagonloads (the sixty-five-foot-deep well atop the hill proved unproductive), lumber had to be cut and trees planted, and the hilltop flattened, all by slave workmen.[21] He kept records of the construction and at one point calculated it had consumed 190,000 bricks and 1,200 feet of flooring planks.[22] His house, built and rebuilt and rebuilt again, "was the greatest creative project of his life," writes historian Thomas Kidd, "and the most persistent drain on his finances."[23]

Monticello was the name he chose—"little mountain" in the Italian he was studying. From this little mountain, he envisioned looking out over miles of the Piedmont countryside, reading and writing in his study, playing music, and contemplating collections of plant specimens and Indian artifacts, strolling through gardens and arbors. "A chateau above contact with man," Henry Adams called Monticello."[24] "It seems as if from his youth," wrote the Marquis de Chastellux after a visit in 1781, "as he had done his house, on an elevated situation, from which he might contemplate the universe."[25] Or as Jefferson himself asked his flirtatious acquaintance Maria Cosway in 1786 to envision how nature had "spread so rich a mantle under the eye? Mountains, forests, rocks, rivers. With what majesty do we rise above the storms! How sublime to look down into the workhouse of nature, to see her clouds, hail, snow, rain, thunder, all fabricated at our feet!"[26] But that was in the future. When he brought his bride, the rich young widow, Martha Wayles Skelton, there in January 1772, only one room had a roof to provide shelter from the rain and snow, for them and for the pianoforte he bought for her. Jefferson's marriage made him even richer, and Martha Jefferson's father's death in 1773 doubled his wealth, leaving him with 10,000 acres of land and 185 slaves—but also with debts that he unwisely failed to discharge.[27] However, those never prevented him from returning again and again, after great achievements or migraine-inducing setbacks, to Monticello, to the house on the little mountaintop that he so painstakingly fashioned and refashioned for more than half a century.

Happily married, respected by his peers and elders, seemingly securely rich and able to dominate his own personal environment, Thomas Jefferson at age thirty was embarked on a life that, in another era, in another country, might have gone unnoticed beyond a circle of friends and admirers. He quickly achieved success as a legislator in Williamsburg. The House of Burgesses, like the House of Commons in London, was something of a meritocracy. It was taken for granted that all members were landed gentry, owners of tobacco plantations, but the legislature's long-serving leaders made careful assessments of the capacities of younger members and were quick to advance those with outstanding ability and strong character to positions of influence. George Washington, first elected at age twenty-six, was quickly singled out as "one of those young men of high ability placed on important committees, even chairmanships, relatively soon after their first appearance in the House."[28] Similarly, Thomas Jefferson, first elected at age twenty-five, "earned his colleagues' esteem with his capacity for hard work, his tact, his mastery of parliamentary procedure, and his talent with his pen."[29] "His rise was swift and smooth," historian Forrest McDonald writes, "as leaders of the provincial elite quickly recognized his abilities and in effect brought him into the ruling groups while he was still in his mid-twenties."[30] Evidently in the

House of Burgesses, as at those intimate dinners at the Governor's Palace, Jefferson employed his wide learning, based on continual disciplined study, and his considerable charm to make favorable impressions on older men, and carefully avoiding, as he would all his life, open disagreement or confrontation. His writings from this period are the first evidence of his gift for the felicitous phrase and persuasive argument and of his ability to write in easily flowing, clear prose, without the overly elaborate subordinate clauses characteristic of his eighteenth-century contemporaries.

His intellectual growth may have been stimulated by the sense that he was coming of age at a historically significant moment. He entered the House of Burgesses just three years after the British Parliament's Stamp Act of 1765 and he was aware that Virginia's leaders and other colonists had protested against what they regarded as taxation without representation. He knew that the Stamp Act had been repealed but that Parliament in the Townshend Acts of 1767 had stubbornly reasserted what it regarded as its right to tax the colonies. To back up their protests, George Mason of Fairfax County, at the prompting of his neighbor George Washington, proposed a non-importation agreement, to persuade Parliament to abolish import duties. The Burgesses, now including Jefferson, in May 1769 passed such legislation prohibiting the import of most goods from Britain starting in September. It had its intended effect: Parliament in March 1770 cut imports on all items except tea. This example of cutting off the lucrative trans-Atlantic trade and luxury imports remained throughout his public career a cherished example to Jefferson, a self-sacrificing measure which had, in his experience, forced an obdurate but trade-dependent Britain to concede. "On Jefferson, the impression of this experience of successful commercial pressure would be lifelong," write historians Stanley Elkins and Eric McKittrick. "All of this may well have strengthened Jefferson's convictions as to the relatively circumscribed function of commerce, and further limited his sensitivity to the impact such a policy might have on a community largely dependent on commercial pursuits."[31]

The issue was not extinguished but continued to smolder. In the spring of 1773, Jefferson, his brother-in-law Dabney Carr, and Richard Henry Lee persuaded the Burgesses to establish a committee of correspondence, for leaders of different colonies to share ideas and coordinate political strategy. In December 1773, the Boston Tea Party—the dumping of shiploads of taxed East India Company tea in Boston Harbor—exacerbated the split between Britain and the colonies. Parliament responded by closing the port of Boston, dispatching troops to Massachusetts, dissolving its elected legislature, and imposing martial law. In Virginia, the House of Burgesses passed a resolution for a day of fasting and prayer. In response, the governor, Lord Dunmore, dissolved the General Assembly. The ousted burgesses, including the thirty-one-year-old Jefferson, marched down Duke of Gloucester Street to the Apollo Tavern, where they adopted a resolution calling for a Continental Congress to assemble in Philadelphia. By late spring, eight other North American colonies joined that call,[32] and the Congress was scheduled to meet in Philadelphia in September.

To prepare for that, Jefferson in August 1774 wrote as instructions to the Virginia delegates a paper subsequently entitled *A Summary View of the Rights of British America*, arguing that Parliament had no authority to tax the colonies and begging the king to work with the colonies' legislatures.[33] It is an impassioned and discursive manifesto, written with Jefferson's characteristic clarity and grace and gift for captivating phrases and metaphors, with arguments veering as far back in history as the Saxon migrations to England and to events as recent as an instruction to the Virginia governor to bar creation of new counties with representation in the House of Burgesses. "The British parliament has no right to exercise authority over us," Jefferson argued. He excused the Boston Tea Party with the threatening observation that "an exasperated people, who feel that they possess power, are not easily restrained within limits strictly regular," and warned that "his majesty has no right to land a single armed man on our shores." Jefferson reminds his readers of the misdeeds of the Stuart monarchs, that Charles I was beheaded and James II ousted by "the glorious revolution." Jefferson was writing when few Americans were ready to assert their independence, and he was still only suggesting some kind of separate status under King George III—a course that might have proved wise and was recommended by the most famous son of the colonies, Benjamin Franklin. But the looming implication of his argument that Parliament had no authority in North America was that the colonies were in some sense an independent polity, and one with an already distinct national character. "These are extraordinary situations which require extraordinary interposition," he exhorts. "Let those flatter who fear; it is not an American art."[34] *A Summary View* was endorsed by Peyton Randolph, a Jefferson relative who was speaker of the House of Burgesses, head of the Virginia delegation to Philadelphia, and chosen there as president of the Congress. This pamphlet, published anonymously in Williamsburg, Philadelphia, and London, but widely attributed to Jefferson, made this young man, "formerly just a regional planter and politician," into "a political and rhetorical figure of Anglo-American renown."[35]

In its meetings in September and October 1774, the First Continental Congress voted for a Continental Association, to launch a boycott of British goods—shades of the Virginia Association of 1769, and a precedent for Jefferson's Embargo of 1807—and called for a second Continental Congress to meet in May 1775, and this time Jefferson was chosen as a delegate. Before that assembly convened, armed warfare broke out, in Lexington and Concord, Massachusetts, on April 19. The Continental Congress unhesitatingly created a Continental Army and chose Jefferson's Virginia colleague George Washington as its commander. He was one of the few delegates with significant military experience and appeared at the session in military uniform. But the selection of a Virginian to command a force made up primarily of New England Yankees reflected a sense that their cause was not a local one. In July, the Congress adopted a petition begging the king to intervene, but in August, George III scornfully rejected this so-called Olive Branch Petition and declared the colonies in revolt.

Over the next months, support for independence grew. In May, John Adams of Massachusetts proposed a resolution for a new frame of government, and in June, Richard Henry Lee of Virginia proposed a resolution declaring "that these united colonies are, and of right ought to be, free and independent states." Jefferson arrived late in Philadelphia and was not initially named to the five-man committee to draft a document declaring independence; he was added only when Lee left to attend to business in Virginia. The committee left initial drafting to Adams and Jefferson, and Adams deferred to his younger colleague because of his "happy talent for composition and singular felicity of expression." Jefferson spent seventeen days in June in his rented rooms writing his draft, and accepted major changes from Franklin and Adams, and between July 2 and 4, the Congress debated the wording. It eliminated arguments directed at Parliament and the British people and retained Jefferson's denunciations of George III. It also deleted, to Jefferson's lasting regret, his sections denouncing the king for encouraging the trans-Atlantic slave trade. On July 4, the amended Declaration of Independence was adopted. Jefferson's words have reverberated throughout American history, setting a standard the nation has striven to meet. "We hold these truths to be self-evident"—that last word was Franklin's substitute—"that all men are created equal, that they are endowed by their creator with certain inalienable rights, that among them are life, liberty and the pursuit of happiness." Could anyone else have done better?

Jefferson's role as the prime author of the Declaration was known to members of the Congress, of course, but not more widely at the time; it became public only in 1784. And it is indicative of the relative importance of the Continental Congress and the state governments that, soon after drafting the Declaration, Jefferson decided to leave Philadelphia and return to Virginia and what was thenceforth called the House of Delegates. He failed to transmit the new constitution he had written for Virginia during the spring of 1776 in time for consideration, and ended up vigorously criticizing the one that was actually adopted. Undaunted, he sought to abolish entail (allowing landowners to require it be inherited only by family members) and primogeniture (by which the eldest son inherited everything in the absence of a will), to reduce the number of crimes punishable by death, to establish scholarships for each school district's best students, to ease manumission (freeing a slave), and to disestablish and defund the state's Anglican Church. The results were mixed: Primogeniture was abolished immediately and entail a few years later, and some death penalties were abolished; manumission was made easier and the Anglican Church disestablished in 1786, but the school scheme went nowhere.

In June 1779, the legislature elected Jefferson governor, a position with few effective powers under the new state constitution. He persuaded the legislature to move the capital from Williamsburg to Richmond, farther from the sea, but it proved vulnerable to the British Army. After his reelection in June 1780, a British Army led by Benedict Arnold invaded Virginia in January 1781, and Jefferson evacuated Richmond, which Arnold briefly occupied. That spring, Jefferson evacuated the capital again, and British cavalry under Lieutenant Colonel Banastre Tarleton flashed through Richmond and rode through Charlottesville to Monticello. Jefferson evacuated the state government over the Blue Ridge to Staunton in the Shenandoah Valley, then returned to Monticello, where he stuffed papers into his saddlebags and rode off on his swiftest horse five minutes before Tarleton's troops arrived, following his family to his Poplar Forest property in Bedford County, some ninety miles away.[36] Jefferson's term as governor expired June 2 and he regarded himself as a private citizen. Since the legislature could not meet to elect a successor until June 12, Virginia was left without a governor for more than a week and Jefferson was widely accused of cowardice. The legislature ordered an investigation to report six months later—which as it happened was after the unexpected American victory in Yorktown in October. Jefferson got himself elected to the legislature, and in response to the report delivered a long speech exonerating himself. He was cleared of all charges and promptly resigned, declaring he was finished with public service. "He does appear to have withdrawn with an overwhelming sense of hurt, and a settled determination to stay with his family, his books, and his ever-evolving Monticello," writes Christopher Hitchens.[37]

This pattern would be seen again in his career—a public setback followed by a retreat to his little mountaintop at Monticello. As biographer Richard Bernstein writes, these "repeated retreats to Monticello—in 1781, 1794, and finally in 1809—make even more sense when we see them not just as flights *from* the remorseless struggles of politics but as flights *to* realms in which he felt safe, admired, respected, and, above all, loved."[38] He had torn down his original house, probably without consultation with his often pregnant wife, and started a new Monticello in 1778, "but the second Monticello became a never-ending operation with incessant delays and unexpected expenses." He experimented in shifting his farms away from tobacco, which soon exhausted the soil, to grain and vegetable crops, and ordered his enslaved laborers to plant hundreds of peach trees "for fruit firewood, and landscaping. Monticello was always something of a showpiece property."[39] His chief preoccupation in these years was the composition of what turned out to be his only book, *Notes on the State of Virginia*. It is a strange book. Jefferson seems to have seized on a mass mailing as an excuse to make use of the contents of his library shelves. In 1780, a French diplomat in Philadelphia, François Marbois, sent out a question-naire to multiple members of the Continental Congress about their states, and a Virginia member sent a copy to Governor Jefferson. At Monticello, which was something of a construction site, and at his country retreat at Poplar Forest, he spent many hours replying to Marbois's twenty-three queries. "He turned with what must have been a sigh of relief from the world of war and politics to a realm always delightful to him, that of scientific and philosophical thought. Released for the time being from the demands of public life, and during a period of enforced idleness after a fall from his horse, he worked rapidly and efficiently, digesting the memoranda which he had brought with him from Monticello, filling in gaps and omissions, effecting in writing a synthesis of much that he had seen and heard and read and pondered during his active life."[40] By December 1781, he reported to Marbois that he had finished and enclosed a manuscript. But he continued to revise and enlarge the manuscript, with information from friends and informants, in the weeks and months following. When he was on diplomatic service in Paris, he arranged for a printing, without an author's name on the title page, completed in May 1785. A French translation was published in early 1787, with the author indicated by initials. Jefferson was dissatisfied with both these versions and arranged for another to be printed, with his name acknowledged, by British printer James Stockdale in London in July 1787.

Notes on the State of Virginia, in this edition prepared and approved by Jefferson, begins with a map, a version of the 1751 map draw by Peter Jefferson and Joshua Fry, as revised by Thomas Jefferson. *Notes* can almost be described as an atlas, a book of maps plus text; in an early chapter describing rivers, Jefferson advises readers that "an inspection of a map of Virginia will give a better idea…than any description in writing."[41] Pages are filled with statistics in tabular form about vegetables, fruits and plants, animals and birds, rainfall and temperatures, population, militia forces and Indian tribes, crimes, public revenues and expenses, and historical sources.[42] Jefferson lived in an age when men of letters could still hope to learn everything about every important subject, and in presenting this material in encyclopedic form, Jefferson presumably was influenced by d'Alembert and Diderot's *Encyclopedie*, first published in Paris in 1751, and the *Encyclopaedia Britannica*, first published in Edinburgh in 1768. Generations before Charles Darwin (who was born in the last full month of Jefferson's presidency, on the same day as Abraham Lincoln), Jefferson was presenting all available information and much intelligent speculation about the development of the Appalachian ridges, about the bones of North America's prehistoric mammoths, and its unique species of elk, hare, and squirrels. He deployed this learning in his attacks on the French naturalist Buffon, who asserted that North America produced only puny and weak animals and plants. He noticed what most Americans of his time and later have ignored, the Indian mounds or barrows, "of which many are to be found all over this country." He was alert to the possibility of climate change and noticed that temperatures in Virginia in his time were warmer than during the seventeenth century, the height of what climate researchers have long dubbed the little ice age.

But *Notes on Virginia* is not just about Virginia. The Jefferson-Fry map is not just a map of Virginia, which in the 1780s included what is now West Virginia and Kentucky. It also includes all of Maryland and Delaware, almost all of Pennsylvania, the western half of New Jersey, and the eastern half of what would become the state of Ohio, which, as Jefferson mentioned, was among the lands ceded by Virginia to the federal government in 1784, while *Notes* was incubating. Most of this land Jefferson had not seen when he began writing in response to Marbois's queries and would never see in the remaining four decades of his life. Jefferson never ventured as far beyond the Blue Ridge as his father had done while surveying the boundaries of Lord Fairfax's grant, and while he famously collected and preserved specimens of plants and fossils, his text included reference to more items than could be found on his carefully farmed land or in his meticulously amassed collections. After pages of statistics, Jefferson brought his felicitous writing style into play in his accounts of spectacular scenery he had witnessed in person—his picture of where the Shenandoah River empties into the Potomac, which then plunges through the Appalachian ridge, and of "the Natural Bridge, the most sublime of nature's works," on land which he purchased from the Crown in 1774 for twenty shillings. "You involuntarily fall on your hands and feet, creep to the parapet and peep over it. Looking down from this height about a minute, gave me a violent head ach."[43] In contrast are the aficionado of Palladio's disgust with vernacular Virginia architecture and with the colonial capital of Williamsburg in particular. "The private buildings are very rarely constructed of stone or brick; much the greatest proportion being of scantling and boards, plaistered with lime. It is impossible to devise things more ugly, uncomfortable, and happily more perishable." In Williamsburg, "The College and Hospital are rude, mis-shapen piles, which, but that they have roofs, would be taken for brick-kilns. There are no other public buildings but churches and courthouses in which no attempts are made at elegance."[44]

Jefferson's mental map, as reflected in *Notes on Virginia*, included only a passing glance at New England and little interest in the Atlantic Ocean beyond a parochial Virginian's prediction, unfulfilled for two centuries, that Norfolk "will probably be the emporium of all trade of Chesapeak bay and its waters."[45] His gaze was constantly directed westward, beyond the most prominent feature on his father's map, the highest Appalachian ridge, beyond which he never ventured—and on how Americans might penetrate beyond it. He described the major rivers, mentioning briefly their connections with the Atlantic, but with more attention to their navigability upstream and how they could be "channels of extensive communication with the western and northwestern country" beyond the mountain chains. Three could provide "principal connections with the Atlantic," he wrote; "the Hudson's river, the Patowmac, and the Missisipi itself." Upriver traffic on the "Missisipi," he noted three decades before the first commercial steamboat, is "so difficult and tedious" that it would be unfeasible, and "there will therefore be a competition between the Hudson and Patowmac rivers for the residue of the commerce of all the country westward of Lake Erié, on the waters of the lakes, of the Ohio, and upper parts of the Missisipi." Like his fellow Virginian George Washington, Jefferson optimistically overestimated the ease of overcoming barriers to navigation on the Potomac and of portaging between its tributaries and the Ohio, and he disparaged any Hudson route because of waters freezing during months-long winters. Writing nearly half a century before the first railroad headed to the interior, he described routes the short portage of "Chickago" between "the lakes" and tributaries of the "Missisipi," spotlighted "the Cayahoga" as one of the few harbors on the southern shore of "Lake Erié," and despite his agrarian bias, made mention of the raw materials of America's industrial revolution—coal, especially "of very special quality" in "Pittsburg"; iron; and limestone, the prime raw materials of the Midwestern industrial revolution. Readers can take his description as anticipating the rise of the great river cities—Pittsburgh, Cincinnati, Louisville, St. Louis—that grew mightily in the middle third of the nineteenth century, and perhaps foreshadowing the rise in the last third of the century of the industrial Great Lakes cities—Buffalo, Cleveland, Detroit, Chicago, Milwaukee. Like Benjamin Franklin, Jefferson appreciated the young nation's rapid population increase, which Franklin pegged at doubling every twenty or twenty-five years and Jefferson at a spuriously precise twenty-seven and one-third.

Like Franklin, Jefferson saw a nation and a continent with a vast supply of land but a limited supply of labor—the contrary of Europe with its plenteous labor but limited amount of land.[46] His "singular passion for space," historian Robert Wiebe writes, "rose out of his horror at Europe's congestion."[47] Although he authorized publication of *Notes* several years after the Treaty of Paris set the Mississippi River as the western border of the United States, he was already looking farther west, noting that there was more water and turbulence in the supposedly tributary Missouri River, up which he would send the Lewis and Clark Expedition in 1804. "What is the shortest distance between the navigable waters of the Missouri, and those of the North River [Rio Grande], or how far this is navigable above Santa Fé, I could never learn." But he does record, with his typical precision and minimal inaccuracy, that distance from Santa Fé to Mexico City, "passing the mines of Charcas, Zaccatecas and Potosi" as 1,550 miles.[48] And in 1806, he would send Zebulon Pike west, via the peak that still bears his name, to Santa Fe, and American troops would reach the halls of Montezuma some forty years later. In *Notes*, he expressed respect for the character and mores of American Indians, speculating that they were descended from ancestors who migrated over a Bering Strait land bridge and urging that their languages be transcribed before they were lost.[49] He was more pessimistic about the prospects of America's enslaved blacks. The most disturbing passages in *Notes* are about slavery, a subject to which he returns in three separate passages.[50] The prophet of liberty described blacks as intellectually inferior to whites, incapable of advancing—a belief he stuck to later even when faced with the talents of the poet Phyllis Wheatley or the architect Benjamin Banneker. The closest he came to making an exception was in his recognition of blacks' musical abilities. Unlike George Washington, who developed respect for the black troops he was persuaded to lead and who freed his own slaves, Jefferson foresaw no possibility that freed blacks could live together peaceably with whites and freed no slaves except for members of the Hemings family. He seemed uncomfortably aware of the tension between American revolutionaries' demands for liberty and their insistence that slaves were their property, and he had written scathingly about Britain's refusal to outlaw the trans-Atlantic slave trade in *A Summary View* and in a deleted portion of his draft for the Declaration of Independence. He supported the manumission bill passed in Virginia in 1786 that facilitated voluntary freeing of slaves. But the 1787 version of *Notes* included no mention of the judicial abolition of slavery in Massachusetts and New Hampshire or the gradual abolition legislation passed in Pennsylvania, Connecticut, and Rhode Island in the years between 1780 and 1784.

In September 1782, Martha Jefferson died after ten years of marriage, extracting a promise that he not marry again. After struggling with grief, her husband returned to public life as a delegate to the Continental Congress in the winter of 1783–84. Britain had finally recognized American independence, and American sovereignty west to the Mississippi River, south to the 31° parallel and north to the Great Lakes, in the Treaty of Paris in September 1783. The Continental Congress was thus presented with the question of what to do with this territory, then inhabited largely by Indians and garrisoned by British troops, but destined for expansion of the rapidly growing American population. There was some urgency since under the Articles of Confederation, Congress could not levy taxes but could raise revenue by selling off western lands. In March 1784, Jefferson, as chairman of a committee established for this purpose, unveiled a plan for the western territories, together with Virginia's relinquishment of its claims based on British colonial grants to land north of the Ohio River. Jefferson's plan provided for western areas to be administered as territories subject to Congress and be admitted in time as full states, of equal status with the original thirteen. His polysyllabic names for the territories were ridiculed, though Illinoia and Michigania were ultimately adopted.[51] But the most notable feature of his legislation was to bar slavery after the year 1800.[52] He hoped, writes Richard Bernstein, "to encourage the spread westward of a republic of individual farmers, each tilling his own land and committed to personal and national independence and liberty."[53] The measure did not come close to passage, though he lamented later that it lost due to the absence of one New Jersey delegate. "'Thus we see the fate of millions of unborn hanging on the tongue of one man, and heaven was silent in that awful moment.'"[54] But his efforts were not in vain. Provisions from his proposal were carried forward in later legislation. Territorial status leading to full statehood became standard practice, except for California, which got statehood immediately. Jefferson's proposal for regular straight-line boundaries within the territories led to the mile-square checkerboard pattern so apparent to cross-country airline passengers on cloudless days.[55] A ban on slavery, however, was omitted in legislation considered, after Jefferson sailed for Paris, in 1785 and 1786 and was only inserted, rather surreptitiously, into the Northwest Ordinance passed in July 1787. Though not enforced rigorously at first, this antislavery provision largely prevented Virginians from bringing slaves, and their anti-anti-slavery politics, across the Ohio River, as they did, in fact, in the adjacent and physically similar lands west of the Mississippi River in Missouri. Instead, as one historian of the Northwest Territory wrote, "The enlightened provisions of the ordinance attracted the thrifty Yankee from New England, the enterprising Dutchman from Pennsylvania, the conscientious Quaker from Carolina and Virginia, and some of the sturdiest pioneer stock from the frontier of Kentucky.[56] The six free states—Ohio, Indiana, Illinois, Michigan, Wisconsin, and Minnesota—created from the Northwest Territory all voted for Abraham Lincoln in 1860 and provided critical manpower and industrial might that enabled the Union to prevail in the Civil

War. One other Jefferson proposal in the Confederation Congress that reached fruition later, when he was secretary of state, was the adoption of a decimal dollar, which spared Americans the bother of calculating sums in pounds, shillings, and pence, as the British did until 1971.[57] His decimal proposal was perhaps an instance, of which *A Summary View* was a far more profound example, of Jefferson's inspired prose inspiring others to follow his lead.

In May 1784, Jefferson was offered the position of minister in Paris, to negotiate trade treaties in Europe. This would be his first and only travel outside the United States, and would last for five years, from August 1784 to September 1789. Once again, as when he avoided military service during the Revolutionary War and as he retreated to Monticello in 1781 and 1794, he found himself outside the arena where grave events were taking place and great issues debated and decided. Acceptance in this case enabled him to escape a Monticello still in mourning for his wife, and it promised a reunion with his colleagues from the five-member committee charged with preparing the Declaration of Independence in June and July 1776, Benjamin Franklin and John Adams. But Franklin and Adams had already performed their great assignment, negotiating the Treaty of Paris, despite the deep distrust that had grown up between them. Soon after he arrived in Paris, he learned that Franklin, at age seventy-nine, was granted his wish to be recalled to Philadelphia, where he would serve in the Constitutional Convention, and that John Adams was leaving for London to take up his duties as the first American minister (ambassador was too grand a title for the young republic) to Great Britain. Jefferson would miss them all, including Abigail Adams, the only woman whose political opinions he seems to have taken seriously, and the seventeen-year-old John Quincy Adams, a prodigy whom Jefferson may almost have seen as a surrogate son.

As it turned out, Jefferson accomplished little as a diplomat. He did succeed, with Adams's help, in renegotiating Dutch bankers' loans to the United States, and persuading the king of Prussia to sign a free trade treaty with the new republic. In 1788, he negotiated a Consular Convention with France, a template for many treaties to come. However, his efforts to modify a French monopoly in tobacco failed. His visit to Britain in the spring of 1786 brought a happy reunion with the Adamses, but a bitterly resented glaring snub from King George III, whose misdeeds he had chronicled in *A Summary View* and the Declaration of Independence. Meanwhile, he missed out on the Constitutional Convention, about whose work he was ambivalent, uncertain whether the loose unity prevailing under the Articles of Confederation needed improvement. His friend and Virginia neighbor James Madison, whose commitment to the new document was total, did try to keep him in touch with the proceedings, and with the struggles over ratification that followed, but the slowness of trans-Atlantic travel meant that neither could provide timely information or advice to the other.

The gulf between Jefferson as a patron of luxuries and as a champion of the common man is nowhere clearer than his five years in Paris, whose 600,000 people dwarfed the 20,000 in America's largest city, Philadelphia. He bought a copy of a new map of the city immediately on its publication and "roamed all over Paris."[58] He delighted especially in the Luxembourg Gardens and the Jardins des Tuileries, admired the paintings at the Salon of 1789 and concerts at the Salle de Machines. He disliked Versailles and had no use for royal ritual, was unimpressed with King Louis XVI, and loathed Marie Antoinette. He settled in at the Hôtel de Langeac, a house with stables and gardens built for a mistress of King Louis XV on the Avenue Champs-Elysées,[59] which he promptly started to remodel and furnish at ruinous expense. He dressed like a French nobleman, ignoring his predecessor Benjamin Franklin's habit of dressing in what Parisians took to be North American backwoods clothes, and he bought lavish clothes for his oldest daughter Patsy and for her younger sister Polly, who arrived later, accompanied by the teenage slave Sally Hemings (the natural daughter of Martha Jefferson's father), and enrolled the two daughters in an exclusive Catholic convent school. He studied French but never bothered to master that language,[60] and he never engaged easily in French conversation.[61] Aside from Lafayette, whom he had met in Virginia in 1781, he developed no intimate relations with any French acquaintances. He spent lavishly on books, paintings, musical scores, wine, and fine clothes—expensive suits, ruffled shirts, and powder for his hair. In the portrait painted by Mather Brown, the forty-something Jefferson looks like a young dandy. He embarked on extended trips. He traveled on diplomatic business to England in March and April 1786, journeying also to Birmingham and Oxford, admiring eighteenth-century landscape architecture at Blenheim Palace, Hampton Court, and Chiswick and the few Palladian buildings he saw—Hagley Hall outside of Birmingham, Inigo Jones's Queen's House at Greenwich, the Covent Garden piazza in London. From February to June 1787, over five months while the Assemblée Nationale was meeting in Paris and the Constitutional Convention was assembling in Philadelphia,[62] he embarked on a personal journey to the south of France, where in Nîmes he admired the Roman Maison Carrée, on which he would model the Virginia Capitol, and to northern Italy though he stopped in Milan, after smuggling out samples of Piedmont rice.[63] But he didn't travel the short distance east to see the villas of Palladio, whose drawings and descriptions he had read in the sixteenth-century architect's *I quattro libri dell'architettura* (*The Four Books of Architecture*). With John Adams, he journeyed in March 1788 to Amsterdam to deal with financial firms and then traveled alone down the Rhine to Frankfurt and Strasbourg until April 1788. Starting when he landed at the port of Le Havre and through all his travels, he took pains to obtain maps and guidebooks of every city on his itinerary, and to orient himself typically climbed to the town ramparts or the highest steeple[64]—the one in the Strasbourg cathedral made it the highest building in the world.

As in *Notes on Virginia*, Jefferson was trying to systematize his knowledge of the world, to understand it from the point of view of a detached and aesthetically minded observer. Angered by the French naturalist Buffon's assurances that North American animals and plants were punier than those in Europe, he urged American correspondents to furnish him with mammoth skeletons and giant animal skins, and sent the results to Buffon.[65] He arranged for his updated *Notes on Virginia* to be translated into French and be published in Paris in 1787, without his name and in a translation not entirely meeting his approval. He also arranged to have the original, together with additional notes, published by a more reliable printer and with his name attached, in London, which appeared a few weeks later.

For all his appreciation of the luxuries of Paris, Jefferson expressed enthusiasm for armed rebellion in America and revolution in France. From Paris he idealized the 1786 Shays debtor rebellion in Massachusetts, even as James Madison recoiled in horror and developed his plans for a stronger federal government to prevent such disorder. Meanwhile, Jefferson was telling Abigail Adams that "the spirit of resistance to government is so valuable on certain occasions, that I wish it to be always kept alive. It will often be exercised when wrong, but better so than not to be exercised at all. I like a little rebellion now and then. It is like a storm in the Atmosphere."[66] To William Smith, Adams's son-in-law, he wrote, "What signify a few lives lost in a century or two? The tree of liberty must from time to time be refreshed with the blood of patriots and tyrants. It is it's natural manure."[67] He was an eyewitness to the convening of the Estates General in Versailles in May 1789 and its amalgamation of the three estates—nobles, clergy, commoners—into a united National Assembly, which proceeded with, as Jefferson wrote Thomas Paine on July 11, "a coolness, wisdom, and resolution to set fire to the four corners of the kingdom and to perish with it themselves rather than to relinquish an iota from their plan of a total change of government.[68] He had immediate news of the sacking of the Bastille on July 14. Eleven days later, he wrote his coquettish friend Maria Cosway, "The cutting off heads is become so much á la mode, that one is apt to feel of a morning whether their own is on their shoulders."[69] In September, he wrote to Madison, who was trying to rally support for the Constitution he had done so much to fashion to provide for an orderly republic, "The earth belongs in usufruct to the living; that the dead have neither powers nor rights over it."[70] In his last letter as he prepared to leave Paris, he told Paine, "Tranquillity is well established in Paris, and tolerably so thro' the whole kingdom; and I think there is no possibility now of any thing's hindering their finally establishment of a good constitution, which will in it's principles and merit be about a middle term between that of England and the United States."[71] Jefferson's prophecy, and his scornful dismissal of Edmund Burke's *Reflections on the Revolution in France*, which accurately predicted the horrors to come, shows him verging on frivolity, insulated from responsibility, acting with reckless disregard of the terror to come. In his enthusiasm for revolutionary violence, as in his gift for the memorable phase, he resembles the younger English poet Percy Bysshe Shelley, another rich man who lived much of his life surrounded by adoring women and dominating others through dazzling conversation. As his critical biographer Conor Cruise O'Brien argues, "For Jefferson, from late 1789 to 1793, the French Revolution was inherently impeccable. It was not a changing set of processes within terrestrial politics. It belonged, along with the Declaration of Independence, in the domain of the sacred and immutable. The French Revolution had become an aspect of 'the true god,' inseparably and eternally part of 'the holy cause of freedom' proclaimed in the Declaration."[72] For Americans, it is fortunate that the influence of the constitutional framework largely established by others, the restraint imposed by the superintendence of George Washington and his own shrewd appreciation of political limits when he was a participant rather than a spectator, prevented this aspect of Thomas Jefferson from prevailing after he arrived back in Virginia in November 1789 and learned he was nominated to be secretary of state.

Jefferson left Paris in September 1789, arrived in Norfolk, Virginia, in November, and learned that George Washington had appointed him secretary of state. It was seven months after Washington had been sworn in as president, six months after John Adams as vice president proposed long-winded official titles which were widely ridiculed, and two months after Alexander Hamilton began taking up his duties as secretary of the Treasury. Jefferson took his time, accepting the nomination in a letter from Monticello in February and arriving at the temporary capital of New York on March 21.[73] This put him at a disadvantage in his struggles against Hamilton in what Washington had hoped would be a united government. Jefferson had known Washington for twenty years, since their time together in the House of Burgesses, but during the more recent years from 1777 to 1781, the general had worked much more closely with Hamilton. Washington ran a tightly controlled administration, meeting frequently with cabinet members and requiring written reports of all important business from them. They were kept on a short leash and in time it became apparent that the president was more in agreement with his former aide than with his fellow Virginian.

There was an obvious personality clash between the emollient Jefferson, who disliked confrontation, and the volatile Hamilton, who was quick to provoke argument. They had principled disagreements on both domestic and foreign policy, and their differences can be seen as a series of conflicts between two geographical visions of the future of America, two maps of future courses they hoped the country would take. Hamilton's map was of lines of commercial voyages ranging across the oceans, made possible by an America equipped with fiscal institutions and commercial enterprises characteristic of the seventeenth-century Dutch Republic and eighteenth-century parliamentary Britain. Jefferson's map looked westward, across the Appalachian chain to Kentucky and Tennessee and over the Potomac to the Ohio River Valley and the Great Lakes, but also with an eye looking southwest to New Orleans and other Spanish territory. Hamilton wanted an America in which banks helped merchants and manufacturers accumulate capital and whose commercial ties would be primarily with Britain. Jefferson wanted a republic populated by yeomen farmers, proprietors of their own lands and masters of their own communities as they spread across the continent, and believed that banks which lent out more money than they held in deposit were inherently fraudulent.[74]

Their first clash was over assumption—Hamilton's plan for the federal government to consolidate continental and state debts, to build a credit rating that would enable America to support an energetic government and to raise sums needed in war. To his surprise, he was stymied in the House by his partner in the Federalist Papers James Madison, now a friend and faithful ally of Jefferson. Jefferson arranged a compromise, over dinner in June 1790: Madison would switch enough votes to pass assumption, and Hamilton would agree that the new nation's permanent capital would be on the Potomac. On this, Jefferson was confident of the support of George Washington, who saw the Potomac as the nation's wide avenue to the west. But Jefferson humiliatingly failed to get Washington's approval in February 1791 when he and Madison opposed Hamilton's proposal for a national bank. Jefferson wrote a legal memorandum arguing that Congress lacked the power to create a bank under a strict interpretation of the Constitution. Under deadline pressure on whether to sign or veto the bill, Washington asked Hamilton for a response. Hamilton argued persuasively that the Constitution's necessary and proper clause authorized acts that were a reasonable means to achieve a constitutionally permissible end. Washington agreed and signed the bill.

These two extraordinarily gifted cabinet secretaries continued to disagree. The young republic was developing, despite its leaders' professed abhorrence, a two-party politics, with officeholders readily classifiable as Republicans and Federalists and what Washington denounced as "self-created" Republican societies. Hamilton used Treasury contracts to get favorable newspaper coverage; Jefferson put the editor of an anti-Hamilton paper on the State Department payroll.[75] Jefferson was an enthusiastic supporter of the French Revolution, despite its increasing violence, and saw it as a congenial fellow republic, despite occasional excesses. Hamilton and Washington feared those excesses and increasingly saw the French regime as tyrannical and incompatible with America's. In July 1791, Jefferson was embarrassed when the publisher of Thomas Paine's pro-French Revolution *The Rights of Man* included Jefferson's letter to him praising the book and seeming to criticize Vice President John Adams's more conservative works. Jefferson sent an apology to Washington, but relations between them suffered permanently and his friendship with Adams ended, not to be revived until after both men left public life.[76] The disagreements escalated in January 1793, the beginning of the Jacobin reign of terror when King Louis XVI was guillotined. Jefferson was unfazed, even by the killings of friendly acquaintances. As he wrote his successor in Paris, William Short, that month, "The liberty of the whole earth was depending on the issue of the contest, and was there ever such a prize won with so little innocent blood? My own affections have been deeply wounded by some of the martyrs to this cause, but rather than it should have failed, I would have seen half the earth desolated. Were there but an Adam & an Eve left in every country, & left free, it would be better than it is now.[77] February 1793 saw the outbreak of war between America's chief trading partner Britain and its treaty ally since 1778 France, a war that lasted with only two short pauses, until 1815, and which moved Americans to take sides even as the leaders of the two contending nations took only minimal notice of American actions. Washington issued a Neutrality Proclamation in April 1793. That same month the Jacobin ambassador "Citizen" Genêt arrived in Charleston and traveled up the Atlantic coast, greeted by cheering Republican societies who saw France's revolution as a benign successor to America's. Genêt was also commissioning privateer ships and threatening to "appeal from the president to the people." This was too much for Jefferson, who reluctantly concurred in Washington's demand that Genêt be recalled. At this point Jefferson, who like Hamilton had urged the aging Washington to accept a second term, decided to resign, and he left Philadelphia in the first week of 1794.

Again after a setback, he retreated to his little mountaintop to contemplate the world. He found his second version of Monticello in poor repair and proceeded to plan and build a third Monticello, one much closer to what the twenty-first-century visitor sees, with a much more Palladian influence, with many more peach trees and landscaping devised with slaves' quarters out of lines of sight—a house built partly for an extended family and for the expected large number of visitors, but clearly centered on the interests and peculiarities of one man.[78] Fleeing from his often unhappy personal contacts and conflicts in New York and Philadelphia, he was on his mountaintop aloof, and in a physical sense remained that way the rest of his life. "During the last thirty years of his life," writes the slyly acerbic Henry Adams, "he was not seen in a Northern city, even during his Presidency; nor indeed was he seen at all except on horseback, or by his friends or visitors in his own house."[79] "Jefferson, in order to function well, required complete authority that was based on habit and consent," writes the later and also sardonic Forrest McDonald. "Far more than the Father of His Country, George Washington, Jefferson in real life was the ultimate paternalist. He took care of his people—his daughters, his sons-in-law, his brother, his slaves, his friends, and every manner of helpless, weak, or ill-fitting person he encountered—and managed their lives gently, kindly, tactfully, and totally. All he asked in return was their absolute devotion, and he got it. He was quite inept at dealing with peers, but when he was master of circumstances, he had no peers."[80]

Jefferson maintained an active correspondence, keeping in touch with Republican allies and admirers. In 1794, he mocked Washington—and Hamilton's—dispatch of troops to quell the Whiskey Rebellion in western Pennsylvania, and in 1795, he urged on Madison's efforts to undermine Washington's Jay Treaty with Britain by denying appropriations—and watched that initiative collapse as commerce boomed and the treaty became more popular. Like other Founders, he continued to disparage political parties, but after Washington's announcement in September 1796 that he would retire, it was clear that Republicans and Federalists, if not fully articulated parties, were in the words of historian Jeffrey Pasley, "rather loose but intense communities of political ideology, emotion and action that took form among politicians, political writers and their audiences."[81] Jefferson and John Adams, once friends but no longer on epistolary terms, were clearly candidates who, in line with expectations, "were not doing much," Pasley writes, but hundreds of lesser known figures carried on haphazardly organized campaigns that "managed to construct remarkably coherent images of the two candidates that connected clearly to the policy issues and cultural tensions of the day, especially those raised by the French Revolution."[82]

It was a close-run election, which Adams won with a bare majority of seventy-one electoral votes, while Jefferson, with sixty-eight, under the Constitution's original system, was elected vice president. He was relieved not to have become president, Jefferson informed friends, and perhaps sincerely, since Washington's successor would have to deal with a hostile revolutionary France. The vice presidency was a part-time job, "honorable and easy," as Jefferson later recollected,[83] limited to presiding over the Senate, which Jefferson did gingerly, busying himself with compiling a Manual of Parliamentary Practice.[84] Today the Manual remains the basis of the parliamentary rules of the House of Representatives, in which Jefferson never served—along with the decimal dollar and the square-mile township grid, one of his underappreciated contributions to American life. Jefferson was embarrassed in 1796 when a letter he had written the year before to the Italian reformer Philip Mazzei was made public, in which he denounced the "Anglican monarchical, & aristocratic party" and "the apostates who have gone over to these heresies, men who were Samsons in the field & Solomons in the council, but who have had their heads shorn by the harlot England."[85] This clear insult of Washington ended all communication between the two. In response to the Alien and Sedition Acts, an increasingly partisan Jefferson authored, behind the scenes, the Kentucky resolutions, claiming a state's right to nullify federal legislation it deems unconstitutional—an argument cited by Southern secessionists in the 1850s and 1860s. But the crisis with France cooled down in 1799, even as Republicans prepared to run Jefferson for president, and as Federalists were split, with Hamilton actually writing a pamphlet denouncing the incumbent. The election of 1800, like the elections of the 1790s once the parties began emerging, was close; Republicans had swept the elections centered in 1794, the Federalists in 1798. But after 1800, there was no close election for a quarter-century. The key to Jefferson's victory was the Republicans' success in elections to the New York legislature, which gave Jefferson twelve electoral votes he had not won four years before. The catch was that Republicans this time, unlike 1796, had enough discipline that their vice-presidential nominee, Aaron Burr, won the same number of electoral votes, seventy-three, as Jefferson, narrowly ahead of Adams's sixty-eight. That sent the election to the House of Representatives, where Republicans lacked the required majority of state delegations. Many Federalists supported a supposedly pliable Burr, but Hamilton, who had known him since the Revolution and interacted with him often in New York, argued that he was unprincipled and should be shunned. Eventually, on the thirty-sixth ballot, seven Federalists abstained, and Jefferson was elected the third president.

Jefferson became president thirty-three years after being elected to the Virginia House of Burgesses. After one-third of a century in and out, but mostly in, public office and political controversy, he was no longer a young man charming his elders and eager for revolutionary change, but an elder himself—sixteen years older than the British Prime Minister William Pitt the Younger, twenty-six years older than the French First Counsel Napoleon Bonaparte—seeking to establish a stable partisan consensus after years of contention and upheaval. He was never an orator and delivered his shrewdly and, as always, gracefully written inaugural speech in an almost inaudible voice. He abhorred disagreement and confrontation and, while capable of forceful argument and caustic phrases in his letters, carefully avoided political topics at his famous dinner parties. "He disliked personal controversy and was always charming in face-to-face relations with both friends and enemies," writes historian Gordon Wood. "But at a distance he could hate, and thus many of his opponents concluded that he was two-faced and duplicitous.[86] He had been less than completely successful in other offices: His governorship ended in ignominious retreat, his reform proposals in the Virginia legislature and Confederation Congress were enacted only through the exertions of others; as a Cabinet member he lost battle after battle for Washington's approval; his Kentucky Resolution was cited in support of breaking up the nation he loved. But as president, at least in his first term, his abhorrence of controversy and gift for indirect persuasion served him—and the nation—well. His inaugural speech was inaudible, but the key words—"We are all republicans, we are all federalists"—were communicated across the nation and his warning against "entangling alliances" echoed Washington's farewell address and eliminated a decade of discord over whether to back France or Britain in their two-decade world war. He glumly but silently maintained Hamilton's funded national debt and national bank. "We can pay off his debt in fifteen years," he said, though he never did, "but we can never get rid of his financial system," which proved very handy when he needed cash to purchase Louisiana. He could abjure a standing army, but established a military school in West Point. He maintained the Federalist's navy, as indeed he had foreseen in *Notes on Virginia*, as necessary to protect America's foreign trade, and dispatched it, without congressional authorization, to the Mediterranean to end the extraction of payments from the Barbary pirate regimes of North Africa.[87]

He imitated Washington's constant supervision of his Cabinet and, like Washington, started off with (and unlike him, finished up with) brilliant secretaries of state and the Treasury, James Madison and Albert Gallatin. He kept control of the majority Republican caucuses in Congress not by issuing commands, but by taking advantage of his superb wine cellar and his ability to converse interestingly on dozens of subjects in constant rounds of White House dinners. He was careful, as historian James Sterling Young determined, to invite groups of Republicans who lived in the same boardinghouse to dinners together, to strengthen partisan and personal solidarity, while inviting opposition members from differ-ent boardinghouses so as to promote intraparty divisions.[88] "Now that he was finally in command, his elusiveness and deviousness," writes historian Sean Wilentz, turned out to be "his protean genius, an indispensable quality for one who would lead a new nation of sovereign squabbling individuals. By allowing different constituencies to see in him what they wanted to see, Jefferson mastered the democratic art of leading while appearing to be a follower, and of following while appearing to be a leader."[89] Or as the far from worshipful historian Forrest McDonald concluded, "In sum, he allowed Congress to function with no overt presidential direction and with only the gentlest of presidential guidance. As to cabinet meetings, he conducted them as a democracy of equals. And yet, almost until the end, he ran Congress more successfully and more thoroughly than did any preceding president and precious few succeeding presidents, and the cabinet always reflected his will except when he had no firm opinion on a matter."[90]

All this came together as Jefferson contemplated the map—and limits—of what he called the "empire of liberty." The hated Jay Treaty in 1795 and the American victory at the Battle of Fallen Timbers in 1796 had led to British withdrawal from the Northwest Territory, out of which the first—and free—state of Ohio was admitted to the Union in 1803. But the American writ did not extend unvexedly to the Mississippi, where the American military commander James Wilkinson was, unknown to Jefferson, in the pay of the Spanish. Jefferson was very much aware that hordes of settlers heading westward in Kentucky, Tennessee, and Ohio had no guaranteed outlet to the sea so long as the lower Mississippi remained Spanish territory. And they would have no security as American territory, Jefferson evidently concluded, when he learned in February 1802 that Napoleon was about to transfer the Louisiana Territory from Spain to France. Jefferson sent his friend the Delaware explosives entrepreneur Pierre du Pont de Nemours over to his minister in Paris, Robert Livingston, with a letter whose shimmering words he intended to be leaked to Napoleon. "There is on the globe one single spot, the possessor of which is our natural and habitual enemy," he wrote. "It is New Orleans." If France takes possession, he went on, "From that moment we must marry our-selves to the British fleet and nation."[91] When the Spanish governor cut off New Orleans from American trade, Jefferson sent James Monroe to Paris to negotiate the purchase of New Orleans and West Florida (which included the portion of present-day Louisiana east and north of the Mississippi River and Lake Pontchartrain). Simultaneously, the French defeat and withdrawal from the rich sugar colony of Haiti persuaded Napoleon to give up on his North American plans, and in March 1803, he offered the entire Louisiana Territory to Livingston. Monroe arrived days later, the two envoys conferred, and on May 2, agreed to pay $15 million for what was vaguely described as the lands drained by the Mississippi and Missouri Rivers. When they asked the famously cynical foreign minister Talleyrand for an exact description of the territory, he blandly replied, "You have made a noble bargain for yourselves, and I suppose you will make the most of it."

A jubilant president's impulse was to do just that. "Jefferson grew up with maps in his head," writes journalist Joel Achenbach, "and they remained there his entire life and into his presidency, when he began filling in the blank spaces,... He understood that rivers not only provide an avenue for exploration, and define political boundaries, but their headsprings"—and here he is writing about the son of Peter Jefferson, who surveyed the headsprings of the Potomac and placed the Fairfax Stone there—"are geographic markers even prior to their discovery—reference points in the blank spaces of the map. The precise location of a headspring may be unknown, but it definitely exists out there *somewhere*, as opposed to, say, a hypothetical volcano."[92] Complications remained, but Jefferson quickly overcame them. He brushed aside Spain's claim that France didn't own the territory and the legal complications about raising the money for the purchase. He dithered more over the objection that the Constitution did not authorize purchase of territory and, remembering the "strict" interpretation on which he urged Washington to veto the national bank, considered proposing a constitutional amendment. But time was wasting, and instead he called Congress into session to ratify the treaty and appropriate needed monies.[93] And he ordered his Virginia neighbor Meriwether Lewis and his co-captain William Clark to set out on the expedition that he had previously persuaded Congress to fund. They were to fill in the map, starting in newly American St. Louis, paddling up the Missouri River to the mountains and through a passage to the Pacific Ocean, establishing good relations with Indians and bringing back samples of plants and animals and fossils which would adorn the entry halls of Monticello.[94]

Aside from Lewis and Clark's return, Jefferson's second term had no such triumphs. Chief Justice John Marshall, a distant cousin (their mothers were both Randolphs and they hated each other), established the principle of judicial review in *Marbury v. Madison* in a way unchallengeable by the administration, and attempts to impeach Supreme Court Justice Samuel Chase and to convict former Vice President Aaron Burr of treason failed. Republicans' chief House leader John Randolph of Roanoke, another relative, turned against the administration on one issue after another. The world war between Britain and France had allowed American merchant shippers to amass fortunes and the neutral nation to prosper by dominating the trade to and from both combatants, but Napoleon's Continental System and Britain's Orders in Council cut off that lucrative trade and resulted in mass seizures of American ships and cargo. As historian Robert Wiebe writes, "Like the rest of their generation, Jefferson and his colleagues could not grasp America's insignificance in Europe's calculations. Napoleon had utter disdain for everything about that bastard republic. Although the United States asked only that France repeal those ocean rules it could not enforce in any case, Napoleon still would not bother.... Various British governments on their part decided that they could get what they needed from American commerce without conceding anything to its government."[95] When Britain pressed its Orders in Council, Jefferson's solution was to go back to the principle of the Association of 1769, four decades before, and bar American ships from sailing abroad in the hope that Britain would respond to economic pressure. He persuaded Congress to pass the Embargo Act in 1807 but, as Treasury Secretary Albert Gallatin, always a more realistic economist than Jefferson, predicted, the act brought economic ruin and political discontent to much of the country and was allowed to lapse the day before Jefferson left office,[96] "a splendid misery," as he called it. "Never did a prisoner released from his chains feel such relief as I shall on shaking off the shackles of power."

Released, he headed to the house on top of the little mountain, and the president, who had seldom visited any other part of the United States except its capitals, never left Virginia again. He had begun in 1806 to build another house, a smaller Monticello, in Poplar Forest in Bedford County, which he visited once or twice a year in the 1810s[97] to get away from the crush of family members and visitors, and the continuing construction projects, at Monticello. In his library there, over the dining table with bottles selected from his ample wine cellar, overlooking the vast Piedmont below from the sawed-off mountaintop, consulting his collections of artifacts and his ever-present maps, he could survey the entire world without leaving the zone which he had created and where he could be assured of total veneration and devotion. Kentucky, Tennessee, and the Southwest, which he had hoped to populate with deferential yeoman farmers was instead a land of casual violence, inveterate gambling, and enthusiastic evangelical religion—not Jeffersonian pastimes. The Northwest Territory, which he had proposed perhaps casually to be barred to slavery and speckled with schools, was peopled increasingly by a New England diaspora, enthusiastic for reforms not to Jefferson's refined tastes either. As for the Northeast, ignored in *Notes on Virginia*, as Gordon Wood writes, "He hated the obsessive money-making, the proliferating banks, and the liberal capitalistic world that emerged in the Northern states in the early nineteenth century, but no one in America did more to bring that world about."[98]

"The world around him, the world he had helped create, was rapidly changing, in ways Jefferson found bewildering and sometimes even terrifying," Wood goes on,[99] and the nation he held together in 1801 and expanded in 1803 seemed in danger of being torn apart by divisions over slavery. He dismissed pleas by Edward Coles, a young aide to President Madison who had inherited a plantation not far from Monticello, who in July 1814, wrote Jefferson "to entreat and beseech you to exert your knowledge and influence in devising and getting into operation some plan for the general emancipation of slavery,...a duty, as I conceive that devolves particularly on you."[100] Two months later, and after the British burning of Washington, DC, Jefferson wrote back, hailing Coles's "solitary but welcome voice," but noting "the general silence which prevails on this subject," and calling Coles's imprecations "like bidding old Priam to buckle the armor of Hector," and pleading inability due to age. "No, I have overlived the generation with which mutual labors and perils begat mutual confidence and influence. This enterprise is for the young, for those who can follow it up and bear it through to its consummation."[101] Later Coles was to free his slaves and buy them land in Illinois, where he was elected governor in 1822 and helped defeat a referendum that might have legalized slavery there.[102] Jefferson's attitude to secession was more equivocal. The author of the Kentucky Resolutions, which many read to justify secession, wrote in 1816 to Treasury Secretary William Crawford, whom he would support for president eight years later. "I have no hesitation in saying, 'let us separate.' I would rather the States should withdraw, which are for unlimited commerce and war, and confederate with those alone which are for peace and agriculture.[103] Perhaps he was just catering to the loathing he shared with his longtime Jeffersonian ally for the policies of Alexander Hamilton, although Hamilton's support for commerce and military preparedness had led to war not when he and his allies were in power, but when Jefferson's and Crawford's were. But Jefferson's positive reference to secession on the basis of issues of the past could indicate an openness to secession on the basis of the agonizing issue he came to expect would be pressing in the future. For he was clearly transfixed and anguished by the controversy over admitting Missouri as a slave state in 1819–20. Still possessed of his gift for the memorable phrase, the slavery issue, he wrote in one letter, "was a fire bell in the night." And "we have the wolf by the ear, and we can neither hold him, nor safely let him go. Justice is in one scale, and self-preservation in the other."[104]

In the entrance hall in Monticello and in his spacious office area beyond, Jefferson mounted Indian artifacts and fossils from the Lewis and Clark expedition. They are mute testimony to the mental maps of the president who, after quickly overcoming his constitutional qualms, extended America's boundaries far westward and sent explorers all the way to the Pacific Ocean. Not all of Jefferson's hopes for the future were realized. Students at his University of Virginia proved less interested in natural sciences and philosophy than in alcohol-fueled rowdiness, and the Virginia he cherished in his only published book was gaining slaves and losing the independent farmers he cherished to the lands across the mountains. His party proved adept at winning elections, and produced three consecutive eight-year presidencies headed by his deferential personal allies and congenial local neighbors, James Madison and James Monroe. But his Republicans ended up acquiescing in Alexander Hamilton's fiscal system, and through the Bank of the United States, which Jefferson and Madison had opposed in the 1790s, they created service academies and a peacetime army and navy. They also skittered back and forth on whether Congress should fund roads and canals—public works and internal improvements originally considered not within the constitutional ambit of the federal government. Jefferson kept aloof from current developments, and when persuaded by Richard Rush to resume correspondence with his onetime friend and then opponent John Adams, he wrote guarded responses to Adams's effusive essays. He sold his library to restock the Library of Congress burned by British soldiers, but he silently abandoned all hopes of paying off his long-accumulated debts and that of a fellow Virginia planter whose request for cosigning loans he felt he could not honorably refuse. He died famously the same day as Adams, July 4, 1826, exactly fifty years to the day of the proclamation of the Declaration of Independence. But while the modest Adams mansion was preserved by the second president's son, now president himself, the meticulously designed and redesigned little mansion on the mountain, Monticello, soon settled into ruin. Jefferson's slaves, except for the children of Sally Hemings, whom he freed, were sold at auction in November 1826. "Valuable historical and portrait paintings, busts of marble and plaister of distinguished individuals, . . . a polygraph of copying instrument used by Thomas Jefferson . . . with various other articles curious and used to men of business and private families" were sold in a five-day sale in January 1827. A lottery to pay off his debts failed. Monticello was sold in 1831 for $7,000.[105] The most successful partisan leader of his age, who from age fourteen lived and worked much as he pleased, ended his life frustrated, as the nation he had done so much to define and shape turned out differently from his plans, unable to preserve the house he built and rebuilt and rebuilt again on top of his little mountain.

Join or Die, the political cartoon commissioned and published by Benjamin Franklin in 1754. This was the first ever political cartoon published in North America and was part of early attempts to make Americans regard the Seaboard colonies as a single unit. *Library of Congress, Prints and Photographs Division*

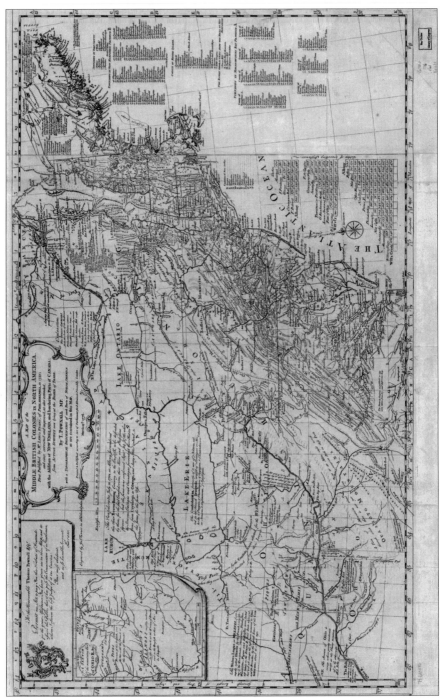

A map of the middle British colonies in North America in 1755. Note the contrast between the relatively accurate rendition of the seacoast and the inaccuracy of areas beyond the mountains. This, and the Fry-Jefferson map, are examples of how what would become the thirteen states were not seen as a single unit by the generation before. *Library of Congress, Geography and Maps Division*

A map of the United States agreeable to the peace of 1783. This shows the theoretical extent of the new republic, including lands beyond the Appalachians over which the Confederation Congress had no effective control. *Library of Congress, Geography and Maps Division*

A map of the United States and part of Louisiana circa 1805. Note the relative accuracy of the rivers flowing into the Mississippi as compared to earlier maps, and also the lack of details indicating non-Indian settlement west of the Appalachians. This is the background on which Treasury Secretary Albert Gallatin made his proposals for federal transportation improvements in 1808. *Library of Congress, Geography and Maps Division*

FOUR

ALEXANDER HAMILTON

Across the Sea Lanes

There is no record of how the thirteen-year-old Alexander Hamilton came to work for the mercantile house of Beekman & Cruger in St. Croix after his mother died in February 1768. Hamilton never told his American contemporaries about his years growing up on the British island of Nevis and the Danish island of St. Croix and mentioned it only in passing to his children. "What we know of Hamilton's childhood," as his biographer Ron Chernow writes, "has been learned almost entirely during the past century."[1] Nevis and St. Croix were among the Caribbean islands that were in the eighteenth century at the geographic fringe of European settlement, but central to the production of a commodity that had become over the preceding century the largest component of world trade: sugar. The taste for sugar, in tea or coffee, in candies, in chocolate, in molasses and rum, swept western Europe in the late seventeenth century and grew multifold in the eighteenth, and the quest for islands capable of growing cane sugar by the governments of Portugal and Spain, England and France, the Netherlands and Denmark was intense. From Madeira and the Canaries, the search ran westward across the Atlantic, to the South American mainland in the northeast of Brazil and to the Caribbean isles.[2] By the middle of the eighteenth century, sugar-producing Saint-

Domingue (present-day Haiti) was the jewel in France's colonial crown and sugar-producing Jamaica in Britain's. French trade with the Americas amounted to one-quarter of all French international commercial operations, and the British trade with the Americas was of a similar magnitude.[3] Smaller Caribbean islands were snapped up by smaller powers. Curaçao was acquired by the Dutch West India Company in 1634. St. Croix, a possession at various times of the Spanish, British, Dutch, French, and the Knights of Malta,[4] was acquired by the Danish West India and Guinea Company in 1733 and then by the Danish crown in 1755, "the beginning of the Golden Days of St. Croix, when sugar or 'white gold' made several planters wealthy, and elaborate estate houses and town houses were constructed throughout the island."[5]

But for the very large majority of people on this booming island, life was dismal and violent. St. Croix in the middle of the eighteenth century was home to about 20,000 black slaves and about 2,000 free whites. Raising and refining sugar was backbreaking work for the slaves, and mortality was so high that new bodies were constantly needed.[6] As a result, the trans-Atlantic slave trade was at its peak during the middle and late eighteenth century. Mortality was high as well among whites, few of whom had immunity to tropical diseases. As for elaborate estate houses, most whites barely scraped by or, like Alexander Hamilton's parents, plunged downward toward disaster. His father, James Hamilton, was the fourth son of the Laird of The Grange in Ayrshire, Scotland. With little chance of inheriting the title, and lacking the university education or business success of his brothers, he set out to the volcanic sugar island of St. Kitts southwest of St. Croix. There he met Rachel Faucette, a descendant of French Huguenots who as a teenager was married off to a supposedly rich St. Croix planter, Johann Lavien. The marriage broke up after the birth of a son, and her husband after dissipating her inheritance had her jailed for adultery. She fled to St. Kitts, where she met James Hamilton, and they moved in together in nearby

Nevis, where their second surviving son, Alexander Hamilton, was born in 1755.[7]

Ten years later they moved to St. Croix, where James pursued a lawsuit, and found that Rachel was barred from remarrying by Lavien's divorce decree. More disasters loomed. In January 1766, James Hamilton won his lawsuit and promptly left St. Croix, never to return to his family. Rachel supported herself by opening a store selling provisions she purchased from the local office of the New York merchant firm Beekman & Cruger. But in February 1768, she died and all her money was inherited by her son by Lavien. Her sister's husband, Peter Lytton, did manage to buy at auction her thirty-four books and give them to her younger son. Sometime in the next year, the thirteen-year-old Alexander went to work for Beekman & Cruger, while his older brother was apprenticed to a carpenter. Then Peter Lytton committed suicide in July 1769 and his father died a month later, with neither leaving anything to the Hamilton sons. "Let us pause briefly," writes Ron Chernow, "to tally the grim catalog of disasters that had befallen these two boys between 1765 and 1769: Their father had vanished, their mother had died, their cousin and supposed protector had committed bloody suicide, and their aunt, uncle and grandmother had all died. James, sixteen, and Alexander, fourteen, were left alone, largely friendless and penniless. At every step in their rootless, topsy-turvy existence, they had been surrounded by failed, broken, embittered people. Their short lives had been shadowed by a stupefying sequence of bankruptcies, marital separations, deaths, scandals, and disinheritance."[8]

Yet at his desk at Beekman & Cruger, a block from the port of Christiansted, Alexander Hamilton was in touch with a much larger and more variegated world, a vast network of trading voyages that spread from Europe to North America, South Asia, Africa, and the Caribbean. In the middle of the eighteenth century, the major nations of Europe tried to preserve monopolies over trade with their distant colonies for ships of their own nationality. Spain jealously limited access to its lands in the Americas and the Philippines to Spanish ships or to a few foreigners authorized for special purposes, like the British traders granted a monopoly contract, the *asiento*, to import slaves from Africa. Thus the Prussian explorer and naturalist Alexander von Humboldt had to obtain official leave from Spain for his expedition to South America in 1799. Portugal had similar restrictions on trading in its far-flung merchant ports, as did their enemies and in some cases their successors from the Dutch Republic. England's Navigation Acts of 1651 and 1660, the products of republican and royal governments, similarly cordoned off English colonies from foreign ships; only after the Act of Union of 1707, joining Scotland to England in the United Kingdom, could Scottish merchants trade in British Caribbean islands and North American colonies.

Such mercantile restrictions did not, however, limit trade in St. Croix, whose Danish rulers lacked the merchant marine to service its needs and the military navy to enforce its restrictions. British, French, Dutch, and Danish ships regularly pulled up to its docks, their captains and crews spoke a multitude of languages and creoles and their bargains were contracted in a dizzying variety of currencies. Beekman & Cruger was a branch of a merchant house based in New York, and both were members of prominent Dutch families with roots going back to Nieuw Amsterdam. Hamilton's boss, Nicholas Cruger's father, was a prominent ship owner in New York and a member of the colony's royal province, his uncle John Cruger was mayor of New York and a member of the Stamp Act Congress, and his brother Henry Cruger was a member of Parliament for Bristol, the west of England port which conducted much of Britain's trade with North America.[9] Ron Chernow in his vivid biography had good reason to write that the teenage Alexander Hamilton "did not operate in an obscure corner of the world, and his first job afforded him valuable insights in global commerce and the maneuvers of imperial powers." St. Croix produced sugar and had to import almost everything else: The young clerk "had to monitor a bewildering inventory of goods. The firm dealt in every conceivable commodity required by planters: timber, bread, flour, rice, lard, pork, beef, fish, black-eyed peas, corn, porter, cider, pine, oak, hoops, shingles, iron, lime, rope, lampblack, bricks, mules, and cattle.... He learned to write in a beautiful, clear, flowing hand. He had to mind money, chart courses for ships, keep track of freight, and compute prices in an exotic blend of currencies, including Portuguese coins, Spanish pieces of eight, British pounds, Danish ducats, and Dutch stivers."[10] According to one friend, "he conceived so strong an aversion" to his clerkship "as to be induced to abandon altogether the pursuits of commerce."[11] But he did not forget the lessons it taught. Years later he told one of his sons that his experience at Beekman & Cruger had been "the most useful of his education," teaching him "method" and "facility."[12]

But surely it taught him something more. It gave him an intimate acquaintance with one end of the dozens of invisible lines marking the passage of merchant ships across the world's oceans from one mercantile anchorage to another. Those lines on the globe marked the commercial connections that made it possible for some still small percentage of mankind to live above the standard of subsistence farming or traditional hunting and gathering. Almost no other job in St. Croix would have given him such a sustained acquaintance of its ocean pathways to the outside world, the avenues to escape what Richard Brookhiser describes as St. Croix's "barren riches and its lack of opportunity."[13] "The community there may have been a planting community, but it was the merchant who brought it to life and gave it whatever touch it had with the outside world," historians Stanley Elkins and Eric McKittrick write. "In no setting, probably, could the cosmopolitan character of the eighteenth-century merchant have been more sharply appreciated."[14] One aspect of the merchant community's cosmopolitan perspective was its dependence on the *lex mercatoria*, the rules and customs, building on free contractual relationships, governing the international exchange of commodities and of bills of exchange, notes, and other negotiable instruments.[15] That the adolescent Alexander Hamilton understood this became apparent when the resident partner Nichols Cruger returned to New York in October 1771 for what turned out to be a five-month visit for medical treatment. The sixteen-year-old Hamilton unhesitatingly took charge, collecting money from reluctant creditors and demanding that the captain of a Cruger-owned ship purchase guns for a voyage to Curaçao. "The adolescent clerk had a capacity for quick decisions and showed no qualms about giving a tongue-lashing to a veteran sea captain," writes Chernow. "He developed an intimate knowledge of traders and smugglers, ... saw that business was often obstructed by scarce cash or credit and ... was forced to ponder the paradox that the West Indian islands, with all their fertile soil, traded at a disadvantage with the rest of the world because of their reliance on only the sugar crop."[16] He showed that he was ready for, indeed that he was itching to take on, adult responsibilities. Hamilton's precocity and eagerness to gain experience resembles that of his almost exact contemporary Wolfgang Amadeus Mozart, with the interesting contrast that while Mozart's genius was recognized and nurtured by his father, a professional musician, from the time he was four, Hamilton's astonishing capacities blazed into light in an atmosphere of darkness and were only dimly appreciated by those around him.

In the months that followed his superintendency, he also showed that he could write energetic and dramatic prose. We do not know the titles of the thirty-four books that his uncle purchased from his mother's estate and presented to him, but they almost certainly included *Plutarch's Lives* and the poetry of Alexander Pope, and may have included more practical volumes such as Malachy Postlethwayt's *Universal Dictionary of Trade & Commerce*. After a violent hurricane struck St. Croix on the last day of August 1772, Hamilton wrote a dramatic account in a letter to his father. Apparently he showed it to a newly installed minister who had befriended him, Hugh Knox, who had it published anonymously in the *Royal Danish American Gazette* in October. It was a local sensation, and one wonders if Hamilton wrote it to impress people, since in his adult life, as Ron Chernow notes, "The endless letters that flowed from his pen are generally abstract and devoid of imagery. He almost never described weather"—even extreme weather—"or scenery, the clothing or manners of people he met, the furniture of rooms he inhabited."[17] But whether the impression he made was calculated, or whether it owed something to the reputation he had achieved as part of what was, after all, a small community, the publication of the letter was quickly followed by a subscription fund set up by Knox and local merchants to send Hamilton to college in North America. The details were long ago lost in time, as was the date of his voyage, which some authorities believe was in October 1772 or, as Chernow speculates, in the early months of 1773. In any case it is agreed that Alexander Hamilton sailed to Boston and quickly made his way to New York. He never returned to the Caribbean or ever expressed any desire to see it again.[18]

Hamilton's destination was never in doubt: New York. This was partly a matter of contacts. New York was the home base of Kortright & Cruger (Beekman left the firm and a member of another old Dutch family joined it) and was also the home of Hugh Knox's Presbyterian associates. But it was not otherwise inevitable. New York was not yet the Empire State it became; it would be only the fifth most populous state in the 1790 Census (after Virginia, Pennsylvania, North Carolina, and Massachusetts), and in colonial times, New York City was much less populous than Philadelphia and not much larger than Boston. But New

York stood out in another respect. It was the only colony whose founders and first settlers were not from the British Isles. The historian David Hackett Fischer's *Albion's Seed* famously describes how settlers from four different British and Irish regions brought their folkways—ways of living ranging from politics to religion to sexual behavior—to different parts of the British North American colonies. But New York, as Fischer acknowledged, was an exception, founded by the Dutch West India Company as Nieuw Amsterdam in 1623, populated by Dutch settlers, and captured by England only in its Second Dutch War in 1664 and relinquished by the Dutch in return for the East Indies nutmeg island of Rum.[19] In the eighteenth century and after Dutch families like the Crugers and Beekmans, Kortrights and Roosevelts continued to be leading New Yorkers, and much of the Hudson Valley between Manhattan and Albany was leased out to tenant farmers by the heirs of Dutch-descended patroons like the Schuylers and VanCortlandts and the Scots-origin Livingstons. The former Nieuw Amsterdam continued to have a Dutch character, favoring commerce with all parts of the world and toleration of every religion and belief, combined with an indifference to principle and scruple. It was "a city where commerce always held an honored place," Ron Chernow writes, and in the 1770s, it "already had a history as a raucous commercial hub, a boisterous port that blended many cultures and religions. Fourteen languages were spoken there by the time Hamilton arrived."[20] Its tolerant atmosphere attracted many French Huguenots (including ancestors of Chief Justice John Jay and John D. Rockefeller) and Jews. As Henry Adams wrote in his classic history of the Jefferson and Madison administrations, "New York cared little for the metaphysical subtleties of Massachusetts and Virginia, which convulsed the nation with spasms almost as violent as those that, fourteen centuries before, distracted the Eastern Empire in the effort to establish the double or single nature of Christ. New York was indifferent whether the nature of the United States was single or multiple, whether they were a nation or a league. Leaving this class of questions to other States which were deeply interested in them, New York remained constant to no political theory."[21] While New England, with its frigid winters, had few slaves in the colonial years and the New England states hastened to abolish slavery in the 1780s, and while Pennsylvania's Quaker founders had principled objections to slavery, New York and neighboring New Jersey before the Revolutionary War were unashamedly slave territory. New York City "still held slave auctions in the 1750s and was also linked through its sugar refineries to the West Indies. Even in the 1790s, one in five New York City households kept domestic slaves, a practice ubiquitous among well-to-do merchants who wanted cooks, maids, and butlers and regarded slaves as status symbols, writes Ron Chernow. "Slaves till the farms of many of the Hudson River estates along with tenant farmers, one English visitor noting that 'many of the old Dutch farmers...have 20 to 30 slaves[, and] to their care and management everything is left."[22]

Lin-Manuel Miranda's musical *Hamilton* characterizes its title character as an immigrant—as an exemplar of those millions who arrived from other countries to New York from its early years to the present. But the eighteen-year-old Alexander Hamilton may not have thought of himself as an immigrant. He was born a British subject, the son of a British father, on the British island of Nevis. It was evidently immaterial that he had been living in St. Croix, a Danish colony but one in which English was the common dominant language of commerce and in which British politics was the subject of intensive coverage in the *Royal Danish American Gazette* starting in 1770.[23] In what was still a small colonial society, his stipend for study provided by his admirers in St. Croix and his letters of introduction from Hugh Knox opened doors of prominent leaders, who were immediately impressed by the young man's ebullient brilliance. He spent several months at the Elizabethtown Academy across the bay in New Jersey and became a regular in the household of William Livingston, a scion of the Hudson Valley patroon family and the first post-colonial governor of New Jersey. He gained an interview with John Witherspoon, president of the Presbyterian-founded College of New Jersey (later Princeton). But Witherspoon refused his request to advance immediately to an upper class, and Hamilton instead enrolled at the Anglican-founded King's College (later Columbia) in New York City, one block west of the Common (current City Hall Park).

At college, he studied hard—and in a Sons of Liberty protest in the Common, he attracted attention in July 1774, delivering a spontaneous speech endorsing the Boston Tea Party, denouncing Britain's closure of the port of Boston, and calling for a boycott of British goods.[24] With British troops stationed in an obviously rebellious Boston, the potential for armed hostilities was obvious—an eventuality that Hamilton seems to have regarded less with dread than delight. In November 1769, at age fourteen, in his first surviving letter, addressed to "his dear friend and look-alike Edward Stevens," he confessed to a vast but undefined ambition and wrote, "We have seen such schemes successful when the projector is constant. I shall conclude [by] saying I wish there was a war."[25] Commerce might provide avenues for slow ascent but war, by unsettling the ranks of society, could open the prospect for sudden advancement to otherwise unreachable heights. "Hamilton came to North America in 1772 [or 1773] as the clouds of war against Britain were beginning to gather," writes economic historian Thomas McCraw. "He had a military frame of mind from the start. For the remaining thirty-two years of his life, first the independence and then the continued safety of his adopted country remained at risk from foreign threats."[26] For all his intellectual prowess, Hamilton yearned also for military glory, as evidenced by his pleas to George

Washington for release from his staff position to active combat and his maneuvering around John Adams to get himself appointed second in command to former President Washington in the army about to be assembled to meet the threat of war with France.

So it is not surprising that while a student still in his teens, Hamilton wrote two anonymous pamphlets published in December 1774 and February 1775, answering the pro-British arguments of forty-five-year-old Anglican minister Samuel Seabury.[27] In their 60,000 words, seemingly written with the same ease as the young Mozart composing a symphony, Hamilton showed a remarkable vision of the future. With unearned acerbity, he condescendingly recommends that Seabury read "Grotius, Puffendorf [*sic*], Locke, Montesquieu, Burlemaqui" and provides his own summary of their work: "The origin of all civil government, justly established, must be a voluntary compact, between the rulers and the ruled." He even waxes poetic about "the sacred rights of mankind" which "are written, as with a sun beam, in the whole of human nature, by the hand of divinity itself; and can never be erased or obscured by mortal power." But he also follows the skeptical philosopher David Hume[28] in arguing that a just system of government must be based on the counterfactual assumption that all men are "knaves," and that "a fondness for power is implanted, in most men, and it is natural to abuse it, when acquired." Writing after the Boston Tea Party but before Lexington and Concord, he asserts his and the Continental Congress's allegiance to the king, while insisting that as for Parliament, "they have no right to govern us." From the thirty-four books he got from his mother, and from the reading he managed to do while improving his Latin and Greek for King's College, the adolescent Hamilton showed a considerable knowledge of history, ticking off one after another of the colonial charters granted to each colony without any authorization from Parliament. He showed also a grasp of the geography of British North America, "this vast continent," which was so very different from the tiny islands he had grown up in. He hails "the boundless extent of territory we [New Yorkers? Americans?] possess, the whole temperament of our climate, the luxuriance and fertility of our soil, the variety of our products, the rapidity of our population, the industry of our country men and the commodiousness of our ports," which "naturally lead to a suspicion of independence." He argues that Americans can increase their production of export products—sheep, "livestock of every kind," grain, flax, hemp, cotton, "skins"—for their own internal market.

The young Alexander Hamilton clearly had developed in his mind a map of a North American commonwealth that could defeat the British militarily and could attain national stature on its own. "Let it be remembered that there are no large plains for the two armies to meet in and decide the contest, by some decisive stroke," he writes, contrasting the relatively narrow geographical margins between the Atlantic and the Appalachian ridges with the expanse of the Northern European plain stretching from France across the Low Countries and through German territories toward Russia in the east, the terrain that had seen so many decisive battles in European wars. He calculates, optimistically as it turned out, that any British military force, though "some of the best troops in the world, with respect to valour or discipline," would be outnumbered by enthusiastic colonials. "Should their soldiery advance into the country, as they would be obliged to do, if they had any inclination to subdue us, their discipline would be of little use to them." Without any previous military experience, and facing circumstances which he never encountered or could have anticipated, he drew on his geographic observations the same military strategy that George Washington would employ. "The circumstances of our country put it in our power to evade a pitched battle. It will be better policy to harass and exhaust the [British] soldiery by frequent skirmishes and incursions than to take the open field with them. Americans are better qualified, for that kind of fighting, which is most adapted to this country, than regular troops." He was optimistic that "Our troops, on the spot, with us, will be much more easily maintained, than those of Britain, at such a distance" and that "France, Spain and Holland," which he forecast accurately would join the colonists in order to weaken Britain, "would find means, to supply us with whatever we wanted." Nor did his vision stop with imagining favorable prospects for a revolutionary war; it extended beyond to what, despite his avowals of loyalty to the king, looked like a future American republic. "There can be no room for doubt, that we may live without the manufactures of Britain, if we are careful, frugal and industrious," the future author of the *Report on Manufactures* asserts—though he does not yet advance the financial policies he would propose to make the young republic commercially venturesome and economically strong. And he evinces no doubt that a rapidly growing America "in fifty or sixty years," that is, in the 1820s, "America will be in no need of protection from Great-Britain. She will then be able to protect herself, both at home and abroad. She will have a plenty of men and a plenty of materials to provide and equip a formidable navy." "This was more than just precocious knowledge," Chernow writes of Hamilton's accurate anticipation of Washington's military strategy. "This was intuitive judgment of the highest order."[29]

New York with its polyglot population and its varied lineages, in contrast to colonial ports like Boston and Charleston with their long-established and interconnected elites, provided newcomers with plenty of avenues in which to rise. But its diverse cultures also made it a cockpit of argument, and on no issue more than whether to protest and sever links with Britain. As the British military historian Piers Mackesy observes, the colonies were split on ethnic lines. "The [Loyalist] Tories were weakest where the colonists were of the purest English stock. In New England they may have been scarcely a tenth of the population; in the South a quarter or third; but in the Middle Colonies including New York perhaps a half." [30] So if Hamilton encountered "tremendous revolutionary ferment" and "some of the colonies' most eloquent agitators and outspoken newspapers" in the city's two square miles south of King's College, he was also exposed to "a vocal Tory population" in which, as he remembered later, "near one half of them were avowed more attached to Great Britain than to their liberty. [31]

Hamilton left no doubt which side he was on. In "the virulent clash of Tories and Whigs" he unstintingly opposed the former and supported the latter, as in his pamphlet denigrating Seabury and denouncing his theories. [32] In April 1775, after news of the armed clashes at Lexington and Concord reached New York, he joined a Patriot militia and intensively studied military drills, tactics, technology, and strategy. Yet in May 1775, when a group of Patriots tried to seize the college's staunchly Loyalist president, Myles Cooper, Hamilton stood outside his door while Cooper escaped to the waterfront, where he fled in a Britain-bound ship. Hamilton had shown himself as "a committed revolutionary with a profound dread that popular sentiment would boil over into dangerous excess." [33] In June 1775, Hamilton witnessed George Washington's arrival in New York on his way from the Second Continental Congress in Philadelphia to his military command in Massachusetts. Through the next six months, he continued his studies at King's, his drills in the militia, his frequent anonymous pamphleteering, and his dispatches to the *Royal Danish American Gazette*. In February 1776, he stepped up to become a captain in a New York artillery unit authorized by the Continental Congress, and drilled his soldiers before General Washington during his brief and disastrous campaigning in and around New York. Even as the army was defeated and came close to annihilation, Hamilton had come to Washington's attention, receiving favorable notice as artillery commander during the retreat across New Jersey and then during Washington's Christmas and New Year's attacks in Trenton and Princeton. In January 1777, Washington asked Hamilton to join his staff as an aide-de-camp. "In fewer than five years," summarizes Chernow, "the twenty-two-year-old Alexander Hamilton had risen from despondent clerk in St. Croix to one of the aides of America's most eminent man."[34]

As Washington's chief aide from March 1777 to February 1781, Hamilton was a front-row witness not only to his military decisions, but to his political struggle to extract enough money from the Continental Congress to keep his army functioning. He also observed the implications of Washington's strategic concentration on recapturing New York City. It was apparent that the British had written off most of New England as a lost cause, but also that they had considerable support in New York—and that their retention of New York made impossible the construction of a new, majority-Patriot nation including both New England and what many then regarded as the middle states of Pennsylvania, Delaware, Maryland, and Virginia. Washington established his winter camps in sites ringing New York City[35]—Middlebrook, New Jersey; Valley Forge, Pennsylvania; Morristown, New Jersey; New Windsor, New York—and was only persuaded to move in the late summer of 1781 south to the Chesapeake Bay in Virginia, after considerable hesitation, with the assurance that the French fleet and French army, with more men than Washington's Continentals, would be heading there as well. After many years of carrying out the strategy envisioned by Hamilton in 1775 and carried out by Washington from that year forward, the surrender of General Cornwallis at Yorktown in October 1781 was a sudden and unanticipated success, although British troops remained in New York until November 1783.

Hamilton's work as Washington's aide was enough to keep him busy during almost every working hour. Yet somehow he managed not just "to meditate on the deeper causes of the surrounding misery," but also through wide reading meticulously noted in his pay book, set about "mastering the rudiments of finance"[36] and the fundaments of republican theory, with a view to setting the course for the new nation when the war was won. These were novel subjects. Republics were rare in the eighteenth-century world, and those that did exist—Venice, Switzerland, the Netherlands—were far smaller geographically than the American states. Sustained economic growth was a rarity as well, experienced only for a few decades in a few countries and commercial cities, and assumed to be as ephemeral as previous growth spurts had been. Nonetheless, in his middle twenties, the military aide Alexander Hamilton imagined not only that the country for whose independence he was fighting might govern itself successfully as a republic, but that that country could generate continued commercial success and economic growth, and he was developing specific plans to bring that about. His thinking can be seen in lengthy letters he wrote to prominent acquaintances who were well positioned to put his plans into operation—James Duane,[37] a rich New York lawyer, son-in-law of the Hudson River patroon Robert Livingston and member of the Continental Congress; and Robert Morris,[38] the very rich Philadelphia merchant who arranged—and made—loans which kept the Continental Army operating. Hamilton apparently dashed off these lengthy and learned missives to the most sophisticated of audiences as readily as his contemporary Mozart in these same years was dashing off symphonies, sonatas, and concertos.

In his September 1780 letter to Duane, after lamenting Washington's difficulty in getting funds from Congress and Congress's inability under the Articles of Confederation from doing more than asking the states for funds, he immodestly set out to describe "the defects of our present system, and the changes necessary to save us from ruin." He based his analysis not just on his bitter contemporary frustrations but also on the experience of other republics ancient and modern—"the old Grecian republics," "the Swiss-cantons" and "the Germanic corps." He lamented not just Congress's lack of power to tax under the Articles of Confederation but also "a diffidence in Congress of their own powers" and an acquiescence in state governments' efforts to run the army. "They should have nothing to do with it." "Without certain revenues, a government can have no power; that power, which holds the purse strings absolutely, must rule." And to rule effectively, government departments should be headed by individuals, not by multi-member boards.

How could these changes to be put into effect? In what Chernow calls his "most startling, visionary leap of all,"[39] Hamilton was the first person known to have advocated for "calling immediately a convention of all the states with full authority to conclude finally upon a general confederation." Congress should be given full powers over finance (including "establishing banks"), foreign policy, and "all that relates to war." His recommendations to this point look very much like what the Constitutional Convention did seven years later, but Hamilton wanted to go farther, to recruit a standing army "at least for three years" and paying military officers half-pay for life. In the letter's last paragraphs, Hamilton considered financing the government, through "four ways through all which must be united—a foreign loan, heavy pecuniary taxes, a tax in kind, a bank founded on public and private credit." He pointed to problems this might entail in a new nation with a colonial economy. Should the government accept tax payments in kind? Should part of the capital for a national bank consist of interests in (notoriously illiquid) land? How to "engage the monied interest" in support of, and in the financing of, the new republic?

These issues Hamilton addressed with more specificity in the next year, in April 1781, in a letter twice as long as his missive to Duane, which he dared to send to Robert Morris, perhaps the richest man in the colonies and preeminent financier of the revolutionary cause. Written six months before, and at a time when no one contemplated the decisive battle of Yorktown, and two months after he had left Washington's staff and was seeking a position as a combat officer, Hamilton showed himself familiar with the particulars of European politics—the recent death of Austrian Empress Maria Theresa, the hostility to the American cause of her son, the Emperor Joseph II, and the character of Spain's King Charles III ("a bigoted prince governed by a greedy confessor"). He showed himself familiar as well with the fiscal policies of states like relatively prosperous Massachusetts ("the mart of the states Northward of Pennsylvania") and with the success, at that point, of the British military offensive in the South ("allow for the loss of Georgia and South Carolina"). His range of knowledge makes it apparent that Hamilton somehow—it is hard to imagine just how—had the time and energy, and access to economic theory and statistical data, to confidently diagnose the new nation's economic condition and to prescribe financial remedies. Long before economists developed the concept of the gross domestic product, Hamilton attempted to measure the size of the economy by the amount of currency circulating and the capacity of the economy to support taxation, concluding that "the proportion of revenue which a nation is capable of affording is about one-fourth of its circulating cash." He added, "This is applicable only to commercial countries," and used the familiar examples of France and Britain plus the Netherlands. It may seem strange that he includes the Dutch Republic as well as the considerably larger France and Britain, but "it was a fact of life in the eighteenth century that any nation seeking to establish public credit must do so in Holland, for Amsterdam was the financial capital of the western world."[40]

From these calculations he concluded that the United States government needed to borrow substantial sums in wartime. To make such borrowings possible would require national taxation, he argued; Congress must impose "an instant, positive and perpetual investiture of an impost on trade, a land tax and a poll-tax to be collected by their own agents." This would require, he admitted in an aside, "a convention of all the states, with full power to alter and amend finally and irrevocably the present senseless and futile confederation." But it would also require—and this is the chief subject of the letter—a national bank. He goes into great detail on terms and conditions: The bank shall pay shareholders dividends of 4 percent and can make loans of 8 percent, it shall redeem all outstanding continental and state debt, and in the process it will produce "a stable currency, an idea fundamental to all practical schemes of finance," and a sufficient amount of circulating currency—something that the colonies had always lacked. It would redeem all outstanding continental and state debt and continue to do so, for "a national debt if it is not excessive will be to us a national blessing; it will be powerful cement of our union. It will also create a necessity for keeping up taxation to a degree which without being oppressive, will be a spur to industry."

Here in a nutshell—a pretty considerable nutshell, since the letter is more than 13,000 words long—is the program which Hamilton, more than anyone else, would put into effect over the next fifteen years: the constitutional convention which he had already proposed to Duane; the consolidation of state and congressional debts, and their perpetuation as a continuing national debt; the passage of federal tariff and excise taxes; and the creation of a national bank. In arguing for the collection of taxes in kind in his letter to Duane, Hamilton had explicitly compared the new nation to "those countries which are not commercial,...Russia, Prussia, Denmark, Sweden." But in his letter to Morris seven months later, he implicitly argued that the United States should be something more. "Most commercial nations have found it necessary to institute banks," he wrote, "and they have proved to be the happiest engines that ever were invented for advancing trade." The colonies had limited economies, providing foodstuffs and raw materials to Britain and its Caribbean colonies and purchasing manufactured goods from England. They had something in the nature of insurance companies, formed by merchants seeking to poll the risks of overseas voyages, but no banks whatever, and a chronic shortage of metallic currency. Barter was standard practice in many transactions, while the financing of planters' exports was handled by factors in England. Hamilton predicted, accurately it turned out, that the circulating currency brought into existence by the national debt and the national bank could foster financial and manufacturing sectors that could rival those of the mother country and her European neighbors.

In retrospect, the late eighteenth century, in various parts of western Europe and coastal North America, saw the world's first sustained economic growth, a rising standard of living not just for elite leaders but for great masses of the society. This was, in the phrase of the optimistic economist Deirdre McCloskey, focusing on growth to come, the great enrichment; or in the words of the more pessimistic economist Angus Deaton, focusing on stagnant preceding centuries, the great escape.[41] Gross economic product, for centuries a straight horizontal line on the graph, was suddenly jutting upward. That movement began in northwestern Europe and was powered forward by mercantile trade. In his days working in and running the house of Beekman & Cruger, Hamilton saw this process from afar, across the shipping routes over which merchants transported the Caribbean's luxury product, sugar, to destinations where increasing numbers could afford it. The focus of this young writer in these wartime letters was on such destinations, and he was urging the new nation that had yet to emerge from the war to learn from their examples. In arguing for a national bank, Hamilton assures Morris that "Venice, Genoa, Hamburgh [sic], Holland, and England are examples of their utility. They owe their riches, commerce, and the figure they have made at different periods in a great degree to this source." He cited two of the remaining Italian city-state republics and the leading Hanseatic League city of Hamburg, and made implicit reference to Holland's leading city, Amsterdam, facing the North Sea from the east, and England's leading city, London, facing it down the Thames to the west. The continental cities in the early 1780s still had their political independence and their merchant-dominated governments, buttressed by civic banking institutions, and Dutch and English trade and prosperity were built on shipping and finance fostered by the Bank of Amsterdam, founded in 1609, and on its offspring and rival, the Bank of England, founded in 1694 under the auspices of Britain's Dutch monarch William III.

Hamilton's admiration for the British model separated him from most of the other Founding Fathers. As Bernard Bailyn, Gordon Wood, and others of the great generation of Colonial American historians have explained, their political theories owed much to English writers such as John Trenchard and Thomas Gordon, the anonymous authors of *Cato's Letters*, and Lord Bolingbroke, the author of *The Patriot King*.[42] These writers and the independent parliamentarians who styled themselves the Country party hated the commercial growth, vigorous speculation, and funded national debt fostered by the bank. The Court party of the Hanoverian kings, led by Robert Walpole, Prime Minister in 1721–42, and managed by the wealthy Duke of Newcastle, a minister for most of the years in 1715–60, was maintained, in their opponents' view, by rampant corruption and bribery. This view of British politics as laced with corruption was shared, to varying extents, by America's Founding five presidents.

Hamilton took a different view. He regarded Walpole's and Newcastle's payments to members of Parliament as necessary lubricants of the engine of state, and he regarded the Bank of England and the funded national debt which it administered as a source of national strength. The Hanoverians' system had put London in the way of becoming Europe's leading financial and commercial center and had put Britain in the way of militarily facing down France, despite the latter having four times the population. These national banks, Hamilton argued, not only spurred economic innovation and growth, but also financed the naval and military forces that protected their independence and their access to the international trade routes running across the ocean which had mesmerized Alexander Hamilton since his adolescent days in St. Croix. "Great Britain is indebted," he wrote Robert Morris, "for the immense efforts she has been able to make in so many illustrious and successful wars essentially to that vast fabric of credit raised on this foundation. Tis by this alone," he added, "she now menaces our independence." Over what historians have called the long eighteenth century, from William III's successful Glorious Revolution in 1688–89 to the Duke of Wellington's defeat of Napoleon at Waterloo in 1815, Britain's capacity to finance the world's dominant navy, to field colonial armies, and to finance European allies enabled it to hold at bay and ultimately defeat a much larger and hitherto dominant France—except in the one war in which Alexander Hamilton was on the other side. Britain's ability to fund itself through the Bank of England and its funded national debt enabled it to build a superior Royal Navy and to fund the members of one continental coalition after another. In the midst of this long century, Hamilton felt confident in assuring Morris that "a national debt if it is not excessive will be...a national blessing." For America, he prophesized, "it will be a powerful cement of our union. It will also create a necessity for keeping up taxation to a degree without being oppressive, will be a spur to industry."

Hamilton evidently developed this vision during his apprenticeship in Beekman & Cruger's office in St. Croix, as he contemplated and at an astonishingly young age managed the voyages of ships unloading and loading their cargo in the port of Christiansted. Hamilton's mental map was a globe crisscrossed by the invisible lines of trade routes, linking the ports which were the Western World's leading centers of commerce and industry, which were also and not coincidentally the most affluent, tolerant, and free places on earth. Without knowing the initial geographical extent of the new nation—an issue not settled in theory until the Treaty of Paris was negotiated in 1783 and remaining unsettled, in fact, until British troops finally retreated from the lands between the Appalachian ridges and the Mississippi River pursuant to Jay's Treaty of 1795—Hamilton understood the United States of America would occupy a much larger space on the map of the world than the city-states of Italy, Germany, and Holland, and much larger geographically than England, Scotland, and Ireland as well. His appreciation of the potential growth of the new American nation at this point was breathtaking. Writing in 1781, at age twenty-six and after just eight years in North America, Hamilton was confident enough to state, "Speaking within moderate bounds our population will be doubled in thirty years; there will be a confluence of emigrants from all parts of the world; our commerce will have a proportionate progress, and of course our wealth and capacity for revenue. It will be a matter of choice, if we are not out of debt in twenty years, without at all encumbering the people." The nation's population did, in fact, more than double by 1811, and despite the efforts of Hamilton's political opponents Thomas Jefferson and James Madison, enough of his system remained in place to finance the purchase of the Louisiana Territory in 1803—an opportunity which flabbergasted Jefferson as much as it did Hamilton—and to pay for the War of 1812. Jefferson had looked forward to an America that would remain almost entirely agricultural, with a yeoman class heading west but somehow remaining deferential to landed leaders like himself. But the land speculators and farmers heading west were not deferential, and along the coasts and internally, at first along the wide and falling rivers but, as the century went on, across the landscape and on the coasts of the Great Lakes, a commercial and industrial America arose, an America that Hamilton's fiscal and financial measures, largely though not entirely envisioned as early as 1780, did so much to foster.

★ ★ ★

Sharing Hamilton's views were the two senior military and financial leaders of the new nation. "At the close of the war," Chernow writes, "Washington had circulated a letter to the thirteen governors, outlining four things America would need to attain greatness: consolidation of the states under a strong federal government, timely payment of its debts, creation of an army and a navy, and harmony among its people. Hamilton would have written the identical list"[43]—and indeed had written most of it in his letter to Duane. Robert Morris was evidently impressed by Hamilton's letter and presumably by his conversations with him over the next few years. In 1788, when he declined Washington's offer to become secretary of the Treasury, he "recommended Hamilton, 'a far cleverer fellow than I am,' Washington was surprised. 'I always knew Colonel Hamilton to be a man of superior talents,' he responded, 'but never supposed that he had any knowledge of finance.' 'He knows everything, sir,' Morris replied. 'To a mind like his nothing comes amiss.'"[44] A similar estimate came from Charles-Maurice de Talleyrand-Périgord, the French foreign minister and ambassador off and on and in different and hostile regimes between 1797 and 1834. In the 1790s, Talleyrand sailed to Philadelphia to escape the guillotine and spent much time with Hamilton, who was fluent in French (much more so than Benjamin Franklin or Thomas Jefferson, who served as ambassadors in Paris). In his long career, Talleyrand had close contact with the leading statesmen of the time—the emperors of Austria and Russia, Napoleon and Metternich, Louis XVI and Louis XVIII, Castelreagh and Charles James Fox. When asked to reflect in his later years on their relative greatness, Talleyrand said, "I consider Napoleon, Fox, and Hamilton the three greatest men of our epoch, and, if I were forced to decide between the three, I would give without hesitation that first place to Hamilton. He divined Europe."[45]

Yet Hamilton never set eyes on Europe. His avowal to his sister-in-law in London that it was his "favorite wish"[46] to visit Europe seems to have been no more sincere than the flirtatious badinage in her letters. Like Washington, who sailed to Barbados with his ailing brother Lawrence, Hamilton made only one overseas voyage, his permanent escape from the Caribbean. At the end of the war, as historian Forrest McDonald writes in his intellectual biography, "Hamilton's personal knowledge of the United States was confined to the small area bounded by Albany, Boston, and Yorktown, and he was really familiar only with the area between Albany and Philadelphia."[47] Wartime service took him from his student quarters in New York to New Jersey, Pennsylvania, and in the Yorktown campaign in 1781, to Maryland and Virginia. His marriage to Elizabeth Schuyler in 1780 took him often to the bailiwick of her father, General Philip Schuyler, scion of a prominent Hudson Valley family, in Albany, and after the war they set up house on Wall Street, then near the northern edge of settlement in Manhattan, and Hamilton set about studying law. New York law, he noted admiringly, more closely resembled English law than any other state's, and he completed a three-year course of study in just nine months.[48] He quickly became known as one of New York's premier lawyers, and one unafraid of controversy, taking on the cause of the property rights of Loyalists.

Amid his busy schedule, and despite the demands of a growing family, he did not abandon his political ideas. He was elected to the Confederation Congress in 1782 and there, in Philadelphia, met James Madison, who though the youngest member when he was elected in 1779 was already playing a major part in legislative debate. There he, like so many other Founders, gained experience in a legislature whose members were incentivized, as historian William Lee Miller writes, to "deal with each other as (more or less) equals, to persuade and deal and compromise and cast votes," and to become "the tactician, the compromiser, the 'skillful organizer who could keep various factions and pressure groups together.'"[49] Both Madison, who had served in Virginia's legislature, and Hamilton learned these skills, despite their bookishness and apparently unsuitable temperaments—Madison's too quiet, Hamilton's too impulsive—and deployed them later, as allies and as adversaries. Serving together only until the end of 1783, they were both dismayed by Congress's ineffectiveness and the shenanigans of the state government. They watched as Congress floundered, moving to avoid mobs, to Princeton in 1782, Annapolis in 1783, Trenton in 1784, and in 1785 to New York City, which the last British troops had evacuated in November 1783. Congress's inability, for lack of unanimous consent by the states, to levy a tariff and New York's internal tariff on goods unloaded there and shipped on to Connecticut and New Jersey led Madison to call for a commercial conference in Annapolis in September 1786. Only five states sent delegates and they took little action except to issue Hamilton's report calling for a convention of all thirteen states to assemble in Philadelphia in May 1787. He had finally set in motion a process that he had been advocating for seven years.

Yet at the Constitution Convention, Hamilton said little at all. Delegates voted by state, and he was outnumbered by two colleagues chosen by Governor George Clinton, who opposed his every idea. He delivered a day-long speech on June 18, presenting a detailed program, calling for representatives elected from districts every three years, senators elected from special districts and serving for life, and a governor chosen by an electoral college and serving for life. It was a replica of the British system of Commons, Lords, and King, with a Republican veneer—which no one else supported. His marker laid down, Hamilton spent all of July and most of August in New York, tending legal business, returning in September to urge adoption of the document despite his stated dissatisfaction with it. Cunningly, the Convention's document provided for approval not by the Confederation Congress or the state legislatures, but by special conventions called in each state, and it provided as well that it would go into effect when it was ratified by nine, not all thirteen, of them. Ratification in New York looked unlikely after the long-serving Governor George Clinton packed the convention with delegates sharing his opposition to the new charter.

Hamilton immediately set out to make the case for the Constitution, recruiting Madison and John Jay to write a series of essays aimed at New Yorkers. They started appearing in newspapers in October 1787 and continued until March 1788; Jay ended up writing only five of what quickly became known as the Federalist Papers while Hamilton wrote fifty-one and Madison twenty-nine. Hamilton, acting as an advocate, submerged any differences with the convention's final product, as he suggested in the last paper that the Constitution "is the best which our political system, habits, and opinions will admit" (Federalist 85). In the papers attributed to him, Richard Brookhiser notes, "his stylist and temperamental fingerprints....Hamilton is flowing, sometimes overflowing, and agitated....He seems always in a hurry, and when he is not moving, he champs at the bit."[50] While Madison's Federalist papers tended to make theoretical arguments for the Constitution's particular form of republican government, Hamilton's papers repeatedly pointed to specific public policies which the Constitution's federal system would—and should—undertake. Or as Brookhiser writes, "Hamilton was driven by problems, Madison by theories."[51] The United States has "an insulated situation" and in its geopolitical situation is an island like Britain (Federalist 8) and needs a navy, he argued (Federalist 24). Happily, he went on, drawing on his mental maps of the new nation's regional economies, the southern states could provide lumber and naval stores for ships, the middle states iron ore and metal fittings, and the "Northern Hive" experienced able-bodied seaman and captains. And he envisioned a republic apparently no longer tied to France by the treaty of 1778. "The right of neutrality will only be respected when they are defended by an adequate power" (Federalist 11). As in his letters in the early 1780s, Hamilton was analogizing the new nation with the city-states and with the larger units, the Dutch republican and the kingdom of Great Britain, whose dominant forces were the great port cities of Amsterdam and London and which led the world in economic growth and personal freedoms. "If we mean to be a commercial people," he wrote confidently, even though political leaders such as Thomas Jefferson wanted Americans not to be a commercial people, "it must form part of our policy to be able to defend that commerce" (Federalist 34). To which he was careful to make mention early on (Federalist 11) of a subject dear to John Adams and other New Englanders, "the fisheries," access to the Grand Banks off Newfoundland and the right to dry out cod on nearby islands' shores. Hamilton also recognized possible difficulties in the republic's land frontier. The Confederation government couldn't force Britain to evacuate the forts in the Northwest Territory, as it had promised in the 1783 Treaty of Paris, and could not secure the Mississippi River frontier with the possessions of Spain. In that connection, he defended the Constitution's authorization of federal regulations of the state militias (Federalist 29), which must have struck some readers as advocacy of the standing army which American revolutionaries decried and many American republicans dreaded.

Hamilton made no secret of the fact that the Constitution's federal government could tax citizens directly by majority vote of Congress and approval by the president. He had not been alone, after all, in criticizing the Confederation government from imposing taxes only through unanimous approval of each state's delegation—which effectively meant no, or almost no, federal taxes. "The federal government must of necessity be invested with an unqualified power of taxation in the ordinary modes," he wrote (Federalist 31), and as a practical matter it must depend on "taxes of the indirect kind, from imposts, and from excises" (Federalist 12). These were, in fact, taxes imposed by the first Congresses, at the recommendation of

Hamilton as the first Treasury secretary. Imposts—tariffs—readily collectible at ports, in line with Hamilton's detailed regulations, and invisible to final consumers, were not unpopular and provided most of the early government's revenue. Excises could be a different story: The tax on whiskey inspired the Whiskey Rebellion of 1794, the military suppression of which Hamilton helped organize and Washington led. Hamilton also telegraphed, though not quite so directly, the argument he would successfully make to Washington in support of his proposal to establish a national bank. "A power to lay and collect taxes must be a power to pass all laws NECESSARY and PROPER for the execution of the power," he wrote (Federalist 33), using all capital letters long before the invention of the caps lock key. Madison similarly argued (Federalist 44) that the necessary and proper clause was essential ("Without the SUBSTANCE of this power, the whole Constitution would be a dead letter"), but in the controversy over the national bank, he and Jefferson took a more strained view. This, however, was the closest Hamilton came in the Federalist Papers to advancing the essentials of the financial system he proposed and largely persuaded Congress to pass. This system—refinancing of national and state government debts, funding the national debt, and establishing a national bank—he had been formulating since his letters to James Duane and Robert Morris, and in his Federalist papers, he carefully lays the groundwork for claiming it was authorized by the Constitution. But in contrast to advocacy of a permanent navy and suggestions of support for a standing army, he was guarded, even opaque, on finance issues.

In contrast, Hamilton's Federalist essays were bold in proclaiming the Constitution's support for a powerful presidency or, as he put it (Federalist 70), "energy in the executive." The Confederation constitution did provide for a president, but one who served for only one year and had very limited powers. The Constitution provided a four-year renewable term with an impressive array of powers. Hamilton's argument was strengthened, of course, by the fact that almost everyone knew that George Washington would be chosen the first president. He had sat, almost entirely silent, as the president of the Constitutional Convention and supported, quietly, ratification of the document, and was universally respected after resigning his military commission in December 1783 and returning to private life in Mount Vernon. Hamilton's analysis of the presidency was not always prescient. The "mode of appointment" of the president, he wrote, "has escaped without severe censure" (Federalist 68). In fact, it misfired in 1800–01, when the vice-presidential candidate Aaron Burr, over Hamilton's opposition, tried to elbow Thomas Jefferson aside, and the Twelfth Amendment was passed to change the process for 1804. He averred that "to a moral certainty," the presidency "will never fall to the lot of any man who is not in an eminent degree endowed with the requisite qualifications" (Federalist 68). He argued that the Senate would have to approve the firing as well as the hiring of major officers (Federalist 77). That argument was, in effect, rejected by the failure of the impeachment of Andrew Johnson in 1868 and in 1926 by the Supreme Court, in *Myers v. United States*, a decision written by former President William Howard Taft. His suggestion that presidents would seldom veto laws passed by Congress (Federalist 73) has frequently proved unwarranted. But Hamilton was also prescient. The Constitution's provision allowing reelection of presidents would, he argued, prevent "the banishing of men from stations in which, in certain emergencies of state, their presence might be of the greatest moment to the public interest or safety" (Federalist 72). Thus voters, despite Washington's precedent of retiring after two terms, reelected Franklin Roosevelt to a third in 1940, when Hitler and Stalin were allied and in control of most of the landmass of Eurasia. His description of the treaty-making power as neither executive nor legislative has been proved out by experience: Woodrow Wilson, who failed to get senators involved, saw his Treaty of Versailles rejected in 1919, while Harry Truman, who worked closely with opposition party senators, got overwhelming approval for the NATO treaty in 1949. "Energy in the Executive is a leading character in the definition of good government," he wrote (Federalist 70). The president's duties, which he specified in his definition of "administration" (Federalist 72), were multiple and consequential: "The actual conduct of foreign negotiations, the preparatory plans of finance, the application and disbursement of the public moneys in conformity to the general appropriations of the legislature, the arrangement of the army and navy, the direction of the operations of war." Washington would give the nation an example, a precedent, of a president seriously engaged in such administration, in active command of a group of, at least initially, sterling appointees, confronting issues of the greatest gravity and moment.

If Washington's election as the first president was as universally expected as it was unanimously approved, his appointment of the thirty-four-year-old Alexander Hamilton was something of a surprise—more than two hundred years later, Hamilton is still the youngest person to hold the post—and he soon became the focus of what was, to him and his contemporaries, surprisingly partisan political conflict. Hamilton was nominated by Washington on Friday, September 11, 1789, confirmed by the Senate the same day, and started working on Saturday by arranging a $50,000 loan to the government from the Bank of New York.[52] He set to work preparing legislation for the First Congress to ponder, setting up what would be the federal government's largest department (with thirty-nine employees!) and its administrative procedures. He had long had in mind the policies he wished to advance, as his letters to James Duane and Robert Morris a decade before showed, and to put them in place, he arranged to have the First Congress request his advice. As historian Gordon Wood summarizes, "He worked his remarkable program out in a series of four reports to Congress in 1790 and 1791: on credit (including duties and taxes), on a national bank, on a mint, and on manufactures. These reports, powerfully written and argued, are the source of most of Hamilton's greatness as a statesman."[53] Ron Chernow tells these stories dramatically in his Hamilton biography, citing historian Forrest McDonald as providing the most thorough analysis of the source of Hamilton's thinking.[54] Hamilton's 40,000-word report on the Support of Public Credit,[55] submitted to Congress in January 1790, asserted that the debt incurred during the Revolution was "the price of liberty" and proclaimed that a funded national debt that commands public confidence "answers most of the purposes of money." He mentioned, but with less emphasis than in the Federalist Papers, that a properly funded debt could enable a government to borrow heavily in case of military need, and asserted that "the creation of debt should always be accompanied by the means of extinguishment." He cataloged the existing $54 million in national debt and $25 million in state debt, and argued that the federal government should assume both debts and pay off bondholders at 100 percent of face value. This provoked strong opposition from James Madison and others, who noted that many original bondholders, including Continental Army soldiers, had sold off debt at far less than face value, and argued that it was unfair to pay speculators full face value. Hamilton replied that it would be impractical to track down the original bondholders, and more important, that failure to pay full value to current bondholders would make it impossible for the government to borrow efficiently or at reasonable cost. And he added complex provisions for a sinking fund and measures to provide initial investors with 6 percent interest but to ratchet that downward to 4 percent, just above the 3 percent at which the Bank of England was able to borrow.

To Hamilton's surprise and dismay, his proposal for funding and assumption of state debts was opposed by his Federalist collaborator James Madison in February 1790. In April 1790, Madison defeated assumption in the House by a 31–29 margin.

To overturn that margin in the House and one in the Senate, Hamilton seized on the other contentious issue in this First Congress: the location of the ten-mile-square federal capital mandated in the Constitution. Hamilton's own preference was New York,[56] at least to remain the temporary capital and hopefully to be chosen as the permanent site. But with only shallow roots in the state and a commitment to forging national loyalty and a national financial system,[57] he understood that to many the city seemed too far north in a time of cumbersome travel, when a central location was considered desirable, that the city's Tory sentiments during the Revolution were by no means forgotten and neither was its atypical polyglot heritage.[58] Encouraged by Thomas Jefferson, who had arrived in March from Paris to take up his duties as secretary of state, he met with Madison for dinner on June 20, and in Jefferson's account, the three agreed to allow assumption to pass and to make Philadelphia the temporary capital for ten years, with the permanent capital on a site on the Potomac River—the preference not only of Madison and Jefferson, but of their fellow Virginian George Washington.[59] Congress in July passed bills setting this arrangement into law. "The sad irony," writes Chernow, a native New Yorker himself, "was that Hamilton, the quintessential New Yorker, bargained away the city's chance to be another London or Paris, the political as well as the financial and cultural capital of the country." But in 1790, New York had not yet become the financial capital of the country; the much larger Philadelphia the next year became the headquarters of Hamilton's national bank of the United States. And Philadelphia, as the home of Benjamin Franklin and of the cultural institutions he founded, had at that time probably the most serious claim to being America's cultural capital. New York's later success as a financial and cultural center owes much to the success of Hamilton's financial system, and it is not clear how the resources of a capital center in a republic, without a royal court or aristocratic patronage, could have made more than a marginal difference, at least over the next century.

The funded national debt, in Hamilton's view, was one means of encouraging an expandable supply of money of stable value. Another, as he had written James Duane and Robert Morris, was a national bank. In response to congressional demand, he produced in December 1790 a second long paper advocating the creation of a national bank.[60] A bank, together with the funded debt, could provide the ready money for commerce and investment that was so glaringly vacant in the colonies. The definitive historian of banking in the early republic quotes Hamilton's "succinct definition of banking" in a 1791 letter to George Washington. "The simplest and most precise idea of a bank is a deposit of coin or other property as a fund for circulating a credit upon which it is to answer for the purpose of money."[61] To overcome Americans' skepticism about banks, which had not existed in the thirteen colonies, he cited their success in "the principal and most enlightened commercial nations"—Italy, Germany, Holland, England, France—and provided an explanation of how they could extend more money in loans than they had taken in as deposits. "Banks become nurseries of national wealth," he argued, "a consequence as satisfactorily verified by experience as it is clearly deducible in theory." He specified that an American national bank, like the Bank of England or the Bank of Amsterdam, should be a private institution, backed by $10 million in private capital, but reporting weekly to the Treasury and with some of its shares purchasable by the federal government. A bill establishing a bank easily passed the Senate in January 1791, but was opposed in the House, once again, by James Madison, who argued that it was unconstitutional. This was in direct contradiction to Madison's argument in Federalist 44 about the Constitution's "necessary and proper" clause: "No objection, the bill passed the House by a solid margin, but similar arguments by Attorney General Edmund Randolph and Thomas Jefferson caused President Washington to consider a veto. At his direction, Hamilton wrote in an astonishingly short time a 15,000-word essay arguing that the Constitution authorized measures that were useful in achieving constitutionally permissible ends, which in the case of a national bank included collecting taxes, borrowing money, regulating interstate commerce, and supporting an army and navy.[62] Washington was persuaded and signed the bill.

Hamilton's forward-looking genius is that he passed over the world's long history of economic stagnation and focused on moments and *loci* of economic growth, with the prescient understanding that what had been unusual and even abnormal could, if buttressed by the right sort of political and legal institution, become habitual and even normal. His mental map of the world was focused on the sea lanes across the oceans connecting the great commercial cities of Europe with the Americas and Asia, and this shaped his foreign policy as well. "In 1790, in a very telling comment," one historian of finance writes, Hamilton "wrote of British Canada as being on 'our left' and Spanish possessions, which then included New Orleans, as being on 'our right.' Such a vision was possible if he was facing east, toward Europe."[63] Hamilton's recognition that America's trade ties with Britain, and the potential for British investment in the United States, shaped his foreign policy of propitiating commercial Britain and risking rupture with revolutionary France.[64] His mental map of the new nation, embedded with detailed knowledge of the economic production of every region, state, and county, developed in the economically depressed 1780s and the economically effervescent 1790s, failed to anticipate the disorderliness of the rushes of trans-Appalachian settlements of the nineteenth century, and in his longstanding open and "fierce" support of the abolition of slavery,[65] he seems not to have anticipated, as few of the Founders did at the time of his death, how sectional differences over slavery would rend the Union. But his appreciation, "better than any other American statesman of his time," of the idea of credit, and how strengthening credit could promote innovation and economic growth[66]—especially by attracting British and other foreign capital to the United States—provided the basis for the industrialization that blazed forward in the second half of the nineteenth century. His plan "to nationalize, monetize, and energize American society," as Forrest McDonald writes, "to make the United States a great nation despite itself,... to liberate and energize a society that slavery and oligarchy had rendered lethargic" did not transpire as or when he expected, nor did it establish a hold on the popular imagination as strong as Thomas Jefferson's agrarian ideal."[67] As the historian of banking Bray Hammond writes, "Alexander Hamilton prepared America for an imperial future of wealth and power, mechanized beyond the handicraft stage of his day, and amply provided with credit to that end."[68] If the America that emerged in the years after his death in 1804 and the end of the British-French world war in 1815 did not resemble, in historian Richard Hofstadter's words, "the seaboard trading republic that Hamilton envisaged, with deference to merchants and bankers,"[69] it was also a nation in which his system of administration and finance was largely preserved by his Jeffersonian critics and opponents, with the potential for almost boundless growth. Less than twenty years after he was left to manage the Beekman & Cruger office in St. Croix, Alexander Hamilton built what turned out to be a firm foundation of a nation whose effervescent productivity and innovative dexterity would make it, not much more than a century later, the most productive and powerful country on earth.

FIVE

JAMES MADISON
West by Southwest

If you wanted to pinpoint the one place in the world where the thinking took place that determined the substance and structure of the Constitution of the United States, you could do no better than to fasten on an upstairs bedroom, not much more than eight by ten feet in size, in a brick plantation house called Montpelier and owned by sixty-four-year-old James Madison Sr., the largest landowner in Orange County, Virginia. In that room in February, March, and April 1786, Madison's thirty-five-year-old son James Jr. read and made notes on the books about republics ancient and modern sent him from Paris by his friend from nearby Albemarle County, the forty-three-year-old Thomas Jefferson, where he represented at the court of the king of France the weak United States government set up by the Articles of Confederation.

From his childhood, James Madison Jr., the oldest of twelve children, was a conscientious, perhaps even a compulsive student. Orange County in the Virginia Piedmont, above the low-lying Tidewater along Chesapeake Bay and the fall line of the river and below the first Appalachian chain, the Blue Ridge, looming hazily on the horizon on clear days, was no longer the frontier in the middle of the eighteenth century but was thoroughly rural and thirty miles upriver from the tiny port of Fredericksburg. Geographically, it was far from the creative intellectual center of the English-speaking world, which was not then in sleepy Oxford or Cambridge, but in the Scottish universities where Enlightenment intellectuals such as Adam Smith, David Hume, Francis Hutcheson, and Adam Ferguson were teaching and writing. But as it happened, Madison's most important teachers were acolytes of the Scottish Enlightenment.[1] In 1762, when he turned eleven, his parents sent him to a boarding school in the Tidewater run by Donald Robertson, a former minister and graduate of the University of Edinburgh and, in Madison's recollection, a man of extensive learning and a distinguished teacher."[2] The curriculum included geography, algebra and geometry, Latin, Greek, and French, and authorities ancient (Homer and Virgil, Xenophon and Thucydides and Cicero) and modern (Locke, Montesquieu, Hume).[3]

After five years, he returned home and was tutored by the local Brick Church minister Thomas Martin, a graduate of the College of New Jersey (now Princeton), headed by the Presbyterian minister John Witherspoon, another graduate of the University of Edinburgh. Madison entered the college in 1769, at age eighteen, and was able to skip the first year after demonstrating he had already mastered the classics. The second-year program, political scientist Jay Cost recounts, included "'a complete system of geography, with the use of globes,' plus 'the first principles of philosophy' and the next year emphasized math and science, 'the higher classics,' and 'a course of moral philosophy.'" Witherspoon supplemented this with lectures to the juniors and seniors on 'history, and afterwards upon composition and criticism,' as well as instruction in French. Students were also required to give public speeches after prayers so 'that they may learn, by early habit, presence of mind, and proper pronunciation and gesture in public speaking.'"[4] An excellent student who was able to graduate after two years, but leery of going home and eager to learn more, Madison got Witherspoon to agree that he remain at his studies for another year. In those three years, he was exposed to glimpses of the American colonies far beyond the Piedmont. At Presbyterian Princeton, Madison was exposed to more diversity of belief and in students' backgrounds than Jefferson had been at Anglican William and Mary. While Jefferson dined with the university president and leading law professor, Madison made friends with an assortment of fellow students—William Bradford, a printer's son from Philadelphia; Philip Freneau, a Huguenot wine merchant's son from New Jersey; and Hugh Brackenridge, a Scot from York, Pennsylvania, who would settle on that state's western frontier.[5] In these interchanges, he was filling in his mental map of the seaboard colonies with information about what the historian David Hackett Fischer calls their "folkways," their particular ways of life, from politics to religion to personal relations, shaped often by what their forebears had brought over from various subregions of the British Isles.[6]

Madison was a small man physically, not much more than five feet tall or weighing more than one hundred pounds, but the conventional picture of him as a sickly, homebound young man was not quite accurate. Montpelier, though the largest house in Orange County, was comfortable and always crowded with members of multiple generations, "a family as large as an oyster bed," in Richard Brookhiser's words.[7] It was built by his grand-father Ambrose Madison, who was murdered (or so a Virginia court ruled) by a slave back in 1732; his widow lived on and was a presence until just before her oldest grandson's departure for Princeton. James Madison Jr., born in 1751, was the first of his generation, twenty years older than his youngest sibling. Perhaps unsurprisingly, he delighted in new environments. Biographer Lynne Cheney, envisioning his summer of 1769 journey to college, describes Philadelphia as "a place full of wonder for a young man from the Virginia frontier,"[8] and when Madison returned home in 1772, he did not stay there long. In May, he accompanied his brother William to a preparatory school in Princeton. In Philadel-phia, he heard the news that the British Parliament had ordered the closing of the port of Boston and suspended the charter of the Massachusetts colony. Back in Williamsburg, this inspired Virginia's House of Burgesses to call for a day of prayer and fasting on June 1, in retaliation for which the assembly was dissolved by the royal Governor Lord Dunmore[9]—events that led directly to the session of the First Continental Congress in Philadelphia in September. But Madison was not yet caught up in these events. He dropped off William in Princeton, and then, apparently alone, decided to travel to New York and Albany. The twenty-three-year-old graduate seems to have had no motive for this journey other than a desire to "see the country" and perhaps visit a portion of America where social conditions were very different from those in Virginia. The beautiful trip from New York to Albany and back, judging from Bradford's note in his letter copybook that Madison was gone from Philadelphia only two weeks, must have been made with good luck on wind and tide.[10] This was not to be the last of Madison's northward wanderings. Historian Jack Rakove notes that in the fall of 1784, after the Treaty of Paris was signed, Madison "resumed his habit of taking annual northward excursions, which allowed him to gather his own political intelligence."[11]

What we see here is a young man of great mental energy with a determination to explore and learn about other places beyond his native Virginia, and not unduly held back by weak health. In an autobiography written after his retirement from the presidency, Madison wrote that he suffered "sudden attacks…something resembling epilepsy and suspending the intellectual functions." Biographer Lynne Cheney, noting that epilepsy was defined then as "convulsive seizures," argues that he suffered "complex partial seizures, which leave affected persons conscious but with his or her comprehension and ability to communicate impaired."[12] She concludes, "The evidence available suggests that this was the pattern of Madison's ailment: fever-related episodes when he was a toddler, then 'sudden attacks' later in his life."[13] This helps to explain why, despite being with his father on the Orange County Committee on Safety, he was excluded from military service in the spring of 1775 after an apparent seizure during training[14]; it could explain as well periods when he removed himself from active life and, perhaps, why his first marriage proposal was rejected. But if so, it also shows the iron determination he brought to his legislative work, which required standing and speaking for hours on end, as a delegate to the Constitutional Convention and his leadership in the House of Representatives in the first four Congresses. Another possible effect, Cheney speculates, is that the stigma of his seizures, together with "the religious view, widely held and fiercely defended, that sufferers were unclean, sinful, even possessed by demons," prompted his fierce conviction that no one should have to accept ideas he did not believe in. At about the same time, in 1773, he was objecting fiercely to the persecution of Baptists by authorities of Virginia's established Anglican Church.[15] His years of exposure to Witherspoon's Presbyterianism and to the various religions of other students at Princeton surely had some effect as well. "During the winter of 1773–74, Madison's thinking underwent a sea change. The young man who embraced traditional views at the beginning became a person who no longer affirmed the religious doctrines with which he grew up."[16]

Orange County and the James Madisons, Senior and Junior, were staunch supporters in the spring of 1775 of the First Continental Congress's boycott of British goods; the young Madison handed a letter of congratulations to Patrick Henry ("Give me liberty or give me death!") as he journeyed nearby, and as a member of the Committee on Safety, he approved the closure of a loyalist Culpeper County parson's church. In the spring of 1776, he was elected by Orange County freeholders to the Virginia Convention, the governing body that replaced the dissolved House of Burgesses and the departed royal governor. It was the beginning of twenty-one years of nearly uninterrupted and distinguished service in a variety of legislative offices. The colonial legislatures, which had survived King James II's policy of shutting them down thanks to the installation of King William III in the events known as the Glorious Revolution of 1688–89, were the universities in which the Founding Fathers learned the practice of politics. As historian William Lee Miller points out, "Virtually all the American Framers and most of the American Founders had a shaping experience in legislative bodies," where "representatives of equal peoples must deal with each other as (more or less) equals, to persuade and deal and compromise and cast votes, and to mingle facts and values, interests and social goods in whatever proportions, and finally to decide collectively on the policy for a people." The legislatures were arenas where people valued "the tactician, the compromiser, the 'skillful organizer who could keep various factions and pressure groups together.'"[17] As a junior member, Madison was mostly quiet but made his mark. On a committee headed by George Mason and charged with creating a state constitution and declaration of rights, he worked through two senior members to substitute for the words "all men should enjoy the fullest toleration in the exercise of religion" for the stronger "all men are equally entitled to the free exercise of religion"[18]—words echoed fifteen years later in the First Amendment to the federal Constitution. The convention determined that it would serve as the state legislature, and its session that fall was joined by Thomas Jefferson, back from Philadelphia and not yet known publicly as the principal author of the Declaration of Independence. Madison and the eight-years-older Jefferson led the move to remove government financing of the Anglican Church; they succeeded only in repealing laws forbidding heresy and requiring church attendance.[19] For the next several years, from Montpelier and, except for most of 1777 when he lost reelection after refusing free drinks to voters, from Williamsburg, Madison watched the progress and, more often, disappointments of the military conflict played out on a field as large as western Europe. He was elected in November 1777 to the eight-member Council of State, which had to approve governors' decisions, so that while still in his twenties, he had to work closely first with Governors Patrick Henry and Thomas Jefferson. In this post, Madison approved Henry's *drang nach West und Sudwest*—the dispatch of thirty men to sail down the river to New Orleans and the commissioning of George Rogers Clark to drive the British out of the western territory north of the Ohio River.[20] Before the Revolutionary War was won, Madison was already thinking of extending the authority of the United States to the west and southwest.

Madison had first met Jefferson in October 1776.[21] Jefferson was eight years older, more than a foot taller, and far more prominent in Virginia. Jefferson was rich in his own right, a married man who designed and redesigned his own houses; Madison was a bachelor who lived in his parents' house and received an allowance from his father.[22] Not until June 1779 did what historian Drew McCoy calls "their stable, long-term partnership in American national politics"[23] begin. It turned out to have a strong basis. Both were assiduous students, Jefferson with a wider range of interests, Madison the more penetrating scholar; both were unorthodox in religion and strong advocates of religious freedom; both came to share an unease about slavery and an impulse toward equality with an uneasiness about overturning Virginia's social order. Their close relationship began when they were daily colleagues, as Lynne Cheney recounts. "Beginning June 1, 1779, Governor Jefferson and Councilor Madison met with other council members in daily sessions that began at ten each morning on the second floor of the Capitol in Williamsburg. In mid-July, as the malarial season was about to begin, Madison left for Orange County, not to return until late October, then, on December 16, 1779, he left the council for good when the House of Delegates chose him to serve in the Continental Congress. Thus the two men worked together on the council only thirteen or fourteen weeks, but it was long enough, in Madison's words, that 'an intimacy took place.'"[24] This intimate relationship continued, sometimes daily, sometimes at long intervals because of the slowness of trans-Atlantic correspondence, often through the somewhat speedier domestic mail, until Jefferson's death forty-seven years and one month later.

Madison entered the Continental Congress in March 1780, and in the months that followed, American fortunes seemed dim. The British had attacked Georgia and South Carolina and captured Charleston, and General Horatio Gates's army was defeated at Camden. General Benedict Arnold betrayed the army in the Hudson Valley and, eluding capture, led British troops in 1781 into raids on Richmond in January and Charlottesville in June. It seemed for an uncomfortably long moment that the new republic might not survive, or that the Carolinas and Georgia would be detached from the Union and remain British colonies. Madison was quickly appointed to committees with pressing business, but he also stayed focused on more distant goals. From the front steps of Montpelier, on clear days, one can see the Blue Ridge hovering above the horizon to the west, fading off to the southwest, and although Madison, like his new friend Jefferson, did not much venture beyond the Blue Ridge and the Appalachian chain that paralleled it, he was very much aware that since the British victory over France hundreds, then thousands, of Virginians and Scots-Irish migrants had headed southwest down the valleys between the ridges and through the Cumberland Gap into the county that Virginians called, and spelled in multiple ways, Kentucky. Madison, historian Jack Rakove writes, shared "the common expectation that the future arc of American migration would swing to the southwest,"[25] and that the chief avenue for the export of their crops would be the Mississippi River. In September and October 1780, amid news of American defeats, Madison wrote John Jay, a New Yorker serving as minister to Spain, urging him to seek the free navigation of the Mississippi River to New Orleans and the Gulf of Mexico that the British had been granted in the 1763 Treaty of Paris.[26] "In a very few years, after peace shall take place, this country will certainly be overspread with inhabitants," he wrote in a draft letter to Jay in October 1780.[27] He expected that they, like the first settlers in Kentucky, would be yeoman farmers and would be seeking markets for their wheat, corn, tobacco, and hemp, and in an era when transportation on downriver rafts was far cheaper than in trans-mountain wagons.[28] He was aware that Spain, in possession of the west bank of the great river, and an ally of France but not of the United States, sought to deny navigation rights and to press claims even to territory east of the river.[29] In his letter, Madison cited the Swiss natural law theorist Vattel for the proposition that free use of natural resources should obtain across international boundaries, but as biographer Ralph Ketcham notes, he shows "a readiness to equate American 'manifest destiny' with natural law. Hence Madison asserted, as though stating a natural right, that vast areas of the American West would be settled inevitably by the energetic peoples of the seaboard states."[30] Other states, seeking Spanish military aid, voted against seeking navigation rights, and in any case no agreement with Spain was reached. Months later, in May 1781, Madison wrote Jay praising his negotiating stance, and Jay replied, "I do not recollect to have ever received a letter that gave me more real pleasure."[31] Thus Madison while still in his twenties, and when other issues were pressing, was alert to American expansion to the west and southwest, that in his view would "in a very few years, after peace shall take place [would be] overspread with inhabitants."[32] The unexpected American victory at Yorktown in October 1781 removed many threats, but the issue of navigation on the Mississippi and possession of the lands beyond would rise again in Madison's career.

In November 1782, Madison found himself working with an even younger member elected by the New York legislature, Alexander Hamilton. Together they proposed an amendment to the Articles of Confederation authorizing a federal impost—import tax—and a requisition of $1.5 million. On the sticky question of how to apportion the burden by states, Madison called for allocation by population; when one proposal called for counting slaves as one-half a free person and another three-fourths; Madison roughly split the difference and suggested three-fifths, the ratio that would be adopted for apportionment of House members at the Constitutional Convention four years later.[33] But the amendment failed for lack of approval by all thirteen states. Near the end of the three-year limit in service in the Confederation Congress, Madison offered a resolution naming the recently widowed Jefferson as American minister in France. After hesitating, Jefferson accepted and set off on a tour of New England, presumably to gauge opinion among the merchants and shipowners whom he would try to interest in trading more with France and less with Britain. In April 1784, Madison, after four months of study in Montpelier, set out 1784 for Richmond and service in the Virginia Assembly. The two had agreed, before Jefferson's departure for France in July 1784, to use code in referring to prominent figures in their exchange of letters, easily intercepted in that era.

The Virginia Assembly did not attract members as distinguished as the House of Burgesses had before the Revolution. In 1784, Madison wrote, anonymously, a long "Memorial and Remonstrance Against Religious Assessments," arguing successfully against Governor Patrick Henry's bill to pay religious teachers, and in 1786, he advanced instead, and squired through to passage, Jefferson's religious freedom bill.[34] His revulsion against the jailing of Baptists in Culpeper County and his education by Presbyterians in Princeton had made him a steely supporter of freedom of religious belief, and his observation of multiple sects in Virginia prompted the shrewd political tactics that enabled him to prevail in an Assembly with an overwhelmingly Anglican membership. The staunch support of Baptists and Presbyterians was the starting point of his "politicking among the denominations," to which the quiet presence of small numbers of Quakers, Moravians, and Lutherans added weight. He was aided when the fast-growing Methodists, technically members of the established church but with a bishop-unfriendly focus, separated from supporters of the Anglican establishment. "The mutual hatred of these sects," Madison wrote Jefferson, as the battle was ongoing, "has been much inflamed by the late Act incorporating [the Episcopalians]. I am far from being sorry for it, as a coalition between them could alone endanger our religious rights, and a tendency to such an event has been suspected." He had come to see, as William Lee Miller argues, the protection of religious liberty depended on "a division and balance—in which the numbers of, and conflict among, religious groups made overbearing combinations unlikely."[35] And so, while Jefferson was in Paris, Madison was able to secure passage in the Virginia Assembly of Jefferson's Bill for Establishing Religious Freedom—one of the three accomplishments Jefferson called for commemorating on his gravestone.

When the legislature was not in session, Madison headed not back home, but to yet another "ramble into the eastern states." In 1784, after running into the French Revolutionary War hero Lafayette in Baltimore, he accepted his invitation to travel with him to Upstate New York. They ventured across New Jersey, paused in New York City, and sailed up the Hudson, "a journey that took them past lovely country homes and the commanding sites where Forts Washington and Lee and Stony Point had once stood. The barge wound through the highlands that curved and narrowed at West Point, where during the Revolution a great chain had been stretched across the Hudson to prevent British ships from sailing farther north." From Albany they traveled overland, "stopping at a Shaker community and observing the sect's 'convulsive dances,'" and marched along the Mohawk valley to Fort Stanwix, to witness the signature of a treaty between the United States and the Iroquois Confederacy,[36] largely pro-British during the Revolution.

★   ★   ★

Thus Madison brought knowledge of much of the new nation as well as book learning to constitution making. Like most of the Founders, he had no firsthand knowledge of life in slave-heavy coastal South Carolina or Georgia nor of the scattered areas of the upcountry Carolinas, and like most other Virginia leaders, he seems to have spent little time in New England, the most culturally and ethnically uniform of the colonies, whose residents George Washington (from his exposure to Yankee soldiers) and Thomas Jefferson (from his very limited acquaintance with Yankee merchants) found argumentative and stiff-necked. But the Middle Colonies, from Virginia north to New York, were for Madison well-trodden and comfortable ground. He found the religious variety and competition of Pennsylvania and New Jersey bracing, and the Indian frontier of the Mohawk valley—after his 1784 journey, he and James Monroe bought a 900-acre lot there for $1,350 and they sold it in 1796 for $5,250[37]—as interesting as the Indian frontier of Virginia. This was the beating heart of the new nation that Madison was determined to hold together not despite but because of its differences, its diversity, its cultural variety, and its enormous physical size. Along the Atlantic Coast, it was 1,000 miles from Portsmouth, New Hampshire, to Savannah, Georgia; in the interior, it was about 1,000 miles from Mount Vernon southwest to the Lower Mississippi River or northwest to the western tip of Lake Superior. This vast expanse was one reason Britain was unable to squelch the American Revolution: too much ground to cover. But it was also one reason that James Madison and other leaders were so uncertain about its prospects: too much country to hold together, at least by a limited Union government without the power to tax, to regulate trade, and to maintain an effective military force.

To hold the new nation together, Madison continued to believe, it must enjoy free navigation of the Mississippi River, its western boundary. But Spain, in possession of the west bank and of the port of New Orleans on the east bank, was not a party to the Treaty of Paris and obdurately refused to yield this right, which Britain had enjoyed, to the United States. Madison continued pressing the issue on John Jay, now the foreign secretary of the Continental Congress, who after years of Spain's refusal was proposing to forgo free Mississippi navigation for twenty-five years in return for trade concessions in Spanish colonies.[38] Madison lobbied the Virginia legislature to oppose Jay's policy and castigated Spain as a nation "who has given no proof of regard for us and the genius of whose Government, religion, and manners unfit them of all the nations in Christendom for a coalition with this country."[39] His mistrust of Spain did not, however, lead to mistrust of Spain's ally France. Madison supported instructing peace negotiators to only seek terms acceptable to the French and the appointment of Benjamin Franklin, Henry Laurens, and Jay as peace negotiators to outweigh John Adams's mistrust of the French, without appreciating that Franklin and Jay would decide it was necessary to join Adams in negotiating directly with the British for fear the French would postpone any treaty until Britain agreed to restore Gibraltar to Spain (something it has not done in the 240 years since).[40] Madison's focus remained on the Southwest. In a letter to Jefferson in August 1784, just after his departure to France, Madison stressed the importance of gaining free navigation of the Mississippi and suggested the use of force might be needed when he "predicted that the safety of Spain's 'possessions in this quarter of the globe must depend more upon our peaceableness than her own power.'"[41] On his impromptu trip to New York in September, even though he knew that George Washington was less interested in navigation on the Mississippi than in making the Potomac the great highway to the interior, he unblushingly lobbied Lafayette on the issue, and the Frenchman obliged. "I am every day pestering the government with my prophetics respecting the Mississippi," he wrote Madison from Paris in March 1785. The Frenchman even took advantage "of the well-known penchant of Spanish officials to read other people's mail. 'I have written letters by post to Madrid and Cadiz to be intercepted and read,' he told Madison."[42] In Congress, meanwhile, Madison was arguing that Jay's current instructions were invalid, since they were approved by only seven state delegations, not the nine required for approval of a treaty. Jay nevertheless defended his offer on the grounds that gaining navigation rights would be easier in the future and that pressing for them would mean war with Spain for which the new nation was unprepared.[43] In March 1786, unable to get information from Jay, Madison sought the Spanish envoy, Gardoqui, who said he had not talked with Jay for months.[44] Meanwhile, in Congress, opinion was shifting, and in August 1786, it voted by seven delegations to five to repeal its earlier instructions and made no mention of the Mississippi at all.[45] The proposed treaty with Spain fell by the wayside. But Madison's perseverance over the issue of navigation on the Mississippi, an issue literally 1,000 miles distant from Montpelier, validates the conclusion of biographer Richard Brookhiser that he was a politician who "would pursue American expansion with single-minded zeal for decades."[46]

Madison was dejected in April 1786 when the New York legislature rejected the tariff measure Congress passed: One state's veto denied the federal government a regular source of revenue. He was dismayed by the issuance of inflationary paper money by several state legislatures, and by the passage of import duties by states with large ports, such as New York and South Carolina, which essentially levied tribute from consumers in nearby states such as New Jersey and North Carolina. He took seriously the English political theorist John Locke's insight that protection of property was fundamental to the protection of liberty, and throughout his life he was worried that politicians representing voters with little or no property would pass "'agrarian laws and other levelling schemes' as well as 'the cancelling or evading of debts, and other violations of contracts.'"[47] During the 1780s, Madison was almost constantly away from Montpelier, which remained his parents' home. He had moved to Philadelphia to serve in the Continental Congress in March 1780, and then after his three terms expired, he was almost immediately elected to the Virginia Assembly in Richmond, where he dominated the sessions.[48] But he was able to spend much of the months from spring to summer in 1786 at Montpelier. In a house filled with members of the large Madison family, the oldest son installed himself, after sparse breakfasts and before evening games of whist, in a small upstairs bedroom, studying the two trunkfuls of books on republics ancient and modern which he had asked Thomas Jefferson to send him from Paris,[49] systematically "reading and note-taking and thinking about the kinds of governments the Americans were forming—republican governments—and about the foundations of politics itself," as William Lee Miller writes. He read Plutarch's *Lives* and Polybius's *Histories*, Diderot's eleven-volume *Encyclopédie Méthodique* and Felice's thirteen-volume *Code de l'Humanité*, to learn the lessons of the Amphitryonic and Achaean confederations, the Swiss Confederation and the United Provinces of the Netherlands and the Holy Roman Empire.[50] He made detailed notes on the histories of these republics and concentrated "upon the vices—the faults and defects and dangerous tendencies" of each. Significantly, he found that "the overriding 'vices' of all of these past confederacies were the jealousies and 'sovereign' defiance of the component parts and the weakness of the central authorities."[51]

In September 1786, he journeyed to Annapolis, to a convention the Virginia legislature had invited delegates from other states "to take into consideration the trade of the United States." Attendance was sparse, but he met there with his former Confederation Congress colleague Alexander Hamilton, who pressed for a convention the next year to make major changes. Madison persuaded him to tone down his language, but even so it was momentous, calling for "the appointment of commissioners to meet at Philadelphia on the second Monday in May next, to take into consideration the situation of the United States [and] devise such further provisions as shall appear to them necessary to render the constitution of the federal government adequate to the exigencies of the Union."[52] From there, writes William Lee Miller, "the traveling legislator and political scientist, went to a number of other places—to Philadelphia, to Mount Vernon to confer with Washington, to Richmond for the Virginia Assembly, to Mount Vernon again, to Philadelphia again—and then finally, in February 1787, to New York, where the old Continental Congress was involved in what would be its last meeting."[53] He spent much time and energy preparing a plan of attack for the Constitutional Convention, but the issue of navigation of the Mississippi River—and expansion to the southwest—remained on his mind; he devoted long passages to the subject in letters to Thomas Jefferson in August 1786, George Washington in December 1786, and Jefferson in March 1787.[54] The vast geographical expanse of the young republic, and the wider distribution of its population expected in the years to come, were central to Madison's thinking as he composed his April 1787 paper on the "Vices of the Political System of the United States" and the specific proposals that became the Virginia Plan that was introduced fifteen days after the opening of the Convention in May 1787. The Virginia Plan included a two-house Congress, a president, a federal judiciary, plus a guarantee of republican forms of government and provisions for ratification and amendment. Not all of this plan was adopted. A compromise was adopted providing for one house to be chosen proportionately to population and the other by equal representation of each state, and Madison's provision for a federal veto of all state legislation failed to win much support. But Madison, with his fund of knowledge about republics in ancient and modern times and about the governance of each of the thirteen states, was the most active and the most influential member of the Constitutional Convention; Hamilton, in contrast, gave one speech advocating proposals which had no significant support, and he spent most of the sessions away from Philadelphia altogether. Compromises were necessary in what was widely recognized as a culturally and economically diverse nation, and in Madison's view, the timing of the convention was particularly conducive to acceptance of the principle of representation according to population. As he wrote to Jefferson in March and to Washington in April, delegates from most states thought it would be favorable to them. "To the Northern States it will be recommended by their present populousness; to the Southern by their expected advantage in this respect."[55]

This was in line with the guiding assumption Madison had developed in his research, that a geographically large republic would better protect liberties and would better hold itself together than a small republic. This ran contrary to received opinion, including the widely accepted view of Montesquieu's *L'esprit des lois*, that "no large state could ever be modelled into" a republic, and as Madison himself noted, at the Convention and in the Federalist papers, the small republics of ancient Greece and modern Europe were weak and ephemeral. As biographer Ralph Ketcham speculates,[56] Madison may have been acquainted with the contrary argument, advanced by the Scottish philosopher and historian David Hume in his 1752 paper "Idea of a Perfect Commonwealth" that, while small republics are prone to turbulence, in large republics would be (there were no live examples when he was writing) the existence of multiple factions and the logistical difficulties of factional collusion would hinder irrational measures. In his "Vices of the Political System," drafted in April 1787 in preparation for the Convention, Madison argued for "an enlargement of the sphere" of a republic. "The Society becomes broken into a number of interests, of pursuits, of passions, which check each other, whilst those who may feel a common sentiment have less opportunity of communication and concert," he wrote. "The great desideratum in Government is such a modification of the Sovereignty as will render it sufficiently neutral between the different interests and factions, to controul one part of the Society from invading the rights of another, and at the same time sufficiently controuled itself, from setting up an interest adverse to that of the whole Society."[57] In other words, size increases diversity, and in Lynne Cheney's summary phrase, "diversity sustains freedom."[58] Madison's mental map, developed over frequent explorations of the states from Virginia north to New York, and his particular sensitivity to the religious diversity, not just as among the different states, but even within Virginia with its established Anglican Church, at a time when religious differences were known to have been a source of the horrifying wars and civil discord of seventeenth-century Britain and Europe, made him exquisitely aware of the diversity of the new nation, and his study of the history of republics made him confident.

In Federalist 10, the first of twenty-nine Federalist papers he wrote, ostensibly to persuade members of the New York convention to vote for ratification, Madison advanced the same views. "Extend the sphere" of the republic, he writes, "and you take in a greater variety of parties and interests; you make it less probable that a majority of the whole will have a common motive to invade the rights of other citizens; or if such a motive exists, it will be more difficult for all who feel it to discover their own strength, and to act in unison with each other." In Federalist 2, one of only five numbers that he wrote, John Jay wrote that "independent America" was "one connected, fertile, widespreading country"

with one united people—a people descended from the same ancestors, speaking the same language, professing the same religion,
attached to the same principles of government, very similar in their
manners and customs." It is odd that Jay, a native of New York,
the most ethnically and religiously diverse of the states, took this
view, perhaps for hortatory reasons. Madison, with his exposure
to so much of the diversity of the new nation, took note of it in
his more numerous and more famous numbers of the Federalist.
In Federalist 10, he describes the different economic interests.
"Those who hold, and those who are without property, have ever
formed distinct interests in society. Those who are creditors and
those who are debtors, fall under a like discrimination. A landed
interest, a manufacturing interest, a mercantile interest, a moneyed interest, with many lesser interests, grow up of necessity in
civilized nations, and divide them into different classes, actuated
by different sentiments and views." In Federalist 41, he paints a
vivid picture of New York and, writing just four years after British
soldiers departed, its vulnerability to naval attack. "Her sea coast
is extensive. The very important district of the state is an Island.
The state itself is penetrated by a large navigable river for more
than fifty leagues. The great emporium of its commerce, the great
reservoir of its wealth, lies every moment at the mercy of events."
The contrast with his native Virginia—like New York, still a holdout
on ratifying the Constitution—did not have to be spelled out to
readers. And in Federalist 51, he adverts, contra Jay in Federalist 2,
to the new nation's religious diversity. "In a free government, the
security for civil rights must be the same as that for religious rights.
It consists in the one case of a multiplicity of interests, and in the
other, in the multiplicity of sects." As historians Stanley Elkins
and Eric McKittrick write, a "major premise" of Madison's—"that
a multiplicity of interests may function as a guarantee of political
stability and against majority despotism...[grew] very logically
out of Madison's earliest responses to the ecclesiastical situation

in Virginia and to his own peculiar determination all through the 1770s and 1780s to pull down the Anglican Church's privileged position there."[59] The degree of "security for civil rights" in both cases "will depend on the number of interests and sects; and this may be presumed to depend on the extent of the country and number of people comprehended under the same government." Geography again, and the mental map of the new nation, a map not static but dynamic, for Madison was probably aware, as Benjamin Franklin and Thomas Jefferson had written, that the population of the states that had been colonies was doubling in less than twenty-five years. A corollary was economic, that the agricultural interest, to adapt Madison's locution, represented a majority of the nation, but that the other interests he pointed to—manufacturing, mercantile, moneyed—would probably grow at accelerated rates and account for a larger share of the nation as time went on. As he wrote in Federalist 56, "At present some of the states are little more than a society of husbandmen. Few of them have made much progress in those branches of industry, which give a variety and complexity to the affairs of a nation. These however will in all of them be the fruits of a more advanced population." But Madison, like his great friend and political ally of forty-seven years, hoped that the passage to that state of things would not be too rapid, while Alexander Hamilton, his partner in setting up the Constitutional Convention and in writing the Federalist papers, wanted to speed it up.

On his journeyings between Virginia and the North, Madison had stopped for extended periods at Mount Vernon, where he counseled George Washington to attend the Constitutional Convention and, after its ratification, urged him to run for president and, after his own election to Congress, at Washington's direction wrote a short inaugural address. These sessions also provided recesses from Madison's stressful activities. At the Virginia convention to consider the

Constitution, Madison spoke frequently, and against the eloquence and scorn of Patrick Henry, but had to excuse himself twice, perhaps fearing a seizure. His advocacy may have been decisive as the convention voted to ratify by only an 89-79 margin. That winter, denied election to the Senate by a hostile legislature, he ran for the House of Representatives, in a district drawn to include anti-Constitution territory. His opponent was James Monroe, a protégé of Jefferson who served as a young solider under Washington at Princeton; they debated decorously and Madison won by 1,308 to 972 votes.[60] In the First Congress, Madison was clearly the leading member of the House of Representatives—though he did not prevail on every issue. He shepherded through to passage a tariff, to provide most of the federal government's revenue, but despite repeated attempts, he did not succeed in imposing a higher tariff on imports from Britain—which he viewed with suspicion if not hatred all of his adult life—than from America's treaty ally, France. He sponsored legislation to set up government departments and argued, contrary to Hamilton's statement in Federalist 77, that the president could dismiss officeholders who had been confirmed by the Senate—a position upheld by presidents and the Supreme Court in the twentieth century. Having argued in Philadelphia and Richmond that there was no need for the Constitution to include a Bill of Rights, he had become convinced in the fights for ratification that one was necessary, and he sifted through dozens of proposed constitutional amendments to produce the first ten amendments, which were passed by Congress and ratified by the requisite number of states by December 1791.

But Madison found himself at odds with the president and his administration on two important substantive matters—on the financial program of Treasury Secretary Alexander Hamilton and, on foreign policy, how to respond to revolutionary France. When Hamilton, confirmed as Treasury secretary in September 1789, presented his report to Congress in January 1790 on funding the national debt, he was surprised to be opposed by Madison. Hamilton wanted the federal government to assume the debts not just of the Confederation but also of the states, to the dismay of states, including Virginia, which had already paid off most of their debts, and he proposed to pay holders of debt the full amount of its original denomination. Madison considered that unfair to soldiers and others who, often in distress, sold their debt for pennies on the dollar, and proposed a scheme of discrimination, paying only part of the current face value. Hamilton argued that this was unworkable and, more important, would defeat his purposes, first, of making debt instruments of steady value a form of money in a country always short of gold and silver and, second, establishing a solid credit rating so that in wartime the government could borrow cheaply. Madison's discrimination scheme was rejected by a wide margin in the House, but Hamilton lacked a majority on assumption, opposed by representatives from Virginia and other low-debt states. The stalemate was broken when Thomas Jefferson, who arrived from France only in March 1790 to become secretary of state, arranged a dinner between the two *Federalist* collaborators, in which Madison agreed to shift enough votes to pass Hamilton's assumption and Hamilton agreed to support a bill establishing the permanent national capital on a site on the Potomac River. On this issue, though not on the finances, Madison knew he had the support of George Washington, who believed that the Potomac could become the great avenue through the Appalachian mountain chains to the developing west.

Why did Madison in 1789 and 1790 oppose so strongly the proposals of the man who had been his great ally in 1787 and 1788? The historian Gordon Wood argues that Madison saw the federal government as a kind of arbiter among the states, preventing violations of property and other rights by faction-controlled state legislatures—stands on which he and Hamilton were in agreement. But Madison's proposals to increase the amount of credit in the economy—credit in the form of public debt, credit in the form of banks loaning out more money than they have cash on hand—ran up against Madison's suspicion, typical among indebted Virginia planters, of creditors who accumulated capital and of banks that lent out more money than the amount of cash they kept in their vaults.[61] Madison's response was to make moral and financial distinctions among those with financial interests. Trade with France was to be encouraged with lower tariffs, while trade with Britain would be discouraged. Original holders of federal securities who had sold low would be partially compensated and speculators—an especially suspect class, in Madison's view—penalized. There may have been an element of jealousy at work as well. From 1786 to 1789, Madison had been Washington's encourager and supporter, his houseguest and his speechwriter, his collaborator in establishing the new government. But on government finances, Washington took Hamilton's side.[62] This may have remained ambiguous up through the first half of 1790, but became clear after Hamilton in December 1790 delivered his required report to Congress on a national bank. His proposal, based on ideas he had floated to financier Robert Morris as a military aide a decade before, was for the government to charter a largely privately owned national bank—in a nation that had no banks before independence and that by 1790 then had only four of them. This was, as Madison saw, an imitation of the Bank of England, established in 1694 (as that was in imitation of the Bank of Amsterdam established in 1600) and a scheme to move the American economy away from its almost total dependence on agriculture toward the growth and instability of a finance-driven commercial and mercantile republic—as Gordon Wood put it, "a modern European-type state with an elaborate bureaucracy, a standing army, perpetual debts, and a powerful independent executive—the very kind of monarch-like war-making state that radical Whigs in England had been warning about for generations."[63] Madison feared that Hamilton's policies would accelerate the transition to an urbanized and commercial America, and to "a time in the distant future when 'a great majority of the people will not only be without landed, but any other sort of property,'" and warned that 'we see in the populous Countries in Europe now what we shall be hereafter.'"[64] Hamilton, as always, was operating from a mental map focusing on the invisible lines of trade routes across the Atlantic and potentially farther around the world. Madison, as always, was operating from a mental map in which almost all American growth for at least a generation of two would—or should—consist of an expansion of small farmers west and southwest of Virginia, filling in the countryside south of the Ohio River and heading east toward the Mississippi and perhaps, as in Jefferson's *Notes*, continuing beyond.

The national bank bill passed both houses of Congress by February 1791, but Washington had qualms: There was nothing in the Constitution about a bank. Madison's fellow Virginians, Attorney General Edmund Randolph and Jefferson, prepared legal memoranda arguing that the bill was unconstitutional and that creating one was not "necessary and proper" to achieve a constitutional goal. Washington, facing a deadline on whether to veto or sign the bill, asked Hamilton for his view. He produced a devastating reply, defining "necessary and proper" expansively, as Madison had in Federalist 44, where he added that "without the *substance* of this power, the whole constitution would be a dead letter." Against their rhetoric and perhaps against their intentions, Jefferson and Madison were in the process of creating an opposition party. In May and June 1791, they made a supposedly "botanical" trip up the Hudson Valley, making contacts with Governor George Clinton, Robert Livingston, Aaron Burr, and other Hamilton opponents. In October 1791, Jefferson subsidized Madison's college friend Philip Freneau with a job as translator at the State Department while he edited the anti-administration *National Gazette*. Even as Madison and Jefferson joined Hamilton in urging Washington to run for a second term, and after Jefferson delayed his planned resignation, Madison started speaking of a Republican party in 1792, and vote-counters speculated about a Republican majority in the House of Representatives when the Third Congress convened in December 1792. In two anonymous articles in the *National Gazette*, Madison justified his partisan approach and predicted the Republican party would "ultimately establish its ascendance."[65]

A neutral analyst could see that the Republicans, as they came to call themselves, were forming what Madison in the Federalist called a "faction," and a faction which would in time include a large majority of the political nation—the very monopoly he worried about in Federalist 10. But in the early 1790s, as Elkins and McKittrick write, "Madison and Jefferson did not see their party as a faction, but rather the avatar of a broad majority, anchored on the general principles of self-government in the pursuit of common interest."[66] Madison feared what he considered, as political scientist Jay Cost put it, "a minority faction: a wealthy and well-positioned group of insiders who had used Hamilton's system of public finance to enrich themselves to the detriment, and perhaps ultimate destruction, of the republic."[67] This was hyperbole, but the stakes seemed high. The Founders had a sense, which turned out to be accurate, that they were creating precedents and setting a course that would have profound effects for America and in the world for hundreds of years. But history did not unfold exactly as either Washington and Hamilton or as Jefferson and Madison expected. One prime reason is that the young republic was caught up in a multi-decade world war between its dominant trade partner and its revolutionary ally, parliamentary Britain and revolutionary France.

★   ★   ★

The conflict between Britain and France, which lasted all but fourteen months of the years between 1793 and 1814, was of grave importance to the young republic, but the United States was of, at most, peripheral and occasional interest to the leaders of Britain and France—even though Madison and his contemporaries "could not grasp America's insignificance in Europe's calculations."[68] American diplomats had difficulty obtaining meetings, much less commitments, from European officials, but for American voters the issues were highly visible and highly divisive. "It was the French Revolution, and particularly the ensuing war," historian Richard Hofstadter writes, "with the demands it made upon American leaders to make decisions about foreign policy that were bound to have either a British or a French bias, that made the party breach unnegotiable and almost irreconcilable."[69] Leading politicians were divided along lines similar to those regarding the Hamilton financial policies. Thomas Jefferson as minister to France had been in Paris the day of the storming of the Bastille and viewed with insouciance if not downright approval of the French revolutionaries' guillotining of government notables and intellectuals, even those he had known personally. James Madison took a less sanguinary view but maintained his opinion that revolutionary France was still a favored ally, in line with the 1778 treaty. George Washington and Alexander Hamilton initially regarded the French Revolution as a variant of their own, but by the time the King was executed in January 1793 and war with Britain declared in February 1793, they had decided the French Revolution had taken a sinister turn. In April 1793, Washington issued a Proclamation of Neutrality declaring the United States "friendly and impartial toward the belligerent powers." Though Jefferson supported it diffidently, Madison privately called it "a most unfortunate error."[70] That same month, revolutionary France's young ambassador, Citizen Edmond Genêt, arrived not in Philadelphia but Charleston, then proceeded at a leisurely place up the coast, commissioning ship captains as privateers. He spoke to cheering crowds at newly formed Republican societies and called on Congress to override Washington's policy. When Hamilton that summer wrote a series of papers under the pseudonym Pacificus, supporting the proclamation and asserting the president's authority over foreign affairs, Madison wrote a series under the pseudonym Helvidius published in August and September 1793. By summer, Jefferson and Madison understood that Genêt's appeals to Congress and the voters were unpopular, and in early August, Washington decided to demand Genêt's recall. Jefferson concurred and, with cabinet approval, wrote the missive to the French government. Genêt, a Girondin out of favor with the new Jacobin leaders in Paris, decided to seek asylum, married the daughter of New York Governor George Clinton, and died forty years later on his farm in Upstate New York.

In December 1793, Jefferson resigned and returned to Monticello, leaving Madison as the leader of the apparent Republican majority in the House. He found himself increasingly critical of Washington's policies. In response to a brief British restriction on trade in the West Indies (to which Congress voted a thirty-day embargo) and continued refusal to remove troops from the Northwest Territory, Washington in May 1794 sent Chief Justice John Jay to negotiate a new treaty in London—an initiative Madison regarded with suspicion. To subdue Indians in the Great Lakes area, Washington sent 3,000 troops to General Anthony Wayne, who in August 1794 won a decisive victory at Fallen Timbers, with the resulting Treaty of Greenville opening up most of Ohio to white settlement. In contrast, Washington refused to send troops to the southwest frontier,[71] the area favored by Madison for western settlement. In the summer of 1794, Hamilton persuaded Washington to lead an army to suppress the "whiskey rebellion," a concerted refusal to pay the excise tax on whiskey in western Pennsylvania. An army of 13,000 was assembled, led westward across the state by Washington in September and October; the rebellion collapsed and Washington eventually pardoned the leaders. Although Madison had supported the whiskey excise in 1791, he was dismayed by what he considered the administration's disproportionate and overly military response.

He was unhappy as well when Washington in a November 1794 address condemned "certain self-created societies"—after which many of the Republican societies closed down.

Madison was even more dismayed by the treaty that Jay brought back from London in early 1795 but whose terms remained secret for months. Britain again promised, as it had in the Treaty of Paris signed twelve years before, to evacuate the Northwest Territory, it regularized American trade with Britain—by a wide margin America's leading trade partner—and it provided limited access by small American ships to British West Indies ports. Issues relating to damages to American shipping and debts owed to expelled British subjects were submitted to arbitration. It was roundly opposed by Madison's Republicans and by popular demonstrations in much of the country; the fear was that it would make the United States an ally of Britain. It was ratified by exactly the required two-thirds margin, 20-10, in the Senate in June 1795. The young Republican Edward Livingston (later secretary of state under Andrew Jackson) got the House to demand Washington turn over all treaty papers, which he refused, and Madison, despite qualms about whether the House had a constitutional role on treaties, decided to oppose appropriations to make the treaty effective. His position was weakened after Thomas Pinckney negotiated the Treaty of San Lorenzo with Spain, which adjusted the boundary of Spanish Florida southward and guaranteed free navigation of the Mississippi River and deposit of goods in New Orleans. This was widely popular in Kentucky and Tennessee, and stirred fears in western Pennsylvania and New York that blocking implementation of Jay's Treaty would spur a British attack or offensives by Indians, preventing settlers there from reaching the now opened Mississippi.[72] The Republican majority in the House still seemed primed to block the treaty appropriation, but as spring approached in 1796, and the nation prospered with increased trade, the anti-treaty majority melted away in April 1796 and the appropriation went through. Madison's campaign against the Jay Treaty ruptured his relations with Washington; they never spoke again. The farewell address Madison had drafted for the president in 1792 was cast aside when Washington asked Hamilton to draft what became his famous Farewell Address, delivered in September 1796. In an era when it was considered ungainly to seek the presidency, Madison remained aloof from the efforts of some Republicans to elect Thomas Jefferson, efforts that were doomed, it turned out, when Federalists won a majority that spring in elections to the New York legislature, which would cast the state's electoral votes. And Madison himself decided not to seek a fifth term in the House. Unlike Jefferson, he had never had friendly relations with John Adams, who won a bare electoral college majority of seventy-one votes, and he evidently saw no need to remain at the side of Jefferson, who with sixty-eight electoral votes was elected vice president and would preside over the Senate for four years. And so in March 1797, he returned to Montpelier with his vivacious wife, Dolley, whom he had married in 1794 after her husband died in a yellow fever epidemic. It was still his parents' house, but Madison built symmetric additions at each end and put a division in the middle so that he and his wife on one side and his parents on the other had what amounted to separate apartments, with a view from the single porch of the mountains heading toward the southwest.

For the next twenty years, the newly created United States was tossed back and forth in the struggle between ancient powers led by strikingly young men—Britain's Prime Minister William Pitt (born eight years after Madison) and his acolytes and France's cynical post-revolutionary Directory and then the hyperactive Napoleon Bonaparte (born eighteen years after Madison). As Jefferson, with his gift for the apt phrase, put it in January 1806, "What an awful spectacle does the world exhibit at this instant, one man bestriding the continent of Europe like a Colossus, and another roaming unbridled on the ocean."[73] The Republicans had championed free trade with belligerent powers—"free ships, free goods," as they put it—and the trade between one belligerent's Caribbean colonies or even Indian outposts with the home country became hugely lucrative for American shipowners. Madison's retirement from Congress and Jefferson's elevation to the vice presidency spared the two leading Republicans from responding to the "quasi war" with France, in which French privateers attacked and seized more than 300 American ships in the Caribbean. American opinion was roused when the three French diplomats demanded bribes from the three American negotiators dispatched by Adams—the so-called XYZ Affair. Adams and the Federalist Congress moved to establish an effective navy, the need for which Jefferson had conceded since *Notes on Virginia*, and at Hamilton's prompting, assembling an army with George Washington technically in command. Federalists also passed the Sedition Act, criminalizing speech against government policy though less stringently than in English common law. Anonymously, Jefferson and Madison responded with the Kentucky and Virginia Resolutions, with Jefferson characteristically more daring and Madison more cautious in suggesting that states could interpose or nullify federal legislation.

The Republicans' nightmare of war with France was avoided finally by Adams's circumspection and the incoming French leader, thirty-year-old First Counsel Napoleon Bonaparte, who agreed to end hostilities in the Treaty of Mortefontaine in September 1800. Six months later, after prevailing in the House of Representatives against his vice-presidential candidate, Aaron Burr, Thomas Jefferson was inaugurated as president and James Madison was appointed and quickly confirmed as secretary of state. Previous administrations were willing to bribe the North African Barbary States not to capture American ships and enslave their crews. Jefferson, despite the Republicans' opposition to the Federalist military and naval buildup,[74] was willing to use the navy (whose funding they had opposed) to attack them successfully. Meanwhile, sudden changes by Napoleon would present opportunities—and threats—to the United States. In October 1800, he secretly persuaded Spain to return the Louisiana Territory to France, to help provision an attack he was launching to regain the formerly lucrative sugar colony of Haiti. When Americans learned about the agreement in 1802, Madison and Jefferson were furious. Madison wrote Robert Livingston in Paris raising the specter of "not less than 200,000 militia on the waters of the Mississippi,"[75] and Jefferson named James Monroe a special envoy and dispatched a message, intended to be revealed to French Foreign Minister Talleyrand. "There is on the globe one single spot, the possessor of which is our natural and habitual enemy," he wrote. "It is New Orleans." If France takes possession, he went on, "From that moment we must marry ourselves to the British fleet and nation."[76] But Napoleon had changed his mind again. French forces in Haiti were devastated by stubborn resistance and yellow fever, and Louisiana seemed now a burden, not an asset. Even before Monroe arrived, Talleyrand offered an astonished Livingston the entirety of Louisiana; he quickly retracted his initial rejection, and in April 1803, he and Monroe agreed, without knowing its exact extent, to purchase it for $15 million. Jefferson's bluff of threatening a British alliance to expel France was not called, and Madison's longtime dream of removing Spain and, *a fortiori* France, as a barrier to southwest expansion was suddenly achieved. He argued later that he had assumed then and continued to believe that the purchase also included West Florida—the current Louisiana parishes east of the Mississippi River and north of Lake Pontchartrain and the current Mississippi and Alabama Gulf Coast counties south of the 31° parallel—an interpretation neither the French nor the Spanish accepted. But Madison and his colleagues remained deeply interested in expansion to the southwest. When the Prussian scientist and explorer Wilhelm von Humboldt returned from his long excursions in Spanish territory—long barred to foreigners—in South America and Mexico, he paid a special visit to Washington to meet with Jefferson, Madison, and Gallatin. For days they bombarded him with questions about Mexico and, with his permission, transcribed his notes and copied his maps, which were far more accurate than any that were publicly available. Jefferson and Madison peppered him particularly with questions about the "the native population, soils, and minerals" in the Spanish territory between the Sabine River, the western boundary of Louisiana, and the Rio Grande—the land that would be known later as Texas—and Humboldt provided "nineteen tightly filled pages" of notes.[77] Tantalizingly close to the American border, inhabited in later decades by several thousand American migrants, Texas would remain a land of interest—and controversy—to Jefferson, Madison, and their successors for the next forty-one years, until its annexation in March 1845.

Jefferson's second term was less successful. In 1805, Britain revived its Rule of 1756, justifying seizure of neutral shipping, and in 1806, Napoleon imposed his Continental System, justifying seizure of neutral shipping.[78] This was devastating to American shipowners who had been carrying on trade between both sides and their Caribbean colonies. Jefferson responded with a non-importation act and by building up the navy—one of many examples of his adopting Federalist policies. Remembering the colonies' boycott of British goods in 1769, Jefferson moved to impose a total embargo in December 1807. Treasury Secretary Albert Gallatin objected that this policy would be ruinous, but Madison was the Embargo's "most enthusiastic supporter."[79] Like Jefferson, he supposed that European powers were dependent on American trade and shipping and, in Richard Brookhiser's words, "all of his adult life...had believed in the power of commercial warfare."[80] "Both could not grasp the contempt for the United States of the young leaders of the embattled great powers," historian Robert Wiebe writes, "the forty-two-year-old Napoleon, now Emperor of the French, and the forty-nine-year-old British

Prime Minister Spencer Perceval." Wiebe goes on, "Napoleon had utter disdain for everything about that bastard republic. Although the United States asked only that France repeal those ocean rules it could not enforce in any case, Napoleon still would not bother. Various British governments on their part decided that they could get what they needed from American commerce without conceding anything to its government.... Only Spain respected the power of the United States, and Spain's opinion no longer counted,"[81] because since Napoleon ousted Charles IV and installed his brother Joseph as king in August 1808, rebels aided by Britain started a civil war, and Spanish colonies in the Western Hemisphere began to eye independence.

Madison, with his eyes on the Southwest, was happy to take advantage of Spain's weakness. In October 1810, he responded to a convention of Americans in Baton Rouge, at the western extremity of West Florida, to take over the territory. Thirty years before, Madison had maintained that Spain's territorial claims depended "more upon our peaceableness than her own power."[82] Thirty years later, that power was negligible and this seemingly most bookish of the Framers had run out of peaceableness. His consistent claim that the Louisiana Purchase included West Florida, illustrated with a map, was dismissed by the French ambassador with contempt: "Maps are not titles."[83] Madison, untroubled, ordered the governor of Louisiana to take possession of West Florida eastward to the Perdido River (the current western boundary of Florida). "Regarded by his contemporaries as a precise, well-balanced, even a timid man, argumentative to satiety, never carried away by bursts of passion, fretful rather than vehement, pertinacious rather than resolute," as historian Henry Adams in one of his delicious passages described him, James Madison is the only American president to have expanded the continental United States not by treaty or declaration of war but by ordering troops to seize it.[84] His motive, he explained to Jefferson, was the "danger of its passing into the hands of a third and dangerous party"[85]—the British. "Since the 1780s, Madison had looked past such issues as impressment and seen a single, overriding goal in British policy: subjugating the United States by swallowing its commerce," writes historian Robert Wiebe. "With remarkable steadiness, he held to the belief that Britain stood alone as America's nemesis."[86]

But Madison's seizure did not impress the British, who continued to seize American ships and to impress sailors on American merchant vessels—carrying them off on the claim they were British subjects and enrolling them in the Royal Navy. And it did not satisfy the young "War Hawks" elected to Congress in 1812—John C. Calhoun of South Carolina, Felix Grundy of Tennessee, and Henry Clay of Kentucky, elected to the Senate in 1807 at the constitutional minimum age of thirty and elected Speaker as he first took his seat in the House in 1811. In June 1812, Congress voted to declare war, by the narrowest margin in history, not realizing that Britain had repealed its offending Orders in Council a few days before. The War Hawks looked longingly at Canada, and Britain's supposed sponsorship of the Indian warrior Tecumseh and his brother the Prophet in the Northwest Territory. Madison was willing, after Congress declared war, to order troops into British territory and launch American ships on the Great Lakes. But success was limited. The few American troops and militia forces led by superannuated Revolutionary War generals failed utterly in the land war, surrendering Detroit and Fort Dearborn (the site of Chicago), blanching at crossing the Niagara River and failing to move toward Montreal. Only the navy, Alexander Hamilton's creation, reluctantly augmented by Jefferson, made gains, capturing a British warship on the high Atlantic, and winning control of lakes on the Canadian border, Lake Erie in September 1813 and Lake Champlain in September 1814. The success in Lake Erie enabled the army's foray into southern Canada that resulted in the death of Tecumseh at the Battle of the Thames. Madison remained "remarkably sanguine" during the war,[87] despite the British offensive that resulted in the burning of the Capitol and the White House in August 1814 and calls for secession in New England and the summoning of a convention in Hartford in December 1814.

Meanwhile, Americans made one gain in what had long been Madison's focus, the Southwest, when in 1813 the 1810 seizure of West Florida was extended eastward to include Mobile Bay. It took longer for Andrew Jackson, land speculator and duelist, former congressman and senator, to get his forces into play. He marched his Tennessee militia to Natchez, then was ordered to march them back, then managed to get authorization to attack the Creeks in Mississippi Territory and defeated them at the Battle of Horseshoe Bend in March 1814, and forced them, including some of his Creek allies, to sign the Treaty of Fort Jackson, renouncing most of the future state of Alabama.[88] Like Madison, Jackson wanted to extend American territory south and west, heading to Pensacola and Mobile, and Fort Jackson eliminated Indian control over much of what soon became the states of Alabama and Mississippi, only shortly after treaties following the death of Tecumseh and defeat of the Prophet eliminated Indian control over much of what soon became the states of Indiana and Illinois. George Washington had had cordial relations with Indians from his first forays into the Ohio Country, and Thomas Jefferson displayed Indian artifacts in the front hall of Monticello; of all the American presidents in the forty years before the inauguration of Andrew Jackson, James Madison was the most assiduous in rolling back Indian sovereignty and opening land for white, and white slaveholder, settlement.

At the end of 1814, Andrew Jackson, like the president he was in his own fashion serving, headed farther southwest, anticipating correctly that the Royal Navy would ferry troops to attack the nation's southern soft spot, New Orleans. There, on January 8, 1815, he wiped out the British expeditionary force and imposed martial law. Just as the declaration of war had been passed in Washington after one of Americans' major grievances had been rescinded in London, so Jackson's victory in New Orleans occurred sixteen days after a peace treaty had been signed in Ghent, Belgium. For most of 1814, the British government had characteristically ignored the treaty negotiations, requiring the subordinate negotiators to make preposterous demands. Only when it became clear that Napoleon had been removed from the scene and installed in what was thought to be permanent exile in Elba did the negotiators receive serious instructions. The outbreak of peace mooted the issues of impressment and restrictions on neutral shipping, and the American non-conquest of Canada and the British non-instigation of Indian revolt in the Northwest Territory made a ratification of the status quo the obvious basis for peace. The considerably more distinguished American negotiators—led by Albert Gallatin, John Quincy Adams, and Henry Clay—who for months in Ghent had stoutly resisted preposterous terms—now secured a sensible result and signed the treaty the day before Christmas 1814. Thus Canada remained British—and the two sides moved quickly to demilitarize the Great Lakes in the Rush-Bagot agreement of April 1817[89]—while the United States was free to expand to the south and the southwest in lands theoretically belonging to the weakened Spanish. This would raise for Americans, if not for Madison in the remainder of his second term, the nettlesome issue of slavery.

The Madison family had a particularly uncomfortable history of involvement with slavery. In 1732, James Madison Sr.'s father, Ambrose Madison, an apparently healthy man at thirty-six, died of what was judged to be poisoning. One slave, the property of a neighbor, was found guilty of the crime and hanged; two Madison slaves were found "concerned" with the crime and sentenced to twenty-nine lashes.[90] This occurred when James Madison Sr. was nine years old and nearly twenty years before his oldest son was born, but the pall of this ghastly episode surely cast a shadow over

Montpelier. It could not have been unknown to the younger James Madison, whose grandmother, Ambrose's widow, encouraged his reading and studied until her death when he was ten.[91] As an adult, as historian Sean Wilentz writes, Madison "fully recognized that slavery violated the fundamental principles of republican government; his writings and speeches contain numerous moral and political condemnations of slavery; he had been willing, as a state legislator, at least to express in private sympathy for emancipationist petitioners in Virginia in 1785 and, like other enlightened Virginians, he opposed continuing the Atlantic slave trade."[92] That issue came to the fore in the Constitutional Convention, when delegates agreed to allow the federal government to outlaw the trans-Atlantic slave trade at some time after ratification (a time first set at the year 1800, then finally at twenty years after the Constitution's adoption). This was one of several compromises Madison reluctantly accepted; delegates from the Carolinas and Georgia threatened to oppose any document that immediately prohibited the slave trade but were willing to accept a delayed prohibition. But the wording was important. According to the notes that Madison kept of the Convention's deliberations, which were not made public until the 1840s, Madison insisted it would be wrong "to admit in the Constitution that there could be property in men." Accordingly, writes Wilentz, "for the slave trade compromise to stand, it could not carry any implied recognition of slaves as property. The convention then revised the subclause on taxing slave imports to include the word person."[93] In the most painstaking examination of this episode, Wilentz argues that the exclusion of "any validation of property in man...was of profound and fateful importance. It rendered slavery solely a creation of state laws. It thereby opened the prospect of a United States free of slavery."[94] In Federalist 54, written five months after the end of the Convention, he addressed the three-fifths clause, which counted "three-fifths of all other persons"—slaves, without using the word—in the apportionment among the states of members of the House of Representatives. It was another classic compromise: Counting slaves as zero would reduce the power of slaveholders in Congress and therefore in the Electoral College, while counting them as full persons would have increased their power. Contrary to the authors' usual practice in the Federalist of affirmatively defending every provision of the Constitution, Madison defended but stopped short of endorsing the three-fifths clause, explaining gingerly that the law considers slaves "in some respects, as persons, and in other respects, as property," and going on to note that "government is instituted no less for the protection of property, than of the persons of individuals."[95]

In the late 1780s, the eventual abolition of slavery was, in Wilentz's words, "a prospect some delegates deeply desired and many more believed was coming to pass"[96]—not an unnatural assumption in a decade which had seen complete or gradual abolition of slavery become law in Pennsylvania, Massachusetts, New Hampshire, Connecticut, and Rhode Island. Madison himself seems to have shared this view, writing in 1790 that "revolutionary ideas of 'Humanity and freedom [were] secretly undermining the institution,'" with the implication that "raising noise" about the issue "could only slow down the inevitable march of progress,"[97] though in 1791, "he would decline to support a gradual emancipation proposal in Virginia lest he give 'a public wound...to an interest' in which his constituents 'had so great a value.'"[98] But Madison shared Jefferson's belief that freed slaves could not practicably live among whites. In 1790, he wrote that colonization—sending freed slaves to live in Africa—"might prove a great encouragement to manumission in the southern part of the US and even afford the best hope yet presented of an end to slavery,"[99] but in time he had to admit that slaves showed no appetite whatever for moving there.

In the meantime the proliferation of the cotton gin and the development of cotton plantations farther south and the Treaty of Fort Jackson opened the fertile black soil of central Alabama and

Mississippi to vast cotton plantations worked by large numbers of slaves. These developments incentivized Virginia planters to sell their slaves "down south," while the Gabriel slave rebellion near Richmond in 1800 prompted passage in 1806 of a Virginia statute that made manumission—freeing slaves—more difficult. In 1776, most white Virginians didn't own slaves, but by 1810, most did,[100] and the slave percentage of Orange County rose from 45 percent in 1790 to nearly 60 percent in 1820.[101] It was against this background that Edward Coles, a young Virginian who was Madison's chief White House aide, in 1814 urged Jefferson and Madison to free their slaves.[102] Jefferson declined in a picturesquely phrased letter,[103] while Madison, whose mother was still living at Montpelier, seemed uninterested.[104] Coles resigned in 1815, freed the slaves he had inherited, and moved them to Illinois, where he was elected governor in 1822 and beat back a referendum to legalize slavery there.[105] Madison, leaving office as Americans were flush with enthusiasm after the War of 1812, followed public affairs more closely than had Jefferson, who left office amid the fiasco of the Embargo eight years before.[106] In 1820, during the controversy over the admission of Missouri as a slave state, in a letter to a Philadelphia journalist Robert Walsh, Madison argued for diffusion—dispersing slaves over many parts of the country and reducing their concentrations along the Atlantic Coast and the cotton plantation belts farther west, where slaves were treated most harshly. "It would 'better the condition of the slaves, by lessening the number belonging to individual masters, and intermixing both with greater masses of free people.'"[107] He argued also that the Constitution's provision allowing Congress to ban the international slave trade after 1807, the clause from which he had excluded the word "slave," did not authorize the provision in the 1820 Missouri Compromise provision barring slavery north of the 36°30' line to the west.[108] This was close to endorsing, more than thirty years ahead of time, Stephen Douglas's 1854 Kansas-Nebraska Act, allowing residents of territories to decide whether to allow slavery, and the Supreme Court's 1857 Dred Scott decision, ruling that slaves could not obtain freedom by residing in a state banning slavery.[109]

Madison took a less jaundiced view of how he and fellow Republicans had accepted many of the Hamilton policies they had opposed so strenuously many years before—what historian George Dangerfield calls "the movement of Virginia Presidents...away from Jeffersonian principles."[110] After failing to get a recharter of the Bank of the United States in 1811, he obtained one in 1816 when the government's difficulty in funding the War of 1812 was glaringly clear. He argued that the bank, having been supported "under the varied ascendancy of the parties," Federalist and Republican, "amounted to the requisite evidence of the national judgment and intention,"[111] and twenty years later, he opposed Andrew Jackson's veto of the recharter of the bank.[112] In the wake of the War of 1812, he supported the standing army and active navy he and fellow Jeffersonians had opposed. Although he vetoed an internal improvements bill on his last day in office in 1817, he was not dismayed by John Quincy Adams's and Henry Clay's support of federal financing of roads and canals.[113] While Jefferson expressed alarm at the prospect of Andrew Jackson as president, Madison, disappointing two of his young correspondents, both the strongly pro-Jackson William Cabell Rives and the strongly anti-Jackson Edward Coles, avoided taking sides and urged friends to approach the election "in a spirit and manner, neither unfavorable to a dispassionate result, nor unworthy of the great and advancing cause of representative government."[114] Despite his authorship of the Virginia Resolutions thirty years before, he disagreed with the theory, advanced by Virginia friends and South Carolina's John C. Calhoun, that states could nullify the so-called "tariff of abominations." He took care also to make the more difficult case that Jefferson, though seemingly an advocate of state nullification in his more radical Kentucky Resolutions, stood against nullification in this case. "Allowances ought also to be made for a habit in Mr. Jefferson as in others of great genius of expressing in strong and round terms, impressions of the moment."[115] As in his framing of the Constitution while Jefferson was in Paris, or in his inability to share that great friend's relish at the bloodshed of the French Revolution, or in his willingness to put aside Jeffersonian dogma on the National Bank, the army and navy, and the Embargo, Madison showed flexibility in adapting to the circumstances of economic development and foreign affairs and to the will of the people, while maintaining a steely determination to uphold the Constitution that he, five decades before his death, he did more than anyone else to write, and to accommodate and facilitate the movement of Americans to the west by southwest.

SIX

ALBERT GALLATIN
Ever Westward

In the waning days of September 1784, George Washington was making a tour of the western country beyond the Appalachian mountains which he had first visited as a sixteen-year-old surveyor for Lord Fairfax three dozen years before. In the intervening years, Washington had made several journeys west of the mountains, leading troops to counter French advances on the Forks of the Ohio River and warning General Edward Braddock of the peril of enemy Indian tactics, surveying lands and in time buying thousands of acres, building roads, and promoting a canal that would connect the Potomac River and the Atlantic Ocean with the valley of the Ohio and the Mississippi beyond. On the banks of the Monongahela River, he met with local settlers to ask their opinions on the best route for a road across the mountains. But before he was finished, a young man, tall but not as tall as Washington, speaking in a thick French accent, interjected, "Oh, it is plain enough, the location just mentioned is the most practicable." George Washington, the account goes on "laid down his pen, raised his eyes from his paper, and cast a stern look" at the speaker, then "continued his interrogations for a few minutes longer, when suddenly stopping, he threw down his pen, turned to Mr. Gallatin, and said, 'You are right, sir.'"[1]

George Washington was fifty-two years old, majestically tall, and intimidatingly solid, widely admired for having led the Continental Army for eight difficult years and, even more, for resigning his commission ten months before and returning as a private citizen to his farm at Mount Vernon. The impertinent young man was Albert Gallatin, twenty-three years old, last surviving son of a long prominent family in Geneva, Switzerland, who had left his comfortable life and, at nineteen, had journeyed to America, to live in the wilds beyond the mountains. He encountered Washington in his own search for lands to buy and, rejecting the older man's offer to become his land agent, would buy his own acres on the Monongahela, just north of the boundary between Virginia and Pennsylvania, two or three years later.

The story is charming and reflects favorably on both men. Gallatin, far from his homeland, is opinionated, confident, and right. Washington, used to deference, is startled and offended, but quickly recognizes and acknowledges that Gallatin is right. As the account has it, "'It was so on all occasions with General Washington,' remarked Mr. Gallatin to me; 'he was slow in forming an opinion, and never decided until he knew he was right.'" He might have added that Washington's offering him the job as land agent was proof of his talent for spotting extraordinarily able young men of remote origins, the talent that had led him to make a twenty-two-year-old officer from the West Indies his top military aide in 1777. His astonishing ability to appreciate and promote men of transcendent ability is witnessed by the fact that this aide, Alexander Hamilton, became one of the shapers of American government as secretary of the Treasury from 1789 to 1795, and that Albert Gallatin, though a critic of Hamilton and thus of Washington's administration, did much to shape and expand the nation as secretary of the Treasury from 1801 to 1814, just as it is interesting that financial policy in the young republic was the product of two men with unusual backgrounds.

But was the charming story of Gallatin's encounter with Washington true? As Henry Adams noted in his 1879 biography of

Gallatin, its details were clearly wrong: The source, the New York bookseller and publisher John Russell Bartlett, places the meeting at the junction of the Kanawha and Ohio Rivers, but as Washington's daily diary makes clear, he did not journey to the Kanawha as he had planned, but because of Indian attacks, had gone no farther west than the Monongahela. And the diary does not mention Gallatin or any such incident. Bartlett did not make Gallatin's acquaintance until the 1840s, when he was an octogenarian living in New York. And if the story's favorable portrayal of both its prominent subjects was in line with Gallatin's retrospective generosity toward political adversaries as well as allies, it also has the air of an old man's muddled memories. The story also highlights an arresting feature of the founding of the United States of America, the fact that the new nation's finances and the course of its commercial and industrial expansion were anticipated and set in motion by its two dominant early Treasury secretaries, both of whom were migrants—the word "immigrants" was not then in common use—to what were technically the British North American colonies.[2] Alexander Hamilton's origins in the West Indies are now more widely known than in the past two hundred years, thanks to Lin-Manuel Miranda's ingenious Broadway show, while not one in a hundred of even historically educated Americans knows Albert Gallatin's name or his origin in the distant city-state republic of Geneva.

Albert Gallatin grew up amid the stony streets and townhouses of Geneva and in the villas in the mountains on the sloping flanks of Lac Leman. Geneva was French-speaking and Protestant, governed by a council of 200 and a smaller council of twenty-five, in whose ranks Gallatins had been prominent for centuries. In religion, eighteenth-century Geneva carried on, in modulated form, the heritage of its Reformation leader Jean Calvin; in politics it was a loosely tied ally of what would become the Swiss Confederation. Geneva was a city of merchants and bankers and watchmakers, of classical learning and busy commerce, of "one of the most unobtrusive, polite, and cultured societies in pre-revolutionary Europe."[3] Eighteenth-century Geneva, historian Henry Adams declared, was "the most intelligent and perhaps the purest society in Europe," where "a far greater number of well educated and informed men were found in that small spot than on almost every other town of Europe which was not metropolis of an extensive country."[4] It was famously the home town of Jacques Necker, the finance minister of Louis XVI who grappled with the debts France incurred in supporting the American Revolution and whose dismissal led to the storming of the Bastille in July 1789.[5]

Geneva was referenced in Julius Caesar's *Gallic Wars*, and it was part of the central zone between modern France and Germany claimed in the year 843 by Lothar, the oldest of the three grandsons of Charlemagne who split his empire: this Lotharingia, from the Low Countries south along the Rhine through the Alps to northern Italy, has been the richest and the most war-torn part of Europe in the centuries since. Geneva, far from being geographically and intellectually isolated, was situated on that strategic ground and, in the eighteenth century, the home territory of the continent's two most acclaimed writers—Rousseau, born in Geneva and a resident from time to time as an adult, and Voltaire, whose house in Ferney just outside the city was out of reach of the French and Catholic authorities he so often outraged. Orphaned by age nine, Gallatin was raised by a family friend, Mademoiselle Catherine Pictet, who enrolled him in the Academy of Geneva, in which he finished first in mathematics, Latin, and "natural philosophy." But his education was not only classical: As a boy, his grandparents often took him to visit their great friend in Ferney, and as an adolescent, he imbibed Rousseau's elegies of the goodness of man and natural life in the countryside.[6] With two school friends, and with the expectation of succeeding to his inheritances at age twenty-five, Gallatin got it into his head to travel to the frontier lands of America, and without telling Mademoiselle Pictet, in 1780, at age nineteen, he set out for Bordeaux and sailed across the Atlantic.

He arrived in Boston, free of British troops since March 1776, at a moment when the wider success of the Revolution was by no means certain. Unlike Hamilton, Gallatin had no interest then or later in military service. He spent the winter in Machias, in Massachusetts's northern province of Maine, and then got a position at Harvard teaching French for two years.[7] In Boston, he met a French merchant who asked Gallatin, now a fluent though heavily accented English speaker, to travel to Virginia and invest in land claims with him. They stopped in New York and Philadelphia and then in Baltimore bought warrants to buy lands in the Ohio River valley. He seems to have been an impressive young man or at least a distinctive one in the still small cities of North America;—in Richmond, he was befriended by John Marshall and Patrick Henry. By this time, political rioting that brought French and Savoyard troops to Geneva extinguished any desire he had to return home,[8] and he determined to settle far west of the seaboard. In April 1784, he headed across the mountains to Pittsburgh and, deterred by Indian attacks from sailing down the Ohio, headed south on the Monongahela to his perhaps apocryphal meeting with Washington in September. In October, he swore an oath of citizenship in Virginia, and in November, he leased land which he later purchased and built his home, Friendship Hill, overlooking the river.

By this time, Gallatin had a firsthand acquaintance with the geography and demography of the newly independent United States of America.[9] He had not liked New England, whose states had seen few immigrants since they were settled by Puritans more than a century before, and whose Calvinist mores created an atmosphere that may have seemed even more restrictive than Calvinist Geneva. His limited funds—more than most newcomers brought, but no fortune—could make him only a marginal player in the mercantile circles of New York, Philadelphia, and Baltimore. He had already, at twenty-five and after only five years in North America, seen more of the different states than most Americans had in their lifetimes, and not just along the seaboard. A desire to set up a living in a seemingly virgin wilderness, inspired perhaps by Rousseau's *Social Contract* (1762) or the Hector St. John de Crèvecoeur's *Letters from an American Farmer* (1782), sent him west of the mountains. A vision of how the seaboard settlements could be linked to the vast interior by linking the Potomac and Ohio Rivers—the same vision that George Washington pursued over the last decades of his life—sent him to the Monongahela valley, freed from Indian attacks since 1769 but still largely unsettled. A sense that America's growth would come from expansion to the vast lands between the Appalachians and the Mississippi was surely part of his motivation. In 1786, with one-fourth of his inheritance, he bought 400 acres along the Monongahela in Fayette County, Pennsylvania, just north of the Virginia line, and built a house he called Friendship Hill. He was right in supposing that this was a strategic location in the young republic, midway between the coastal plains and not far south of the new town of Pittsburgh, between the Potomac and the Ohio. He hoped to attract Swiss settlers as tenant farmers and built a town called New Geneva on the river, with a boatyard and glassworks.[10]

His hopes were never fulfilled, and many years later, he sold the property, which he admitted was unprofitable. But his land proved to be an excellent base for a political career. "In those days," wrote Henry Adams, looking back from the last decades of the nineteenth century, "except perhaps in New England, the eastern counties of Virginia and South Carolina, there was a serious want of men who possessed in any degree the rudimentary qualifications for political life.[11] Gallatin, with his knowledge of classics, finance, and law, clearly did, and gave him the opportunity to become one of the most effective political operators and policy innovators of those in the generation coming of age in the wake of the Founders.

He attended sessions on revising Pennsylvania's state constitution in 1789 and was elected to the legislature in 1790, 1791, and 1792. By his own account, he was influential there through "my great industry and to the facility with which I could understand and carry on current business." He wrote the report of the Ways and Means Committee, sponsored withdrawal of the state's paper currency and supported chartering the Bank of Pennsylvania on the model of Hamilton's Bank of the United States.[12] Gallatin's first clash with the policies of Alexander Hamilton came over the excise tax on whiskey, widely opposed in western Pennsylvania, where many farmers found distilled liquor easier to transport over the mountains than raw grain. In 1792, Gallatin chaired a meeting in Pittsburgh where the tax was denounced mightily—in "sentiments...violent, intemperate, and reprehensible...my only political sin."[13] He did not support the armed rebellion and attacks on revenue offices in 1794, but also felt that Hamilton's leading an army over the mountains excessive. Lending credence to Gallatin's praise of his work as a legislator was his election, by the Pennsylvania Legislature, to the US Senate in November 1793. But his eligibility was challenged on the grounds that he had not been an American citizen for the required nine years, and he was expelled in February 1794. Later that year, however, he was elected to the US House of Representatives.

In the House, Gallatin quickly became a leader of the Republicans opposing Alexander Hamilton's financial policies. He opposed how Hamilton had financed the Bank of the United States and advocated paying off the national debt rather than funding the debt permanently. He argued that credit provided by the bank would not be treated as investment capital, but simply used for consumption of luxuries.[14] He created the House Ways and Means Committee and wrote a 170-page *Sketch of the Finances of the United States* in 1796, which he updated again in 1800.[15] He claimed not to oppose Jay's Treaty with Britain outright, but criticized it for not stopping

"British intrigues with Indians" and the impressment of American seamen into the Royal Navy[16] and supported his colleague James Madison's attempt to undermine it by denying appropriations to carry it out. In 1796, George Washington announced his retirement and Madison announced that he, too, would leave office and return to his Virginia home. With Thomas Jefferson politically quiescent, presiding over the Senate as vice president but taking no lead public role, Gallatin in his second two terms in the House was de facto leader of the Republican minority in Philadelphia. After 1796 and the retirement of George Washington, Gallatin became de facto leader of the minority Republicans as the republic faced a war scare from France. His foreign policy verged on pacifism. "I think every war except a defensive one to be unjustifiable," he wrote his wife in 1793. "We are not attacked by any nation." Although he conceded that the obstreperous French ambassador, Citizen Genêt, was "totally unfit for the place he fills. His abilities are but slender; he possesses some declamatory powers, but not the least shadow of judgment." Yet he still believed revolutionary France's "cause to be that of mankind against tyrants."[17] He opposed Federalists' demands for the creation of a large army and navy and called for postponing them until they could be accomplished without increasing the national debt.[18] He opposed the Federalists' Alien and Sedition Acts deftly and managed to modify them somewhat.[19]

Thomas Jefferson and his Republicans were the great beneficiaries of First Counsel Napoleon Bonaparte's decision to make peace with the United States in the Treaty of Mortefontaine in September 1800. For four years, the Republicans had been a beleaguered minority in Congress and at risk of seeming unpatriotic, then suddenly they were able to face the presidential race on equal terms and win—though Jefferson had to undergo the ordeal of having a Federalist House break the electoral vote tie between him and his running mate, Aaron Burr. After twelve years in which George Washington had difficulty finding high-quality appointees to replace his original cabinet secretaries, and in which John Adams had a hostile cabinet during almost all his term, Thomas Jefferson had a harmonious relationship with Secretary of State James Madison and Secretary of the Treasury Albert Gallatin, who both served a full eight years. Jefferson and Madison had a close relationship going back to the fall of 1776, and Madison and Gallatin had the gift of talking Jefferson out of his "romantic ideology" into more practical policies. While Jefferson entertained members of Congress with nonpolitical discourse over gourmet dinners accompanied by French wine, Gallatin, whose house was across the swamp east of the White House but just 150 yards from the Capitol, was well positioned to lobby legislators.[20] And unlike Jefferson and Madison, he remained in Washington in the hot summer months, sending his wife and children to her family in New York and visiting Friendship Hill, which he loved and she loathed, only three times (1803, 1806, and 1810) in his thirteen years as Treasury secretary.[21] Gallatin had demonstrated his mastery of financial issues and his capacity for hard work, and never hesitated to indicate when he disagreed with the president.[22] This became apparent when Jefferson assigned him to examine Treasury accounts for "the blunders and frauds" of Hamilton. Gallatin, to his surprise, found "no blunders, no frauds," but rather "the most perfect system ever formed."[23] Nor did Gallatin share Jefferson's repugnance for the Bank of the United States, whose creation he and Madison had so stoutly opposed. In his *Sketch of the Finances*, he recognized the utility of the Bank and its branches in various cities to transfer government funds.[24] Gallatin and Jefferson were agreed, however, on fundamental policies: "reduce both taxes and spending, impose tighter control over specific appropriations, and thwart the growth of a standing army and a strong navy."[25] The hope was that over eight years they could eliminate the national debt. They failed to reach that goal, but during Gallatin's time as secretary, the debt was reduced from $83 million in 1801 to $45 million in 1812.[26]

Jefferson came to office during a lull in the two-decade struggle between royal and mercantile Britain and revolutionary and Napoleonic France. Jay's Treaty with Britain in 1795 had reduced tensions that might have led to war between Britain and the United States, and the Treaty of Mortefontaine in 1800 reduced similar tensions with France. The struggle gave American ship owners the opportunity to make huge profits shipping goods under a neutral flag but subjected them to the risk of interception by either of the rival powers. The Treaty of Amiens between Britain and France, negotiated in October 1801 and signed in March 1802, and in effect until May 1803, was the one pause in this two-decade world war. During these years, Gallatin, devoted to holding down federal spending and reducing the national debt, opposed building up a standing army or strong navy. If Hamilton, the first Treasury secretary, cast his eyes eastward, basing his policies on a vision of seaboard America connected over oceanic trade routes with Britain and other European nations and their Caribbean colonies, Gallatin, the third Treasury secretary and the first cabinet member from west of the Appalachian mountains, cast his eyes westward, basing his policies on a vision of agricultural America expanded ever to the west. As early as 1802, he was urging Jefferson to sponsor an exploratory expedition across the Mississippi and west to the Pacific Ocean, "to acquire as much information as possible about the region's topography, its Native American population, the potential for expanding the nation's fur trade"—Gallatin through his wife's family became a friend of the New York–based fur trader John Jacob Astor[27]—and the use of the Pacific ports.[28] In October 1802, when the Spanish intendant in New Orleans blocked the right of deposit there to Americans, contrary to the Pinkney Treaty of 1795, Gallatin, like Jefferson and Madison, saw this as a mortal threat to the future of the United States. Anticipating that Spain would transfer Louisiana to France under a notorious secret treaty signed in

1800, Jefferson and Madison dispatched James Monroe to Paris to negotiate with Napoleon's government the purchase of New Orleans. When he arrived, Monroe was astonished to find that Napoleon, whose military expedition to regain the lucrative sugar colony of Haiti had failed, had offered to sell not just New Orleans but all of the poorly defined Louisiana Territory to the United States. Without instructions, Monroe and envoy Robert Livingston agreed. It was up to Gallatin to find the $15 million. He had the Treasury issue $11 million in 6 percent bonds redeemable in fifteen years and enabled the French to sell them to Hope & Company in Amsterdam and Baring Brothers in London; through this transaction he began a long friendship with Sir Alexander Baring, who as Lord Ashburton negotiated the Webster-Ashburton Treaty of 1843. In the meantime, and against Jefferson's objections, he set up a branch of the Bank of the United States in New Orleans to provide financial backing for what he envisioned as a growing economy.[29]

Gallatin's desire for westward expansion was advanced by the completion of the Louisiana Purchase in April 1803 and the unpublicized dispatch of Lewis and Clark in May 1804 and furthered by the visit of Prussian scientist and explorer Alexander von Humboldt to Washington in June 1804. Humboldt had just completed an extended exploration of Spain's Western Hemisphere colonies, normally off limits to foreigners, in South America and Mexico. At meetings in the White House, Jefferson, Madison, and Gallatin peppered him with questions about the peoples, the crops, the climates, the minerals of Latin America, and allowed them to copy his maps—much more accurate than any others available—and transcribe his extensive notes. Humboldt replied in a rapid mixture of English, German, French, and Spanish, which Gallatin presumably understood more fully the others—and the Americans showed a particular interest in Tejas, the lands lying just to the west of the southern portion of the Louisiana Purchase.

Humboldt was a "very extraordinary man," Gallatin wrote his wife, whose knowledge was "astonishing," and listening to him was "a great intellectual treat."[30] But not just a source of abstract pleasure: The Jeffersonians' interest suggests that even immediately after the United States doubled its territory to the then unknown borders of the Louisiana Purchase, its leaders, Gallatin not least among them, were contemplating more expansion to the west.

But the connections between this vast expanse, roughly half the size of Europe, were still minimal. George Washington had promoted a canal connecting the Potomac to a branch of the Ohio, and a private company chartered by the Pennsylvania legislature had built a turnpike from Philadelphia to Lancaster a decade before, but even so, most inhabited parts of the young republic were not much more closely connected to others than they were to Europe. In his second inaugural address in March 1805, Jefferson, anticipating that the revenue coming in from tariffs and land sales would eliminate the national debt, called for "the revenue 'thereby liberated' might, 'by a just repartition among the states, and a corresponding amendment to the constitution,' be applied to river clearance, canal and road building, the arts, manufactures, education, and 'other great objects within each state.'"[31] This was in line with Gallatin's thinking: In 1802, he had proposed a federally funded road across the Appalachians, connecting the basins of the Potomac and the Ohio, which "would fulfill a dream hatched twenty years earlier in his decision to settle at Friendship Hill,"[32] and in 1806, the route of a road from Cumberland, Maryland through Fayette County, Pennsylvania, to Wheeling, Virginia (now West Virginia), on the Ohio River, was approved by Congress.[33] This was justified, to Jeffersonians who doubted the constitutionality of federal road building, by the fact that the route was interstate and by a provision in the Ohio statehood act. Only ten miles of road were built by 1813, but it reached Wheeling in 1818, and it became known, as it became clear there would be no more federal roads in the antebellum republic, as the

National Road, extending from Baltimore to St. Louis, on a route followed in large part by the US 40 and paralleled by Interstate 70 in the twentieth century.[34]

Gallatin, however, was thinking nationally, not just locally. In March 1807, the Senate, at Gallatin's urging, requested a report on roads and canals, "internal improvements" in the language of the day, when only a few steamboats had been sighted and no one anticipated railroads. "The assignment took advantage of Gallatin's skill at painstaking research and leveraged his passion for geography, politics, and land planning, economics, and infrastructure, providing the perfect showcase for his talents," writes his admiring biographer Nicholas Dungan. "After a year's hard work, he presented his report to the Senate on April 12, 1808."[35] None of its provisions was adopted immediately and Gallatin's estimate that the total program would cost $20 million was considered astronomical.[36] Thanks to the Embargo Act pushed by Jefferson (and opposed, in internal councils, by Gallatin), in December 1807, federal spending in calendar year 1808 declined sharply from previous years. And subsequent federal legislation was blocked by vetoes by Presidents James Madison (of a less specific bill on his last day in office in 1817), James Monroe (of a toll house to finance repairs on the National Road in 1822), and Andrew Jackson (of a road from Maysville, Kentucky to Lexington, Kentucky in 1830). But in time, all of Gallatin's proposals[37] have been carried out in one form or another, often by technological developments unanticipated in 1808. To cross the Appalachian mountains, the prime transportation barrier in the early republic, he proposed sets of canals and roads connecting river systems on either side of the mountains: the Susquehanna with the Alleghany, the Potomac with the Monongahela, the James with the Kanawha, the Santee with the Tennessee. Some of these canals were built, but all these routes were serviced, before or after the Civil War, by railroads built by railroad corporations chartered by states and financed by state governments and by private investors.

Another proposal, for a canal around the falls of the Ohio River at Louisville, was built by a private corporation and opened in 1830.[38] Gallatin proposed canals connecting the Hudson River with Lake Ontario and Lake Champlain; instead, New York Governor DeWitt Clinton in 1817 pushed through legislation for the hugely successful Erie Canal, which was completed in 1825 and made New York City the main Atlantic port for much of the trans-Appalachian West. His proposal called for a canal around Niagara Falls; its purpose, to allow navigation around the falls, was accomplished when the Canadians in 1829 opened the Welland Canal, west of the Niagara River, connecting Lake Erie and Lake Ontario.[39] Some of his proposals for canals radiating from ports on the Atlantic (Boston, Philadelphia, Baltimore, Charleston) or inland waters (Detroit, St. Louis, New Orleans) were carried out at the behest of state governments or financed by private corporations. Some of his proposals had to wait for the twentieth century: His "Great canals, from north to south, along the Atlantic Coast" anticipated the Intracoastal Waterway,[40] and his "great turnpike road from Maine to Georgia" foreshadowed US 1 and Interstate 95. Gallatin's *Report on Roads and Canals*, like Hamilton's *Report on Manufactures*, anticipated a degree of centralized federal financing and control which proved to be impossible in the rapidly decentralizing antebellum America, in which Americans were surging westward in waves beyond control and creating new technologies uncontemplated by national elites. What is striking about Gallatin is the extent to which he anticipated the nation's needs and the course of its growth, and how he adapted and modified both Alexander Hamilton's system of national finance and Thomas Jefferson's philosophy of minimal national government to foster that growth and adapt to internal and external circumstance.

The *Report on Canals and Roads*, though not carried out, can be seen as the capstone of Gallatin's career, though he lived on, active and perceptive, four decades more. He opposed loudly

Thomas Jefferson's economically disastrous and strategically ineffective Embargo Act, and warned Jefferson and Madison that "government prohibitions do always more mischief than has been calculated, and it is not without much hesitation that a statesman should try to regulate the concerns of individuals, as if he could do it better than themselves."[41] But he had to admit that the alternative of going to war was unattractive, because administration policies which he had long supported left the United States with little in the way of an army or navy. When Madison succeeded Jefferson to the presidency, Gallatin hoped to be appointed secretary of state, but his frankness and dispatch had made him many enemies within Republican ranks,[42] and he remained increasingly frustrated at Treasury.[43] He urged the recharter of the Bank of the United States in 1811, but it was opposed by old-time Jeffersonians and by Federalists and Republicans with ties to the many new state-chartered banks which resented regulation by the national bank.[44] Madison only tepidly supported recharter, and it failed in the Senate by the tie-breaking vote of Vice President George Clinton—the only time in history a vice president defeated an administration measure. Gallatin supported going to war against Britain in 1812 but struggled with how to pay for it. His hopes of raising capital for coastal merchants ran up against the fact that cities' marine insurance companies would claim much available capital to compensate merchants for losses. His estimates of needed bond issues rose from $10 million to $50 million, and with the Bank of the United States no longer available to purchase government bonds, interest rates had to be raised from 6 to 8 percent. In March 1813, he wrote Madison, "We have hardly enough money to last till the end of the month." But in April 1813, he was able to raise $16 million from a syndicate headed by Philadelphia merchant Stephen Girard, New York fur trader John Jacob Astor, and Philadelphia financier David Parish, all of whom like Gallatin had emigrated from Europe to North America.[45]

The next month, Madison appointed him to the commission negotiating peace terms with Britain, although between travel to St. Petersburg and Amsterdam, the American negotiators did not all arrive and begin negotiating until July 1814 in Ghent. Britain deliberately sent low-ranking diplomats and offered insultingly unacceptable terms like the establishment of a British protectorate for Indians in the Northwest Territory. But through his contacts with Sir Alexander Baring, Gallatin knew the British were weary of war and was able to warn Secretary of State James Monroe that they would be attacking New Orleans.[46] Gallatin had to soothe tempers among the five-member American delegation, as the diligent John Quincy Adams would be irritated while rising at five o'clock in the morning to see Henry Clay returning from a night of gambling, and each of those two had demands the British were unlikely to accept. Clay demanded a renunciation of the right of navigation on the Mississippi River that Britain had obtained in the 1783 Treaty of Paris, while Adams demanded renewed recognition of the American right to fish for cod and dry fish ashore in the Grand Banks near Newfoundland, which his father, John Adams, had obtained in that same treaty. Gallatin suggested that both nations' negotiators submit draft treaties, so as to set aside issues on which they were at or close to agreement, and he persuaded Clay and Adams that silence on their key issues would achieve the results they desired.[47] The British would have no practicable way to navigate the Mississippi, and Americans could assert their rights to the fisheries on the basis of the previous treaty. Nor did the United States have to insist on ending the impressment of seamen; with the Napoleonic Wars over temporarily (Napoleon was then in exile in Elba), Britain would have no need for more sailors. The British Foreign Minister Lord Castelreagh, finally addressing the negotiations, gave sudden orders to renounce British demands and accept the status quo, and the two sides reached agreement and signed the Treaty of Ghent on Christmas Eve 1824.[48]

Gallatin, after turning down John Jacob Astor's offer to make him a partner,[49] spent the next decade as a diplomat after returning briefly to Geneva for his first visit in thirty-six years. During 1815 and 1816, he was part of a team renegotiating a commercial treaty with Britain, with most past disputes mooted because of the end of the world war between Britain and France.[50] From 1816 to 1823, he was Minister to France, where he enjoyed Paris greatly. In 1824, he supported the old Jeffersonian and current Treasury Secretary William Crawford for president; despite that, John Quincy Adams appointed him Minister to Britain in 1826 and he served an unpleasant year in London.[51] Returning to the United States, in 1828, to the great satisfaction of his wife, he sold Friendship Hill, which he admitted to his son was "a troublesome and unproductive property, which has plagued me all my life," and at age sixty-seven, moved to New York City.[52] It was his wife Hannah's beloved hometown and now, after breathtaking growth, the largest city in the United States. He worked as president of Astor's National Bank of New York, supported free trade and recharter of the Second Bank of the United States, was president of the New-York Historical Society, and was a cofounder of New York University. He wrote a paper in 1830 recommending a currency based on a fixed ratio of gold to silver and a single national bank issuing paper currency and conducting open market operations for the Treasury—much like the system the United States would have after passage of the Federal Reserve Act in 1914[53]—and in 1832, opposed Andrew Jackson's veto of the recharter of the Second Bank of the United States, which he had come to believe was important in regulating state banks.[54]

But even in New York, in a townhouse on Bleecker Street in Greenwich Village, his mind still turned to the west. In 1823 in Paris, Alexander von Humboldt, learning that Gallatin was interested in Indian languages, suggested that he write an essay on the subject. The resulting essay, though unpublished, was cited in the introduction to *Atlas Ethnographique*, by Adriano Balbi, published in Paris

in 1826. When Gallatin returned to the United States, he began collecting and recording vocabularies of Native American languages
and prompted the War Department to circulate a pamphlet with
some six hundred Indian words. "Toward the end of 1831," writes
Gallatin biographer Nicholas Dungan, "George Folsom, the chair
of the publications committee of the American Antiquarian Society,
based in Worcester, Massachusetts, having seen the reference in
the introduction to Balbi's *Atlas*, wrote to Gallatin to ask if he had
anything further to offer on the subject." Gallatin, approaching
seventy and amid his duties as a bank president, went to work. In
1836, when he turned seventy-five, the Society published his 422-
page study, *A Synopsis of the Indian Tribes Within the United States
East of the Rocky Mountains and in the British and Russian Possessions of North America,* with an ethnological map and numerous
Native American vocabularies.[55] He pursued these studies further,
and in 1842, at eighty-one, he and John Russell Bartlett founded
the American Ethnological Society, to foster "inquiries generally
connected with the human race."[56] In his last decade, before his
death at eighty-eight in 1849, Gallatin had become reluctant to
support national expansion, opposing the annexation of Texas as
he had opposed slavery throughout his career, questioning the use
of threats to persuade Britain to recognize American acquisition of
the Oregon Territory up to the 54°40' line (President James Polk
settled for the 49° parallel Gallatin had negotiated for years before)
and vehemently and in a pamphlet with a circulation of 90,000
opposed the war with Mexico.[57] Like Martin Van Buren and Henry
Clay, both of whom tried and failed to be elected president in 1844,
and like John Quincy Adams and Abraham Lincoln, who as House
members voted against the declaration of war in 1846, Gallatin felt
that the United States had moved far enough west already—and
perhaps that further movement might provoke civil war. But he
could take pride in the fact that he had foreseen and forwarded the
peaceful westward expansion of the young republic in his last years,

until his death. He was buried in Trinity Church's graveyard, near Alexander Hamilton's grave, and the two graves, like their statues on the grounds of the Treasury Department in Washington, seem to look in opposite directions—Hamilton's to the east, toward the ocean and Europe, and Gallatin's always to the west.

NOTES

INTRODUCTION: MENTAL MAPS

1 Jerry Brotton, *A History of the World in 12 Maps* (New York: Penguin, 2012), p. 4.

2 Kathryn Schulz, "Why Animals Don't Get Lost," *New Yorker*, March 29, 2021, www.newyorker.com.

3 Deirdre Mask, *The Address Book: What Street Addresses Reveal About Identity, Race, Wealth and Power*, Kindle loc. 879.

4 Michael Barone, *Our First Revolution: The Remarkable British Upheaval That Inspired America's Founding Fathers* (New York: Crown Forum, 2007).

ONE – BENJAMIN FRANKLIN: JOIN OR DIE

1 Edmund S. Morgan, *Benjamin Franklin* (New Haven: Yale University Press, 2002), pp. 64–65.

2 Benjamin Franklin, *Autobiography*, ed. E. Boyd Smith (New York: Henry Holt, 1916), p. 39.

3 Walter Isaacson, *Benjamin Franklin: An American Life* (New York: Simon & Schuster, 2003), pp. 26–35, 40–51.

4 Ibid., pp. 94–101.

5 Gordon S. Wood, *The Americanization of Benjamin Franklin* (New York: Penguin, 2004), pp. 44–45.

6 Isaacson, pp. 103–6; Wood, p. 45.

7 Isaacson, pp. 147–48; pp. 45, 48.

8 Isaacson, pp. 105–6, 123–26; Wood, pp. 45, 59.

9 Morgan, pp. 21–22, 49–50, 59; Isaacson, pp.109–13.

10 Wood, pp. 52–54.

11 "How Ben Franklin Established the US Post Office," history.com, August 10, 2020.

12 Wood, p. 52.

13 Isaacson, p. 126.

14. Wood, p. 54.

15 Wood, pp. 52–54.

16 Isaacson, p. 127.

17 Wood, pp. 61–62.

18 Isaacson, pp. 129–33.

19 Ibid, pp. 133–45.

20 Ibid., pp. 133–45. Quotation on p. 135.

21 Morgan, p. 72.

22 Isaacson, p. 157.

23 H. W. Brands, *The First American: The Life and Times of Benjamin Franklin* (New York: Random House, 2002), pp. 245–47; Morgan, pp. 75–77.

24 Morgan, p. 75.

25 Gary B. Nash and Billy G. Smith, "Notes and Documents: The Population of Eighteenth Century Philadelphia," in *American Historical Review*, July 1975, p. 366.

26 Morgan, pp. 146, 81.

27 Isaacson, p. 147.

28 Wood, p. 81.

29 Isaacson, p. 150.

30 Ibid., p. 464.

31 Ibid., p. 150.

32 Brands, p. 247.

33 Ibid., p. 244.

34 Barnet Shecter, *George Washington's America: A Biography Through Maps* (New York: Walker & Co., 2010), pp. 22–29; E. M. Sanchez-Saavedra, *Description of the Country: Virginia's Cartographers and Their Maps 1607-1881* (Richmond: Virginia State Library, 1975) pp. 29–32.

35 James Thomas Flexner, *George Washington: The Forge of Experience* (New York: Norton, 1965), p. 55; Ron Chernow, *George Washington* (New York: Penguin, 2010), pp. 31–32.

36 Wood, p. 81.

37 Quoted by Isaacson, p. 158.

38 Ibid., p. 156.

39 Morgan, *Franklin*, p. 82; Wood, *Franklin*, pp. 72–73;

40 Patrick Spero, *Frontier Country: The Politics of War in Early Pennsylvania* (Philadelphia: Penn Press, 2016), p. 110.

41 Accounts of the Albany Plan of Union draw on Isaacson, pp. 158–62; Morgan, pp. 82–92; Wood, pp. 72–78; Brands, pp. 233–38.

42 Ron Chernow, *Washington: A Life* (New York: Penguin Press, 2011) p. 44.

43 Isaacson, p. 159; "Join or Die: The Story Behind Ben Franklin's Iconic Woodcut," mrnussbaum.com, n.d.

44 David Hackett Fischer, *Albion's Seed: Four British Folkways in America*, Vol. 1 (New York: Oxford University Press, 1989).

45 Spero, pp. 110–11.

46 Isaacson, pp. 159–61; Morgan, pp. 84–85; Wood, pp.74–75.

47 Franklin, p. 147.

48 Ibid., p. 147, quoted by Isaacson, pp. 161–62.

49 Morgan, p. 86.

50 Brands, p. 238.

51 Morgan, p. 93.

52 Isaacson, pp. 166–69.

53 Ibid., pp. 169-72.

54 Colin Dueck, *Offshore Balancing* (Washington: American Enterprise Institute, 2022), pp. 17–23.

55 Ibid., pp. 26–27.

56 Morgan, pp. 150–59.

57 Ibid., p. 159.

58 Ibid., pp. 159–219, quotation at pp. 218–19.

59 Isaacson, pp. 305-7; Samuel Flagg Bemis, *The Diplomacy of the American Revolution*, 2d ed. (Bloomington: Indiana University Press, 1957), pp. 197–98.

60 Morgan, pp. 97, 238.

61 Ibid., pp. 237–40.

62 Bemis, pp. 50, 49.

63 A classic account of the negotiations is Bemis, pp. 203–56. See also Morgan, pp. 285–94, and Walter Stahr, *John Jay: Founding Father* (New York: Hambledon & Continuum, 2006), pp. 144–72.

64 Bemis, pp. 255–56.

65 Morgan, pp. 302–5, 312.

TWO – GEORGE WASHINGTON: WEST BY NORTHWEST

1 Hugh Fairfax, *Fairfax of Virginia: The Forgotten Story of America's Only Peerage* (London: The Fairfax Family, 2017).

2 James Thomas Flexner, *George Washington: The Forge of Experience* (New York: Norton, 1965), p. 23.

3 Joel Achenbach, *The Grand Idea: George Washington's Potomac and the Race to the West* (New York: Simon & Schuster, 2004), pp. 77–78.

4 Fairfax.

5 Barnet Shecter, *George Washington's America: A Biography Through Maps* (New York: Walker & Co. 2010), p. 26.

6 Noemie Emery, *George Washington: A Biography* (New York: Putnam, 1976), p. 51.

7 Flexner, p. 35; and Ron Chernow, *Washington: A Life* (New York: Penguin Press, 2011), p. 20.

8 Stanley Elkins and Eric McKittrick, *The Age of Federalism: The Early American Republic, 1788-1800* (New York: Oxford University Press, 1995), pp. 35–36.

9 James Thomas Flexner, *Washington: The Indispensable Man* (New York: Norton, 1974), p. 40.

10 Richard H. Brown and Paul E. Cohen, *Revolution: Mapping the Road to American Independence, 1755-1783* (New York: Norton, 2015), p. 7.

11 Ibid., p. 15.

12 Schecter, pp. 34–35.

13 Flexner, *George Washington: The Forge of Experience*, p. 55; Chernow, p. 31.

14 Schecter, pp. 22–29.

15 E. M. Sanchez-Saavedra, *Description of the Country: Virginia's Cartographers and Their Maps 1607-1881* (Richmond: Virginia State Library, 1975) pp. 29–32.

16 Chernow, p. 32.

17 Schecter, p. 44.

18 Chernow, p. 44.

19 Ibid., p. 60.

20 Ibid., p. 79.

21 Ibid., pp. 79, 123.

22 Ibid., p. 323.

23 Elkins and McKittrick, p. 38.

24 Schecter, p. 6.

25 Chernow, p. 149.

26 Ibid., p. 183.

27 Daniel Walker Howe, *What Hath God Wrought: The Transformatioon of America, 1815-1848* (New York: Oxford University Press, 2007), p. 617.

28 Piers Mackesy, *The War for America*, 1175–1783 (Lincoln: University of Nebraska Press, 1993), pp. 78ff.

29 Brown and Cohen, pp. 82–84.

30 Ibid., pp. 82–87.

31 Schecter, pp. 2–3, 18, 21.

32 Chernow, p. 156.

33 Alan Taylor, *American Revolutions: A Continental History*, 1750-1804 (New York: Norton, 2016), p. 162.

34 Flexner, *George Washington: The Forge of Experience*, p. 332.

35 Brown and Cohen, p. 87.

36 John Ferling, *Almost a Miracle: The American Victory in the War of Independence* (New York: Oxford University Press, 2007), pp. 324, 442–43, 450, 444–45, 503–5.

37 Ibid., p. 524.

38 Chernow, pp. 111–12, 116.

39 Achenbach, p. 124.

40 Schecter, p. 195.

41 Ibid.

42 Elkins and McKittrick, pp. 217–20.

43 See Nathaniel Philbrick, *Travels with George: In Search of Washington and His Legacy* (New York: Viking, 2021), in which the author and his wife follow Washington's routes.

44 Achenbach, p. 185.

45 Adams, p. 55.

46 Chernow, pp. 757–62.
47 Elkins and McKittrick, pp. 250–51.
48 Robert H. Wiebe, *The Opening of American Society: From the Adoption of the Constitution to the Eve of Disunion* (New York: Random House, 1984), p. 70.
49 Elkins and McKittrick, pp. 377-80, 388–96.
50 R. R. Palmer, *The Age of the Democratic Revolution: A Political History of Europe and America, 1760-1800* (Princeton: Princeton University Press, 1959), p. 398.
51 Samuel Flagg Bemis, *Pinckney's Treaty: America's Advantage from Europe's Distress* (New Haven: Yale University Press, 1960), pp. 245–54; Elkins and McKittrick, pp. 439–40, 483.
52 Elkins and McKittrick, table on p. 382.
53 Ibid., pp. 415–32 436–39, quotation on p. 439.
54 Flexner, *Washington: The Indispensable Man*, pp. 349–50.
55 See Philbrick, pp. 204–5; and Michael Knox Beran, "A Portrait of Washington's Greatness—and His Limitations," *National Review*, nationalreview.com, January 25, 2021.
56 Chernow, p. 20.

THREE – THOMAS JEFFERSON: FROM THE TOP OF THE LITTLE MOUNTAIN

1   Thomas Jefferson, *Notes on the State of Virginia*, ed. William Peden (Chapel Hill: University of North Carolina Press, 1982), p. xviii, n. 24.
2   Jefferson, p. 18.
3   Ibid.
4   Ibid., p. 29.
5   Ibid., p. 30.
6   Ibid., p. 23.
7   Ibid.
8   Dumas Malone, *Jefferson the Virginian: Jefferson and His Time*, Vol. 1 (Boston: Little Brown, 1948), p. 21.
9   Ibid., p. 32.
10 Ibid.
11 Joel Achenbach, *The Grand Idea: George Washington's Potomac and the Race to the West* (New York: Simon & Schuster: 2004), p. 42.
12 John Ferling, *John Adams: A Life* (New York: Oxford University Press, 1992), p. 269.
13 Ron Chernow, *Alexander Hamilton* (New York: Penguin Press, 2004), p. 312.
14 Henry Adams, *History of the United States During the Administrations of Thomas Jefferson* (Kindle ed., 2017), vol. 1, pp. 86–87.
15 Malone, pp. 73, 78.
16 Ibid., p. 61.
17 R. B. Bernstein, *Thomas Jefferson: The Revolution of Ideas* (New York: Oxford University Press, 2003), p. 5.

18 Malone, pp. 98–101; Thomas S. Kidd, *Thomas Jefferson: A Biography of Spirit and Flesh* (New Haven: Yale University Press, 2022), p. 47.

19 Malone, pp. 89–91.

20 Wood, pp. 103–4.

21 Kidd, pp. 49–50.

22 Ibid., p. 93.

23 Ibid., p. 49.

24 Adams, pp. 86–87.

25 Bernstein, p. 51.

26 Kidd, p. 50.

27 Malone, pp. 160–61.

28 Stanley Elkins and Eric McKittrick, *The Age of Federalism: The Early American Republic, 1788–1800* (New York: Oxford University Press, 1993), p. 38.

29 Bernstein, p. 16.

30 Forrest McDonald, *Alexander Hamilton: A Biography* (New York: Norton, 1979), p. 203. Compare Elkins and McKittrick, p. 203.

31 Elkins and McKittrick, p. 209.

32 Katherine Horan, "First Continental Congress," George Washington's Mount Vernon, mountvernon.org.

33 "A Summary View of the Rights of British America by Thomas Jefferson (1774)," Encyclopedia Virginia.

34 Ibid.

35 Kidd, pp. 61–62.

36 Kidd, p. 103.

37 Christopher Hitchens, *Thomas Jefferson: Author of America* (New York: Harper-Collins, 2005), pp. 42–43.

38 Bernstein, p. 108.

39 Kidd, p. 177.

40 Peden, *Introduction to Jefferson, Notes*, p. xiv.

41 Jefferson, p. 5.

42 Ibid., pp. 38–42, 50–52, 66–70, 74, 83–84, 89, 94–95, 102–7, 144–45, 173, 179–96.

43 Ibid., pp. 19, 24–25; "Natural Bridge (Virginia)," Wikipedia, n.d.

44 Ibid., pp. 152, 153.

45 Ibid., p. 109.

46 Ibid., pp. 83, 85.

47 Robert H. Wiebe, *The Opening of American Society from the Adoption of the Constitution to the Eve of Disunion* (New York: Random House, 1984), p. 135.

48 Jefferson, pp. 15–16, 8–10, 109.

49 Ibid., pp. 84–85, 58–64, 92–102.

50 Ibid., pp. 87, 137–43, 162–63.

51 Achenbach, p. 41.

52 Harlow Lindley et al., *History of the Ordinance of 1787 and the Old Northwest Territory* (Marietta, Ohio: Northwest Territory Celebration Commission, 1937).

53 Bernstein, p. 52.

54 Kidd, p. 114.

55 Ibid., p. 114.

56 Lindley, p. 29.

57 Malone, pp. 416–18.

58 George Green Shackelford, *Thomas Jefferson's Travels in Europe, 1784–1789* (Baltimore: Johns Hopkins University Press, 1995), p. 16.

59 Rice, *Jefferson's Paris*, pp. 51–54; Shackelford, p. 11.

60 Conor Cruise O'Brien, *The Long Affair: Thomas Jefferson and the French Revolution, 1785–1800* (Chicago: University of Chicago Press, 1996), pp. 34-37. "If Thomas Jefferson had wanted to speak French, he would have learned to speak it" (p. 36).

61 Dumas Malone, *Jefferson and the Rights of Man* (New York: Little, Brown, 1951), p. 6.

62 O'Brien, pp. 42–43.

63 Malone, *Jefferson and Rights*, p. 123.

64 Shackelford, p. 9. Malone, *Jefferson and Rights*, p. 115.

65 Malone, *Jefferson and Rights*, pp. 100–5.

66 O'Brien, p. 40.

67 Bernstein, p. 70; O'Brien, p. 42.

68 O'Brien, p. 60.

69 Kidd, p. 152.

70 Ibid., p. 151.

71 O'Brien, p. 63.

72 Ibid., p. 81.

73 Ibid., pp. 69–70.

74 Thomas McCraw, *The Founders and Finance: How Hamilton, Gallatin, and Other Immigrants Forged a New Economy* (Cambridge: Harvard University Press, 2012), p. 351.

75 Bernstein, p. 102.

76 Ibid., p. 92.

77 O'Brien, pp. 145–47.

78 Bernstein, pp. 108–10.

79 Adams, pp. 86–87.

80 McDonald, p. 32.

81 Jeffrey L. Pasley, *The First Presidential Contest: 1796 and the Founding of American Democracy* (Lawrence: University Press of Kansas, 2013), p. 6.

82 Ibid., p. 11.

83 Bernstein, p. 158.

84 Ibid., pp. 117–18.

85 Ibid., p. 121.

86 Wood, Kindle locs. 5138–159.

87 Hitchens, p. 155.

88 James Sterling Young, *The Washington Community*, 1800–1828 (New York: Columbia University Press, 1966), p. 128.

89 Sean Wilentz, "America Made Easy: McCullough, Adams, and the Decline of Popular History," *The New Republic*, July 2, 2001.

90 McDonald, Jefferson, p. 166.

91 McDonald, Jefferson, pp. 63-65.

92 Joel Achenbach, *The Grand Idea: George Washington's Potomac and the Race to the West* (New York: tk publisher: 2004), p. 42.

93 McDonald, pp. 68–74.

94 Bernstein, Jefferson, p. 143.

95 Robert H. Wiebe, *The Opening of American Society From the Adoption of the Constitution to the Eve of Disunion* (New York: Random House, 1984), p. 177.

96 Gordon S. Wood, *Empire of Liberty* (New York: Oxford University Press, 2009), loc. 3609.

97 Kidd, p. 264.

98 Wood, *Empire of Liberty*, locs. 5138–159.

99 Gordon S. Wood, *Revolutionary Characters: What Made the Founders Different* (New York: Penguin Press, 2006), p. 111.

100 Kurt E. Leichtle and Bruce G. Carveth, *Crusade Against Slavery: Edward Coles, Pioneer of Freedom* (Carbondale: Southern Illinois University Press, 2011), p. 45.

101 Ibid., p. 46.

102 Ibid., pp. 46–48; Suzanne Cooper Guasco, *Confronting Slavery: Edward Coles and the Rise of Antislavery Politics in Nineteenth Century America* (DeKalb, Northern Illinois University Press, 2013), pp. 4–5.

103 Andrea Wulf, *Founding Gardeners: The Revolutionary Generation, Nature, and the Shaping of the American Nation* (New York: Random House, 2011), pp. 85, 249.

104 Kidd, pp. 270, 315.

105 Alan Pell Crawford, *Twilight at Monticello: The Final Years of Thomas Jefferson* (New York: Random House, 2008), pp. 247–54.

FOUR – ALEXANDER HAMILTON: ACROSS THE SEA LANES

1 Ron Chernow, *Alexander Hamilton* (New York: Penguin Press, 2004), p. 27.

2 Sidney W. Mintz, *Sweetness and Power: The Place of Sugar in Modern History* (New York: Penguin, 1985), pp. 35–42.

3 Alexander Mikaberidze, *The Napoleonic Wars: A Global History* (New York: Oxford University Press, 2021), p. 22.

4 *Encyclopaedia Britannica*, 11th ed. (New York: The Encyclopaedia Britannica Co., 1911), vol. 23, p. 1019.

5 Karen C. Thurland, *The Sugar Industry on St. Croix* (Bloomington, Indiana: AuthorHouse, 2014), p. 9.

6 Mintz, pp. 52–57.

7 I take Ron Chernow's view that Hamilton was born in 1755, not 1757, as he stated when he entered King's College in New York in an apparent attempt to meld with classmates who matriculated well before turning eighteen. Chernow, *Hamilton*, pp. 16–17.

8 Ibid., p. 26.

9 Ibid., pp. 29–30.

10 Ibid., p. 26.

11 Ibid., p. 30.

12 Richard Brookhiser, *Alexander Hamilton, American* (New York: The Free Press, 1999), p. 20, citing Robert A. Hendrickson, *The Rise and Fall of Alexander Hamilton* (New York: Van Nostrand Reinhold Co., 1981), p. 29.

13 Brookhiser, p. 14.

14 Stanley Elkins and Eric McKittrick, *The Age of Federalism: The Early American Republic, 1788–1800* (New York: Oxford University Press, 1993), pp. 128–29.

15 Forrest McDonald, *Alexander Hamilton: A Biography* (New York: Norton, 1979), p. 122.

16 Chernow, p. 31.

17 Ibid., p. 333.

18 Brookhiser, p. 14.

19 See Russell Shorto, *The Island at the Center of the World: The Epic Story of Dutch Manhattan and the Forgotten Colony That Shaped America* (New York; Random House, 2004); Giles Milton, *Nathaniel's Nutmeg: The True and Incredible Adventures of the Spice Trader Who Changed the Course of History* (New York: Farrar, Straus and Giroux, 1999).

20 Chernow, p. 48.

21 Henry Adams, *History of the United States During the Administrations of Thomas Jefferson* (Kindle ed., 2017), vol. 1, p. 69.

22 Chernow, p. 212.

23 Ibid., p. 33.

24 Ibid., p. 55.

25 Ibid., p. 30.

25 Thomas McCraw, *The Founders and Finance: How Hamilton, Gallatin, and Other Immigrants Forged a New Economy* (Cambridge: Harvard University Press, 2012), p. 359.

26 "The Farmer Refuted: or A more impartial and comprehensive View of the Dispute between Great-Britain and the Colonies, Intended as a Further Vindication of the Congress," February 23, 1775, Founders Online, founders.archives.gov.

27 See McDonald, pp. 35–38.

28 Chernow, p. 61.

29 Chernow, p. 194.

30 Piers Mackesy, *The War for America, 1175–1783* (Lincoln: University of Nebraska Press, 1993), pp. 78ff.

31 Chernow, p. 48.

32 Ibid., pp. 63–64.

33 Chernow., p. 85.

34 Chernow, pp. 107, 110.

35 "List of Washington's Headquarters During the Revolutionary War," Wikipedia, n.d.

36 Ibid., p. 110.

37 "From Alexander Hamilton to James Duane, [3 September 1780]," Founders Online, founders.archives.gov.

38 "From Alexander Hamilton to Robert Morris, [30 April 1781]," Founders Online, founders.archives.gov.

39 Chernow, p. 139.

40 McDonald, p. 155.

41 Deirdre McCloskey, *Bourgeois Equality: How Ideas, Not Capital or Institutions, Enriched the World* (Chicago: University of Chicago Press, 2016); Angus Deaton, *The Great Escape: Health, Wealth, and the Origins of Inequality* (Princeton: Princeton University Press, 2013).

42 Bernard Bailyn, *The Ideological Origins of the American Revolution* (Cambridge: Harvard University Press, 1967); Gordon Wood, *The Creation of the American Republic, 1776–1787* (Chapel Hill: University of North Carolina Press, 1969).

43 Chernow, p. 294.

44 Ibid., p. 293, quoting McDonald, p. 128. McDonald, however, writes that Morris's recommendation is "an old story, based on secondhand recollections."

45 Chernow, p. 466.

46 Ibid., p. 333.

47 McDonald, p. 72. Chernow notes that when he traveled to Annapolis in 1786, "After his nomadic youth and wartime roaming, Hamilton had retained little wanderlust and now traversed scenery he had last viewed as a soldier" (Chernow, p. 223).

48 Chernow, pp. 169–70.

49 William Lee Miller, *The Business of May Next: James Madison & the Founding* (Charlottesville: University Press of Virginia, 1992), pp. 10–11.

50 Brookhiser, p. 69.

51 Ibid., p. 53.

52 Chernow, p. 288.

53 Gordon Wood, *Revolutionary Characters: What Made the Founders Different* (New York: Penguin Press, 2006), p. 133.

54 Forrest McDonald, *Alexander Hamilton: A Biography* (New York: Norton, 1979).

55 "Report Relative to a Provision for the Support of Public Credit [9 January 1790]," Founders Online, founders.archives.gov.

56 Chernow, p. 275.

57 McCraw, p, 363.

58 Chernow, p. 326.

59 Ibid., pp. 328–29.

60 "Final Version of the Second Report on the Further Provision Necessary for Establishing Public Credit (Report on a National Bank), 13 December 1790," Founders Online, founders.archives.gov.

61 Bray Hammond, *Banks and Politics in North America from the Revolution to the Civil War* (Princeton: Princeton University Press, 1957), p. 69.

62 Chernow, pp. 351–57.

63 McCraw, p. 360.

64 Robert H. Wiebe, *The Opening of American Society: From the Adoption of the Constitution to the Eve of Disunion* (New York: Random House, 1984), pp. 70–71.

65 Chernow, p. 22.

66 McCraw, pp. 351, 354–55.

67 McDonald, pp. 231, 227, 216.

68 Hammond, p. 121.

69 Richard Hofstadter, *The Idea of a Party System: The Rise of Legitimate Opposition in the United States, 1780–1840* (Berkeley: University of California Press, 1969), p. 171.

FIVE – JAMES MADISON: WEST BY SOUTHWEST

1 For a summary of the influence of the Scottish Enlightenment, see Stanley Elkins and Eric McKittrick, *The Age of Federalism*, Kindle ed. (New York: Oxford University Press, 1993), pp. 84–87.

2 Lynne Cheney, *James Madison: A Life Reconsidered* (New York: Viking, 2014), p. 21.

3 Jay Cost, *James Madison: America's First Politician* (New York: Basic Books, 2021), p. 19.

4 Ibid., pp. 20–21.

5 Cheney, p. 24.

6 David Hackett Fischer, *Albion's Seed: Four British Folkways in America* (New York: Oxford University Press, 1989).

7 Richard Brookhiser, *James Madison* (New York: Basic Books, 2011), p. 10.

8 Cheney, p. 23.

9 Ibid., p. 40.

10 Ralph Ketcham, *James Madison: A Biography* (Charlottesville: University Press of Virginia, 1971, 1990), pp. 59, 60; cf. Cheney, p. 40.

11 Jack Rakove, *A Politician Thinking: The Creative Mind of James Madison* (Norman: University of Oklahoma Press, 2017), p. 34.

12 Cheney, p. 4.

13 Ibid., p. 18.

14 Ibid., pp. 51–52.

15 Ibid., pp. 6, 30–33.

16 Ibid., pp. 39–43.

17 William Lee Miller, *The Business of May Next: James Madison & the Founding* (Charlottesville: University Press of Virginia, 1992), pp. 10–11.

18 Cheney, pp. 58–59.

19 Ibid., pp. 63–64.

20 Ibid., pp. 65–67.

21 Rakove, p. 104.

22 Cheney, pp. 69, 293.

23 Drew R. McCoy, *The Last of the Fathers: James Madison and the Republican Legacy* (New York: Cambridge University Press, 1989), p. 52.

24 Cheney, pp. 72–73.

25 Rakove, p. 76.

26 Brookhiser, p. 64.

27 Cheney, p. 84.

28 Ibid., pp. 84–85.

29 Ketcham, pp. 95–96.

30 Ibid., pp. 96–97.

31 Ibid., p. 98.

32 Cheney, p. 85.

33 Cheney, pp. 94–95.

34 Ibid., pp. 108–10.

35 Miller, pp. 12–13.

36 Cheney, p. 112.

37 Ibid., pp. 115–16.

38 Ketcham, p. 177.

39 Ibid., p. 178.

40 Samuel Flagg Bemis, *The Diplomacy of the American Revolution*, 2d ed. (Bloomington: Indiana University Press, 1957), pp. 203–56.

41 Gordon S. Wood, *Empire of Liberty* (New York: Oxford University Press, 2009), p. 366.

42 Cheney, p. 113.

43 Walter Stahr, *John Jay: Founding Father* (New York: Hambledon & Continuum, 2006), pp. 211–12.

44 Cheney, pp. 122–23.

45 Stahr, pp. 212–17.

46 Brookhiser, p. 64.

47 McCoy, p. 193.

48 Rakove, pp. 7–8.

49 Ketcham, p. 184; Miller, pp. 14–17.

50 Ketcham, pp. 183–85.

51 Miller, pp. 14, 16.

52 Cheney, pp. 119.

53 Miller, pp. 201–21.

54 Jack N. Rakove, ed., *James Madison: Writings* (New York: Literary Classics of the United States), pp. 55–57, 60, 65–67.

55 Madison, *Writings*, pp. 65, 81.

56 Ketcham, p. 187.

57 Madison, *Writings*, p. 79.

58 Cheney, p. 41.

59 Elkins and McKittrick, p. 83.

60 Chris DeRose, *Founding Rivals: Madison vs. Monroe, the Bill of Rights and the Election That Saved a Nation* (Washington: Regnery History, 2011).

61 Thomas McCraw, *The Founders and Finance: How Hamilton, Gallatin, and Other Immigrants Forged a New Economy* (Cambridge: Harvard University Press, 2012), p. 351.

62 Elkins and McKittrick, p. 92.

63 Wood, pp. 98–99.

64 Ibid., p. 626.

65 Richard Hofstadter, *The Idea of a Party System: The Rise of Legitimate Opposition in the United States, 1780–1840* (Berkeley: University of California Press, 1969), pp. 80–86.

66 Cost, p. 211.

67 Ibid.

68 Robert H. Wiebe, *The Opening of American Society From the Adoption of the Constitution to the Eve of Disunion* (New York: Random House, 1984), p. 177.

69 Hofstadter, p. 88.

70 Wood, p. 182.

71 Ibid., p. 132.

72 Cheney, pp. 258–62.

73 Wood, p. 621.

74 Ibid., p. 630.

75 Cheney, p. 305.

76 McDonald, pp. 63–65.

77 Andrea Wulf, *The Invention of Nature: Alexander von Humboldt's New World* (New York: Random House, 2015), pp. 117–19.

78 Wood, p. 646. The "net effect…all neutral commerce [was] illegal and liable to seizure by one power or the other."

79 Ibid., p. 650.

80 Brookhiser, p. 171.

81 Wiebe, p. 177.

82 Wood, p. 366.

83 Brookhiser, p. 165. Henry Adams, loc 3495 (summons to surrender) to loc 3601 (the United States were "filching a petty sand heap").

84 Henry Adams, *History of the United States of America During the Administration of James Madison* (New York: Scribner, 1891), Kindle loc. 3495–601, quotation at 3537.

85 Cheney, pp. 367–68.

86 Wiebe, pp. 181–82.

87 Wood, pp. 697–98.

88 Peter Cozzens, *A Brutal Reckoning: Andrew Jackson, the Creek Indians, and the Epic War for the American South* (New York: Knopf, 2023).

89 The agreement was made at the British Legation on the 2400 block of L Street N.W., the site of my Washington apartment.

90 Cheney, p. 13.

91 Ibid., pp. 20–21.

92 Sean Wilentz, *No Property in Man: Slavery and Antislavery at the Nation's Foundation* (Cambridge: Harvard University Press, 2019), p. 97. See also Drew McCoy, pp. 260–61.

93 Wilentz, pp. 97–98.

94 Ibid., p. 1.

95 Miller has an insightful discussion of the "peculiar" Federalist 54, pp. 171–75.

96 Wilentz, p. 1.

97 Wood, p. 526.

98 Wilentz, p. 97.

99 Wood, p. 541.

100 Ibid., p. 526.

101 McCoy, p. 273.

102 Kurt E. Leichtle and Bruce G. Carveth, *Crusade Against Slavery: Edward Coles, Pioneer of Freedom* (Carbondale: Southern Illinois University Press, 2011), p. 45.

103 Ibid., p. 46.

104 Ketcham, pp. 551–52.

105 Ibid., pp. 46–48; Suzanne Cooper Guasco, *Confronting Slavery: Edward Coles and the Rise of Antislavery Politics in Nineteenth Century America* (DeKalb: Northern Illinois University Press, 2013), pp. 4–5.

106 McCoy, p. 29.

107 Brookhiser, p. 232.

108 McCoy, pp. 108–14.

109 Ibid., pp. 261–62.

110 George Dangerfield, *The Era of Good Feelings*, 2d ed. (Chicago: Ivan R. Dee, 1989).

111 Brookhiser, p. 191.

112 McCoy, pp. 81–82.

113 Ibid., pp. 115–19.

114 Ibid., p. 126.

115 Brookhiser, pp. 240–43.

SIX – ALBERT GALLATIN: EVER WESTWARD

1 Henry Adams, *The Life of Albert Gallatin*, 1879 (New York: Good Press, 2022), pp. 47–49. See also Nicholas Dungan, *Gallatin: America's Swiss Founding Father* (New York: New York University Press, 2010), p. 36.

2 On the importance of immigrants in establishing financial policies and institutions in the early republic, see Thomas K. McCraw, *The Founders and Finance: How Hamilton, Gallatin, and Other Immigrants Forged a New Economy* (Cambridge: Harvard University Press, 2012), pp. 301–2.

3 George Dangerfield, *The Era of Good Feelings*, 2nd ed. (Chicago: Ivan R. Dee, 1989), p. 6.

4 Adams, pp. 9, 16.

5 R. R. Palmer, T*he Age of the Democratic Revolution: A Political History of Europe and America, 1760-1800* (Princeton: Princeton University Press, 1959), p. 111.

6 Adams, pp. 17–18; McCraw, p. 182; Dangerfield, p. 6.

7 McCraw, pp. 184–85.

8 Adams, p. 41.

9 McCraw, pp. 188–90; Bray Hammond, *Banks and Politics in North America from the Revolution to the Civil War* (Princeton: Princeton University Press, 1957), pp. 164–65, 205.

10 McCraw, pp. 190–92; Adams, pp. 50–55.

11 Adams, p. 56.

12 Adams, pp. 55–72; McCraw, pp. 195–202; Hammond, pp. 165–66, 206.

13 Stanley Elkins and Eric McKittrick, *The Age of Federalism* (New York: Oxford University Press, 1992), p. 462; Adams, p. 77; McCraw, p. 100–3.

14 Elkins and McKittrick, pp. 777–78; McCraw, pp. 205–13.

15 Dungan, pp. 62–65; Adams, pp. 120–21.

16 McCraw, p. 204.

17 Adams, pp. 85–86, 90.

18 Ibid., pp. 129–32; Elkins and McKittrick, p. 890.

19 Elkins and McKittrick, p. 591.

20 McCraw, pp. 228.

21 Ibid., pp. 266–67.

22 Ibid., p. 234.

23 Ibid., p. 232; Richard Brookhiser, *James Madison* (New York: Basic Books, 2011), p. 191.

24 Dungan, p. 78.

25 McCraw, p. 231.

26 Ibid., p. 238.

27 Ibid., p. 200.

28 Ibid., p. 245.

29 Dungan, p. 78.

30 Andrea Wulf, *The Invention of Nature: Alexander von Humboldt's New World* (New York: Random House, 2015), pp. 117–19.

31 John Van Atta, *Securing the West: Politics, Public Lands, and the Fate of the Old Republic, 1785–1850* (Baltimore: Johns Hopkins University Press, 2014), p. 78.

32 McCraw, p. 253.

33 John Austin Stevens, *Albert Gallatin, American Statesman Series, Vol. XIII* (Boston: Houghton Mifflin, 1898), p. 207.

34 George R. Stewart, *U.S. 40* (Boston: Houghton Mifflin, 1953), pp. 91, 94, 106.

35 Dungan, p. 78.

36 McCraw, pp. 253–54.

37 Van Atta, *Securing*, p. 76; McCraw, pp. 254–58; Stevens, *Gallatin*, pp. 207–8; Henry Adams, *The Administrations of Thomas Jefferson: The Second Administration*, Kindle ed. (Madison & Adams Press, 2017), p. 1196.

38 "Louisvile and Portland Canal," Wikipedia, n.d.

39 "Welland Canal," Wikipedia, n.d.

40 "Intracoastal Waterway," Wikipedia, n.d.

41 Richard Brookhiser, *James Madison* (New York: Basic Books, 2011), p. 172.

42 Robert H. Wiebe, *The Opening of American Society from the Adoption of the Constitution to the Eve of Disunion* (New York: Random House, 1984), pp. 170–71.

43 McCraw, pp. 286–87.

44 Ibid., p. 293.

45 Ibid., pp. 300–2.

46 Ibid., pp. 309–10.

47 Dangerfield, p. 90.

48 Henry Adams, *A History of the United States in the Madison Administration* (New York: Scribner's, 1891), Vol. V, locs. 19374–430; Dangerfield, pp. 5–7, 85; McCraw, pp. 308–14.

49 Dangerfield, p. 6.

50 McCraw, pp. 313–14.

51 Ibid., pp. 315–18; Dangerfield, p. 374.

52 McCraw, p. 318.

53 Dungan, p. 154.

54 Hammond, p. 304–5.

55 Dungan, pp. 159–61.

56 "About," American Ethnological Society, americanethnologist.org, n.d.

57 McCraw, pp. 322–24.

INDEX